Preparing for Exaltation

Teacher's Manual

Published by
The Church of Jesus Christ of Latter-day Saints
Salt Lake City, Utah

Cover: *The Resurrection,* by Harry Anderson

English approval: 9/95

Contents

Introduction

Purpose of the Course

This Sunday School course is designed to help 12- and 13-year-olds understand our Heavenly Father's plan of salvation and apply gospel truths that will lead them to eternal life. It discusses the steps in our eternal journey and the requirements and guides that the Lord has revealed for our progress through mortality. Individual lessons explain the basic doctrines, principles, and ordinances of the gospel.

A chart of the plan of salvation is included at the back of the manual (picture 1 in the picture section). You may want to make a larger copy of the chart so it can be seen more easily by the entire class. Save this chart, and use it often throughout the course as you discuss various aspects of the plan of salvation.

Scan the table of contents and browse through the manual to become familiar with all the lesson subjects. Seeing the overall design will give you better perspective as you prepare and present each lesson.

Preparing to Teach

You will always need certain equipment in the classroom: a chalkboard (or whiteboard), chalk (or erasable markers), an eraser, and your own set of scriptures. Therefore, these items have not been listed in the "Preparation" section of the lessons.

Class members should bring their own copies of the scriptures, but you may want to bring a few extra copies (these can be obtained from the meetinghouse library) so those who do not bring their own can participate fully in the lesson. You may also want to bring scripture marking pencils for class members to use (remind class members to mark only in their own copies of the scriptures, not library copies or other borrowed copies).

Each lesson begins with a statement of the purpose of the lesson—what you are trying to help class members know or do. At the end of each "Preparation" section, in italics, is a note to the teacher. These short statements are provided to help you understand the importance of the lesson topic as it relates to youth. Other notes, also in italics, appear intermittently throughout the manual. These notes provide guidance in using various teaching methods suggested in the lessons.

Each lesson has an "Enrichment Activities" section containing additional activities, discussion material, and stories. If class members need added activity to keep their attention, select one or two of these activities to use as part of the lesson.

The picture section at the back of the manual contains several pictures suggested for use in the lessons. Other suggested pictures are available from the meetinghouse library or in the Gospel Art Picture Kit.

Presenting the Lessons

Begin and end each lesson with prayer.

Do more than lecture. Invite class members to participate in discussions and activities. Encourage class members to read, mark, and study the scriptures. Let class members discover for themselves the glorious principles that Heavenly Father has given us as part of his plan of salvation.

Remember that the doctrines, principles, and ordinances of the gospel can prepare us for exaltation only when we apply them to our lives. Encourage class members to live according to the principles that are discussed in class.

Inviting the Spirit

The Lord has said, "The Spirit shall be given unto you by the prayer of faith; and if ye receive not the Spirit ye shall not teach" (D&C 42:14). Help class members feel and recognize the influence of the Holy Ghost so they can be prepared to apply the principles they learn. These suggestions can help you invite the Spirit into your class:

1. Pray. While preparing to teach, pray for the Holy Ghost to help you understand the doctrines and principles being taught and the needs of class members. During class, pray in your heart for the Spirit to guide you and to touch class members. Remember that the Holy Spirit is the teacher in your class.

2. Use the scriptures. Encourage class members to bring their scriptures each week, and show them that the doctrines and principles discussed in the lesson are based in scripture. Help class members learn to use footnotes and other study aids in the scriptures.

3. Bear your testimony. Testify whenever the Spirit prompts you, not just at the end of the lesson. Bear testimony of the Savior. As appropriate, invite class members to bear their testimonies.

4. Use sacred music. The hymns of Zion can help prepare class members to feel the Spirit. Youth may be reluctant to sing in class, but you can use other methods to bring the hymns into the classroom. Class members could read and think about the words to a hymn while someone plays it, or you could invite an individual or small group to sing a hymn. You could also play recordings of hymns.

5. Express love. Let class members know that you love them. Express your love for Heavenly Father and for the Savior.

6. Share personal experiences. Demonstrate to class members that your testimony is based in experience with living the gospel. Share simple, everyday experiences that have helped you understand gospel principles such as the importance of prayer or the blessings that come from keeping the commandments. Encourage class members to share, as appropriate, their insights, feelings, and experiences that relate to the doctrines and principles being taught.

Sometimes you or a class member may feel prompted to share a spiritual experience. Remember that these experiences are sacred and should not be shared casually, but "with care, and by constraint of the Spirit" (D&C 63:64). Follow the promptings of the Holy Ghost regarding which experiences you should share, and remind class members to do the same.

Using the Scriptures

Included in each lesson are suggested scriptures for reading and marking. Read the scriptures aloud, or have class members read them. Class members should follow each verse as it is read, marking words and phrases that you suggest or that they feel are meaningful.

When you ask class members to read a scripture passage, you may want to write the reference on the chalkboard so that everyone can find it easily and so the person reading will know where to stop.

Asking and Answering Questions

The success of your lessons will depend largely on your use of questions. As you prepare your lessons, think of ways to help class members go beyond standard, superficial responses. Many questions in the manual encourage class members to consider how a doctrine or principle applies to their lives. Encourage class members to give sincere thought to these questions. Do not be concerned if class members are silent for a few seconds after you ask a question. Allow them time to think of responses. If they do not seem to understand a question, you might need to rephrase it or provide more context.

Encourage class members to ask questions about the lesson, and create an environment where they can do so without embarrassment or fear of ridicule. You should not feel embarrassed if a class member asks a question that you cannot answer. Instead of making up an answer or giving your own opinion, admit that you do not know and offer to try to find an answer for the class member.

Using Quotations

Many lessons include quotations from latter-day Church leaders. Use these quotations to direct class discussion, clarify doctrine, and emphasize that the Lord continues to reveal his will in our day. In addition to the quotations in the lessons, you may use other appropriate statements from prophets, apostles, and other Church leaders. The best sources for these are recent general conference issues of the *Ensign* (May and November) or the International Magazines (July and January).

Helping Class Members Who Have Disabilities

Be sensitive to class members who have disabilities. Know their needs and abilities, and include them in class activities as much as possible. Before class, help these members prepare to read or comment. Provide a place for people in wheelchairs, and ask class members to speak loudly so that everyone can hear.

A Loving Father— An Eternal Plan

1

Purpose	To help class members understand how knowing God's eternal plan can help us make daily decisions with an eternal perspective.

Preparation

1. Prayerfully study the scriptures indicated on the plan of salvation chart, found on page 3 or in the picture section of the manual.

2. Draw on a large piece of paper or on the chalkboard an outline of the plan of salvation chart (page 3 or picture 1 in the picture section of the manual). Do not include any of the words yet. If you draw the chart on a piece of paper, save it for use in other lessons.

3. Make a copy of the "Mortality Maze," found on page 7, for each class member or pair of class members. If it is not feasible to make copies, draw the maze on a large piece of paper or on the chalkboard so that class members can work together to solve it.

4. Materials needed:
   a. Pens or pencils for class members to use in doing the maze.
   b. A set of scriptures and a scripture marking pencil for each class member. Encourage class members to bring their own scriptures to class each week.

Note to the teacher

It is often difficult for young people to see beyond their everyday experiences and understand how such events are part of our Father in Heaven's plan for them. Help class members understand that Heavenly Father loves them and that the plan of salvation is evidence of his love.

Suggested Lesson Development

Our Earth Experience Is Part of the Plan of Salvation

Story and discussion

Read the following story told by Bishop H. Burke Peterson, who was a member of the Presiding Bishopric:

"My parents and grandparents were born and raised in Utah. However, my mother and father began their married life in Phoenix, Arizona. That is where my three brothers and I were raised. Almost every summer my father and mother would take all of us to Utah . . . to enjoy the association with our cousins and other relatives.

" . . . One spring before school was out I asked my father if I could go to Salt Lake City to work and then return to Phoenix at the end of the summer to be with my family and begin school again. After thinking it over, my parents decided it would be fine. When school was out in May, Dad took me with him to the [bus station] and, since I had no money of my own as yet, bought me a ticket to Salt Lake City. I was somewhat taken back when I found out that he had purchased for me a one-way ticket instead of a round trip. He said he would take the responsibility to see that I arrived in Salt Lake City but it would be up to me to do what was necessary while I was there to purchase the ticket for a return home to Phoenix at the end of the summer. As you can imagine, I was most anxious to come back home after my work experience as I had burning in my memory the happy experiences we had always enjoyed in our home. I enjoyed the association with and loved my three brothers and was most happy and comfortable being with my parents.

"When I arrived in Salt Lake City I immediately set about to find work. This I was able to accomplish, and as soon as my first paycheck was given to me, guess what I did. First I paid my tithing, and then I took the rest of the money to the bus depot downtown in Salt Lake City and purchased a return trip ticket to Phoenix. I wanted to be sure that when summer was over there would be nothing to stand in the way of my returning home. I loved my home very much. For the rest of the summer I was particularly mindful of taking good care of myself and doing everything necessary to insure my return home to Phoenix. More than anything else I wanted to enjoy again the experience of being with my family."

- Have you ever had an experience where you were away from your family and home and were anxious to return?

Give class members a few moments to comment, and then read Bishop Peterson's comments on the story:

"We all had an experience similar to this long ago before we came to this earth. We were in a gathering where we were being instructed by our Father in heaven concerning the earth he had prepared for us. . . . He let us know that the decision to come here would be ours, and if this was our wish, he would see to it that we arrived into this mortal experience safely. Like the experience I had in Phoenix as a boy, our Father in heaven would provide a one-way ticket for us. Whether or not we returned again to him at the end of our mortal experience on earth would depend upon the things we did while we were here" ("Return Trip Ticket Home," *New Era,* Apr. 1974, 5).

Explain that this year in Sunday School, class members will learn about Heavenly Father's plan for us, Jesus Christ's role in that plan, and what we must do to return to them when our earth life is over.

The Plan of Salvation Is Heavenly Father's Plan for Us

Chart discussion   Show the plan of salvation chart you have drawn.

- What do these boxes and circles represent?

If class members do not immediately realize that the drawing represents the plan of salvation, label one or two of the boxes or circles. Then ask class members to fill in the rest of the chart, helping them as needed. Explain that this diagram answers three universal questions: Where did we come from? Why are we here? Where are we going after this life?

- Which box or circle represents where we are right now? (The circle labeled "mortality.")

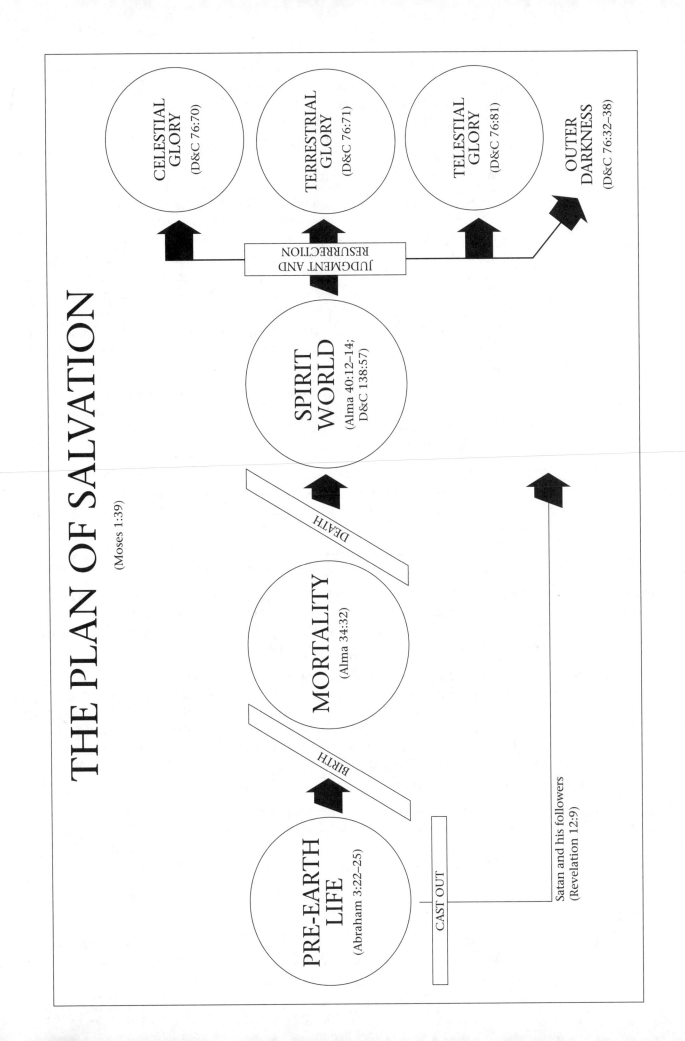

THE PLAN OF SALVATION

(Moses 1:39)

PRE-EARTH LIFE
(Abraham 3:22–25)

CAST OUT

Satan and his followers
(Revelation 12:9)

BIRTH

MORTALITY
(Alma 34:32)

DEATH

SPIRIT WORLD
(Alma 40:12–14;
D&C 138:57)

JUDGMENT AND RESURRECTION

CELESTIAL GLORY
(D&C 76:70)

TERRESTRIAL GLORY
(D&C 76:71)

TELESTIAL GLORY
(D&C 76:81)

OUTER DARKNESS
(D&C 76:32–38)

Point out that our earth life is only part of our eternal existence. We lived before we came to earth, and we will live after we die. Briefly review the plan of salvation as illustrated on the chart, and tell class members that they will be learning about it throughout the year.

Scripture discussion

Have class members turn to Moses 1:39. Ask one of them to read the verse aloud.

- What does God tell us his work is?

Point out that the scripture names two things as God's work—to bring to pass immortality and eternal life. Explain that these two words do not refer to the same thing. Immortality is a state of being resurrected, of being free from physical death. This blessing will come to all people. Eternal life is living with Heavenly Father and Jesus Christ in the celestial kingdom. This blessing—which is also called exaltation—comes only to those who keep the commandments and make the necessary covenants. (You may want to point out that the title of this course of study is "Preparing for Exaltation." The lessons that will be taught in Sunday School this year focus on how we can prepare to live with Heavenly Father and Jesus again.)

- How does it make you feel to know that Heavenly Father's most important work is helping you return to live with him again? (Invite class members to answer this question to themselves if they do not wish to share their feelings with the class.)

Explain that Heavenly Father's plan of salvation provides a way for us to gain a body, learn by experience, show that we will obey his commandments, and return to him stronger and wiser. Emphasize that this plan is given because of Heavenly Father's great love for us.

Knowing the Plan Helps Us Make Wise Decisions

Activity

Give each class member or pair of class members a pen or pencil and a copy of the "Mortality Maze" (or have all class members work together on a large copy of the maze). Explain that the objective is to draw a continuous line from "Birth" to "Death," passing through the center ("Fulfill the purpose of life").

When class members finish the maze, explain that in life, as in this maze, we must make many decisions about which way we should go. However, when we understand that life on earth has a purpose and is part of Heavenly Father's plan, we can begin to make correct decisions. (You may want to point out that there is a second path from "Birth" to "Death," but this path does not go through the center. Likewise, some people finish their earth life without understanding or fulfilling its purpose.)

Stories and discussion

Read or have a class member read the following stories. Discuss with class members how being aware of God's plan could influence the decisions of the person in each story. Help class members see how a knowledge of God's plan can help them better understand themselves and the decisions they will have to make in life.

Paul

All his life, Paul had planned to go on a mission. From the time he was very young, his parents had taught him the importance of serving the Lord in this

4

way. He had built a substantial savings account, which he called his "mission money." It had never occurred to him that he might do anything else.

As Paul grew older, however, it became harder for him to save money for a mission. Any money he earned seemed to be spent before he got around to putting any in his savings account. In addition, he saw many expensive things he wanted to have. Paul began to doubt whether he wanted to spend so much money and time on a mission.

• What does God expect of Paul?

• How could understanding the plan of salvation help Paul make a correct decision about serving a mission?

• What difference will this decision make in Paul's progress toward eternal life?

Note to the teacher   *Good questions cause class members to think. Avoid asking questions that can be answered with a simple "yes" or "no." (See* Teaching—No Greater Call, *105–6.)*

Melissa

Melissa had many friends in her ward until she began attending a new school. She made new friends at the school, and soon her new friends became very important to her. She saw her old friends in the ward less and less, and she began to feel that she had outgrown them. Her new friends seemed more exciting and mature and seemed to be doing adventurous things she had never done before.

One day Melissa attended a party at the home of one of her new friends. Everyone she thought was important was there. As the party progressed, the activities became much different from what Melissa was accustomed to. Even people she would never have expected such conduct from were drinking, and some were using drugs. Melissa wanted to have fun and be accepted by these people who were so important to her, but she was very uncomfortable. When one of her friends offered her an alcoholic drink, she thought maybe it wouldn't hurt to drink just one.

• What do you think Melissa should do? Why?

• How could understanding the plan of salvation help Melissa make the right choice?

• If you were to talk to Melissa privately, what might you say to her to help her make the right decision?

Carl

Carl played basketball and played it well. But he did not do as well in schoolwork. Because of his interest in basketball, he devoted little time to studying for his classes. Carl's parents told him that if his grades were poor, he would no longer be able to play on the basketball team. Carl didn't know what to do. Then a possible solution appeared. Mike, a member of Carl's basketball team, mentioned that the same thing had happened to him. He solved his problem by cheating on tests. He was able to get good grades without studying. Mike suggested that Carl do the same thing. Carl knew it was dishonest, but it seemed like such a simple solution to his problem.

- What could Carl do to solve his problem without cheating?

- How could a testimony of the plan of salvation help Carl decide what to do?

Understanding the Plan of Salvation Makes a Difference

Discussion

Ask class members to think about some of the decisions they face each day.

- How can understanding and having a testimony of the plan of salvation help you with your daily decisions?

Invite class members to explain how understanding that Heavenly Father has a plan for them could help them with a decision they have faced or are facing. If appropriate, share an experience in which knowing the plan of salvation helped you make a good decision in a difficult situation.

Testimony

Testify that because Heavenly Father loves us, he has given us a plan to help us return to live with him. Knowing this plan can help us make wise decisions. Explain that the best way to make a decision is to think of the eternal consequences of each choice and choose that which will lead back to Heavenly Father.

Encourage class members to keep in mind the plan of salvation when making choices.

Enrichment Activities

You may want to use one or more of these activities during the lesson.

1. If it is available, show "Man's Search for Happiness," a thirteen-minute segment of the *Come unto Me* videocassette (53146), to explain the plan of salvation.

2. Display a road map.

   - What is this? Why would someone use this?

   Explain that life is like a journey. Heavenly Father knew that we would need directions to help us find our way back to him, so he provided the plan of salvation as a kind of map for us to follow.

   - How can we "read" this map and know what we must do to reach our destination of living with Heavenly Father again? (Answers may include by studying the scriptures, following the prophets, and listening to our teachers and parents as they teach us about the gospel.)

   - How would our lives be different if we did not have this map, or plan?

3. Invite a recently returned missionary to come to class and share an experience he or she had with teaching the plan of salvation in the mission field.

4. Sing with class members "I Am a Child of God" (*Hymns,* no. 301; or *Children's Songbook,* 2).

Mortality Maze

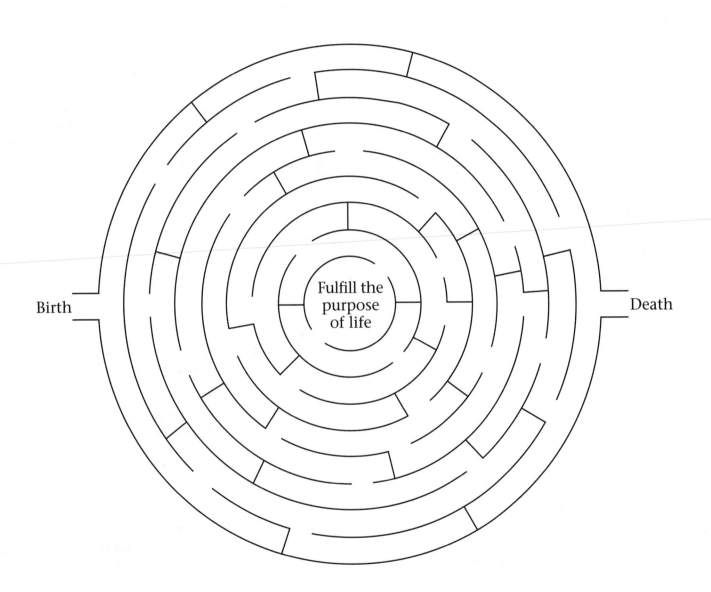

Birth

Death

Fulfill the
purpose
of life

Lesson 2

Agency: The Power to Choose

Purpose	To encourage class members to continue to use their agency wisely, as they did in the premortal life when they chose to follow Heavenly Father's plan.

Preparation

1. Prayerfully study 2 Nephi 2:27; Moses 4:1–4; 7:32; Abraham 3:24–28.

2. Materials needed:
   a. The plan of salvation chart you created for lesson 1 (if you drew the chart on the chalkboard for lesson 1, draw it on a piece of large paper now, or show the copy of the chart in the picture section of the manual). Make sure all the labels and scripture references are now included on the chart. Save this chart for use in future lessons.
   b. A pen or pencil and a piece of paper for each class member.
   c. A set of scriptures and a scripture marking pencil for each class member. Continue to encourage class members to bring their own scriptures to class each week.

Note to the teacher

President Spencer W. Kimball, twelfth President of the Church, described agency as the "basic gospel law" (The Teachings of Spencer W. Kimball, *ed. Edward L. Kimball [1982], 38). So important is this law that Heavenly Father has always protected it. Before we came to this earth he cast Satan out because Satan sought to destroy our agency. Heavenly Father allows us to use our agency in this life even though he knows many of us will use it unwisely. President David O. McKay, ninth President of the Church, said, "Next to the bestowal of life itself, the right to direct that life is God's greatest gift to man"* (Gospel Ideals *[1953], 299). Help class members understand the importance of this great gift.*

Note that although the term "free agency" is often used, the correct, scriptural term is simply "agency" (see D&C 29:36; see also page 11 of this lesson).

Suggested Lesson Development

Agency Is the Power to Choose Good or Evil

Activity

Give class members pens or pencils and paper. Ask them to think of the choices they have made so far today and list as many as they can in one minute. At the end of a minute, invite them to share some of the choices on their lists. Then ask:

• Which of your choices today do you think was the most important?

Have class members circle this item on their list. Invite a few volunteers to tell which choice they circled and why they feel it was most important.

• Where did you get your ability to choose?

Have a class member read aloud Moses 7:32. Suggest that those who are using their own scriptures mark this verse (class members should not mark in library copies or borrowed copies of the scriptures).

Explain that Heavenly Father has given us agency—the power to choose between good and evil. But agency is more than just the ability to do what we want; agency is one of the most basic and important of all gospel laws.

Quotation

Have a class member read the following statement from Elder Richard G. Scott of the Quorum of the Twelve Apostles:

"Your agency, the right to make choices, is not given so that you can get what you want. This divine gift is provided so that you will choose what your Father in Heaven wants for you. That way He can lead you to become all that He intends you to be. That path leads to glorious joy and happiness" (in Conference Report, Apr. 1996, 33; or *Ensign,* May 1996, 25).

Note to the teacher

Invite class members to become familiar with the teachings of the General Authorities by listening to them at general conference or by reading their messages in the Church magazines. These men are appointed by the Lord to teach us and help us along the path toward exaltation.

Story

Explain that for us to have and use agency, several conditions must exist. Write *Principles of Agency* on the chalkboard. Then tell the following story:

Teresa had been away for the summer. During her first day back at school she noticed something different about the way some of her friends treated her. They seemed distant, even a bit unfriendly. Teresa missed the easygoing relationship they used to have.

A few days later Teresa found her friends smoking behind the school. When she approached them, they invited her to join them.

Teresa was shaken. She didn't know what to do. She wanted to get along with her friends again, but she knew that what they were doing was wrong. What would her friends say if she refused to join them?

Chalkboard discussion

Write *1. Law* on the chalkboard below "Principles of Agency."

• What commandment, or law, is involved in this story? (The Word of Wisdom.)

Write *2. Knowledge of the law* on the chalkboard.

• Does Teresa have knowledge of the law?

• Why is it essential to our agency that there be laws (or commandments) and that we know what these laws are?

Write *3. Opposition—good and evil* on the chalkboard.

• What choices does Teresa have? What will Teresa do if she chooses good? What will she do if she chooses evil?

Write *4. Freedom of choice* on the chalkboard.

• Is Teresa free to choose what she will do?

At this point, the chalkboard should look like this:

```
┌─────────────────────────────────────────────┐
│                                               │
│  PRINCIPLES OF AGENCY                         │
│                                               │
│  1. Law                                       │
│  2. Knowledge of the law                      │
│  3. Opposition—good and evil                  │
│  4. Freedom of choice                         │
│                                               │
│                                               │
│                                               │
│                                               │
│                                               │
└─────────────────────────────────────────────┘
```

Explain that these four principles are the foundation on which agency is based. (Leave this list on the chalkboard for the remainder of the lesson.)

Our Premortal Choices Affected Mortality

Scripture and chart discussion

Display the plan of salvation chart. Have class members read and mark Abraham 3:24–26 as you study it together and review the chart.

Help class members understand that in verse 24, the one "like unto God" was Jesus Christ and that he made the earth for us.

- According to verse 25, why were we sent to earth? Why is agency necessary for us to accomplish this purpose?

- What is the "first estate" mentioned in verse 26? (Point to "Pre-earth Life" on the plan of salvation chart.)

- What is the "second estate"? (Point to "Mortality" on the chart.)

Explain that we are here on earth because of choices we made during our first estate, or pre-earth life.

Scripture discussion

Help class members read, mark, and understand Abraham 3:27–28 and Moses 4:1–4.

Explain that when Heavenly Father asked whom he should send, Jesus volunteered to be the Savior of the world and help fulfill Heavenly Father's plan. Lucifer (Satan) also volunteered, but he demanded conditions that would have violated Heavenly Father's plan. Heavenly Father chose Jesus.

- What was wrong with Satan's proposal to save us? (See Moses 4:3; he wanted to take away our agency and force us to do right; also, he wanted Heavenly Father's glory for himself.) What happened to Satan because of his rebellion against Heavenly Father's plan? (See Abraham 3:28; Moses 4:3–4.)

- Point out that one of the reasons Satan was cast out was because he "sought to destroy the agency of man" (Moses 4:3). Why is agency so important? Why would it be bad for us to be forced to keep the commandments, as Satan wanted?

- What important choice did we make in the pre-earth life? (We chose to follow Heavenly Father and Jesus instead of Satan.) How do we know we made this choice? (We have physical bodies; those who followed Satan will never have the opportunity to have bodies. They did not keep their first estate.)

Quotation

Have a class member read the following statement by Elder Boyd K. Packer of the Quorum of the Twelve Apostles:

"In the great council in heaven, God's plan was presented: the plan of salvation, the plan of redemption, the great plan of happiness. . . . The adversary rebelled and adopted a plan of his own. Those who followed him were denied the right to a mortal body. Our presence here confirms that we sanctioned our Father's plan" (in Conference Report, Oct. 1993, 27; or *Ensign,* Nov. 1993, 21).

Refer to the principles of agency listed on the chalkboard, and emphasize that these principles applied also to our first estate. We made one of the wisest choices of our eternal existence when we chose to follow Heavenly Father instead of Satan. That decision set an example we can follow today.

We Are Responsible for Our Choices

Chalkboard discussion

Add to the list on the chalkboard 5. *Responsibility for choices.* Explain that the final principle necessary for agency is our responsibility for the results of our own choices.

- We sometimes hear a person say, "Someone (or something) *made* me do it." Will God ever accept that as justification for our choices? Why or why not?

Quotation

Have a class member read the following statement by Elder Packer:

"We are free to obey or to ignore the spirit and the letter of the law. But the agency granted to man is a *moral* agency (see D&C 101:78). We are not free to break our covenants and escape the consequences" (in Conference Report, Oct. 1990, 108; or *Ensign,* Nov. 1990, 84).

Discussion

Emphasize to class members that when we make choices, we must accept the consequences. We are free to choose our actions, but we are not free to choose the consequences of our actions. The consequences of unwise choices can put us in a position where our choices, and thus our freedom, are greatly limited.

- Some people think that when we obey the commandments we give up our freedom. Do you agree or disagree? Why?

- How do we lose freedom by making bad choices? How do we gain freedom by making good choices?

- How have you seen this happen in your own life?

Invite class members to talk about situations they have seen or experienced where a bad choice led to loss of freedom or a good choice led to more freedom. (One example is the choice whether or not to obey your parents. Choosing to disobey could lead to greater restrictions, while choosing to obey could lead to greater trust and privileges.)

Emphasize that wise use of agency keeps all our choices open and improves our ability to choose. You may want to share a personal experience in which your righteous use of agency led to more freedom and a greater ability to choose.

Our Choices Are of Eternal Significance

Discussion

Refer back to the story about Teresa and ask:

- How could Teresa's choice affect her daily life? How will it affect her eternal life? Which is more important for Teresa to consider as she decides what to do?

- How might Teresa's friends react if she decides not to smoke with them? How can we gain strength to choose what is right even if it makes us unpopular?

Scripture discussion

Have class members read and mark 2 Nephi 2:27.

- According to this verse, what is our main choice in this life? (To choose liberty and eternal life or captivity and death.)

- How do we choose liberty and eternal life? What choices have you made this week that lead you toward liberty and eternal life?

- How does breaking the commandments of God lead to captivity and death?

- What are some seemingly small choices we face each week that, if made improperly, could gradually lead to captivity and spiritual death? (Answers may include whether or not to pray daily, attend church meetings each week, obey your parents, be completely honest in your schoolwork.)

Testimony

On the chalkboard opposite the five points you have listed, write *Do I righteously use my power to choose?*

Testify that each of us possesses the gift of agency, the freedom to choose between good and evil. We exercised our agency wisely to earn the right to come to earth. Now, in this life, we are responsible for each choice we make. Making righteous decisions puts us on the path toward eternal exaltation.

Encourage class members to consider their choices carefully and ask often, "Do I righteously use my power to choose?"

Enrichment Activities

You may want to use one or more of these activities during the lesson.

1. If *Family Home Evening Video Supplement* (53276) is available, show "True to the Faith," a nine-minute segment.

2. Write the following statement (from Conference Report, Oct. 1990, 108; or *Ensign*, Nov. 1990, 84) on the chalkboard:

"The laws of God are ordained to make us happy." —Elder Boyd K. Packer

- How can obedience to laws make us happy?

Discuss with class members how they have seen this to be true in their own lives or the lives of their family members or friends.

You may want to give class members pens or pencils and cards on which they can copy Elder Packer's statement to take home.

The Fall of Adam and Eve

Purpose	To teach class members that the Fall of Adam and Eve allowed each of us to enter mortality.

Preparation	1. Prayerfully study Genesis 1:28; 2:16–17 (Moses 2:28; 3:16–17); 2 Nephi 2:19–20, 22–25; Moses 4:6–12.
	2. Materials needed:
	a. The picture Adam and Eve Leaving the Garden of Eden (picture 3 in the picture section of the manual; 62461; Gospel Art Picture Kit 101).
	b. A set of scriptures and a scripture marking pencil for each class member. Continue to encourage class members to bring their own scriptures to class each week.
Note to the teacher	*The decision of Adam and Eve to eat the forbidden fruit was not a sin, as it is sometimes considered by other Christian churches. It was a transgression—an act that was formally prohibited but not inherently wrong (see Dallin H. Oaks, in Conference Report, Oct. 1993, 98; or Ensign, Nov. 1993, 73). The Fall was necessary for us to progress toward exaltation. We have to experience mortality to become like our Father in Heaven, and Adam and Eve fulfilled their mission to make this possible. Help class members appreciate that the Fall of Adam and Eve enabled each of us to receive a body and come to earth to gain experience in choosing between good and evil.*

Suggested Lesson Development	**The Callings of Adam and Eve**
Discussion	• Imagine you were given the opportunity to live in a world where sickness, sorrow, sin, pain, and death were unknown. Would you like to live in such a world?
	Point out that when Adam and Eve were first placed on the earth, they lived in such a world. In the Garden of Eden there was no sorrow, pain, or death. However, Adam and Eve made a choice they knew would require them to leave the Garden of Eden. (Display the picture of Adam and Eve leaving the garden.) This lesson will discuss why they made that choice and how their choice has affected all of us.
	Explain that Adam and Eve were chosen in the premortal life for a special mission.
	• What was their mission? Why were they chosen to do this?
	Help class members realize that Adam and Eve were chosen to be the first people on earth because of their faithfulness. They were among the "noble and great" of our Heavenly Father's children (see Abraham 3:22). Adam (then known by the name of Michael) helped create the world and was one of those who led the righteous spirits to victory in the war against the rebellious Lucifer.

The Fall

- What commandments did God give Adam and Eve in the Garden of Eden?

Have class members read Genesis 1:28 (or Moses 2:28) and Genesis 2:16–17 (or Moses 3:16–17) to discover two commandments given to Adam and Eve by Heavenly Father: to multiply and replenish (fill) the earth and to refrain from eating the fruit of the tree of knowledge of good and evil.

Explain that Adam and Eve could not keep both these commandments. If they chose to eat the fruit, they would be cast out of the Garden of Eden. But if they did not eat the fruit and remained in the garden, they would not be able to have children (to "multiply and replenish the earth"). Because the Garden of Eden was a place of innocence, while Adam and Eve lived there they could not change or progress in any way, including having children (see 2 Nephi 2:22–23).

Read or have a class member read the following statement by Elder Russell M. Nelson of the Quorum of the Twelve Apostles:

"To bring the plan of happiness to fruition [fulfillment], God issued to Adam and Eve the first commandment ever given to mankind. It was a commandment to beget children. A law was explained to them. Should they eat from 'the tree of the knowledge of good and evil' (Genesis 2:17), their bodies would change; mortality and eventual death would come upon them. But partaking of that fruit was prerequisite to their parenthood" (in Conference Report, Oct. 1993, 46; or *Ensign,* Nov. 1993, 34).

- What happened to Adam and Eve in the Garden of Eden?

Have class members tell what they know about the Fall. Then have a class member read Moses 4:6–12 aloud (you may want to have class members take turns reading one verse each).

- What did Satan say would happen if Eve ate the fruit of the tree of knowledge of good and evil? (See Moses 4:10–11.) Why did he tell Eve this? (See Moses 4:6; emphasize that Satan did not know that eating the fruit was a necessary part of God's plan for Adam and Eve.)

- Which part of Satan's argument was true? (See Moses 4:11.) Which part was not true? (See Moses 4:10.) What are some ways Satan combines truth and lies today to persuade us to do what he wants?

- Why did Eve and then Adam eat the fruit?

Help class members understand that Adam and Eve acted with understanding and used freedom of choice. They realized that if they did not eat the fruit, they would not be able to have children and they would not be able to learn to make righteous decisions. They wisely chose to eat the fruit.

- What are the effects of the Fall on Adam and Eve's descendants, including us?

Label two columns on the chalkboard: *Before the Fall* and *After the Fall.* Have class members develop a list of conditions before the Fall and a list of conditions after the Fall. Following is an example with some suggestions:

14

BEFORE THE FALL	AFTER THE FALL
No mortal experience	Mortal experience
No testing or probation	Testing and probation
No mortal body	Mortal body
Limited choices	Unlimited choices
No work	Work
No judgment	Judgment
No sin or opposition	Sin and opposition
No repentance needed	Repentance
No joy or pain	Joy and pain
No need for a Savior	The Savior and his Atonement
No opportunity for exaltation	Opportunity for exaltation

Scripture discussion

Have class members read 2 Nephi 2:22–25. Suggest that class members mark verse 25 (remind class members not to mark in library copies or borrowed copies of the scriptures).

- What would have happened to Adam and Eve if they had not eaten of the forbidden fruit? (They would have remained in the Garden of Eden without progressing; they would have known no joy because they knew no misery; they would have had no children. Also, God's plan of salvation would have been frustrated.)

- What would have happened to us if Adam and Eve had not eaten the fruit? (Because they would not have had children, we would not have had the opportunity to be born on this earth.)

Have class members look at 2 Nephi 2:25 again.

- How is the Fall of Adam and Eve essential to your eternal joy? (The Fall enabled us to be born on earth, where we can learn and progress toward exaltation and eternal joy.)

Testimony

Testify that Adam and Eve made a deliberate choice to partake of the forbidden fruit. Their choice did not come from a desire to disobey the Lord, but from a desire to gain wisdom. Because of this choice, we have the opportunity to come to earth and learn, as Adam and Eve did, how to choose good over evil. Express your gratitude for Adam and Eve and the choice they made.

Encourage class members to follow Adam and Eve's example and choose good over evil.

Enrichment Activities

You may want to use one or more of these activities during the lesson.

1. Invite the mother of a newborn baby to come to class to show her baby to the class and share her feelings about the privilege of bringing a new spirit into mortality. Explain to class members that this would not have been possible if Adam and Eve had not chosen to partake of the fruit.

2. If *Old Testament Video Presentations* (53224) is available, show "The Fall," a seven-minute segment, instead of reading the quotation from Elder Nelson.

3. Explain to class members that they were among the righteous spirits with Adam in the premortal world. Help them realize that they are like Adam and Eve.

Write two headings on the chalkboard: *Adam and Eve* and *Me.*

Begin by listing on the chalkboard one way we are like Adam and Eve. Discuss this similarity, and then have class members list as many other similarities as they can. Discuss each similarity as it is added to the list. The finished chalkboard will look something like this:

ADAM AND EVE	ME
Spirit children of God	Spirit child of God
Given agency to choose between good and evil	Given agency to choose between good and evil
Used agency to follow God	Using agency to follow God
Special mission— first man and woman	Special mission— held back until last dispensation

As you discuss the final item under "Me," you may want to use the following statement from Elder Ezra Taft Benson (Elder Benson was a member of the Quorum of the Twelve Apostles when he made this statement; he later became the thirteenth President of the Church):

"For nearly six thousand years, God has held you in reserve to make your appearance in the final days before the Second Coming of the Lord. . . . God has saved for the final inning some of his strongest children, who will help bear off the Kingdom triumphantly. And that is where you come in, for you are the generation that must be prepared to meet your God" ("In His Steps," in *BYU Speeches of the Year, 1979,* 59–60).

Encourage class members to continue to be like Adam and Eve, following their righteous examples.

The Atonement of Jesus Christ

Purpose	To help class members gain an appreciation for the Atonement of Jesus Christ and its role in enabling us to gain exaltation.

Preparation	1. Prayerfully study John 1:1–3, 14; 3:16; 2 Nephi 9:7–9, 21–22; Doctrine and Covenants 19:16–18; Moses 4:2.
	2. If it is available, prepare to show "The Mediator," an eleven-minute segment of *Book of Mormon Video Presentations* (53911). If the videocassette is not available, prepare to read or tell in your own words the story by Elder Boyd K. Packer in the fourth enrichment activity.
	3. Materials needed: a. The pictures Jesus Praying in Gethsemane (picture 4 in the picture section of the manual; 62175; Gospel Art Picture Kit 227); The Crucifixion (62505; Gospel Art Picture Kit 230); Burial of Jesus (62180; Gospel Art Picture Kit 231); The Resurrected Jesus Christ (picture 9 in the picture section of the manual; 62187; Gospel Art Picture Kit 239). b. A set of scriptures and a scripture marking pencil for each class member. Continue to encourage class members to bring their own scriptures to class each week.
Note to the teacher	*The Atonement of Jesus Christ is at the center of the gospel. Through the Atonement, we have the opportunity to repent and gain exaltation. Giving class members an understanding of the Atonement is a challenging assignment that can only be fulfilled with the help of the Spirit. As with all lessons, seek direction from the Spirit as you prepare and teach this lesson (see* Teaching—No Greater Call, *13).*

Suggested Lesson Development	**Jesus Christ Gave His Life for Us**
Story	Using your own words, relate the following true story: On a cold, wintry day in 1982, an airplane crashed into a bridge in Washington, D.C., and landed in the Potomac River. Most of the people on the plane were killed immediately, but six people got out of the plane and hung on to its tail while two men in a helicopter threw them a life preserver. The water was very cold, and it was hard to hang on to the plane. The rescuers were afraid that the passengers might lose their grip and drown before they could be pulled out and carried to safety. The rescuers noticed that one man seemed to be more alert than the others, so they lowered the life preserver to him. But every time they did this, he passed the life preserver to someone else so the other person could be rescued first. When the other five people were safe, the helicopter went back for the man, but he was gone. (See Roger Rosenblatt, "The Man in the Water," *Time,* 25 Jan. 1982, 86; see also Thomas S. Monson, *Ensign,* May 1983, 56.)

Discussion	• What do you think of this man's actions? What might you have done in this situation? What Christlike qualities did this man demonstrate?
Picture presentation	Display the four pictures of Jesus Christ. Explain that the man in the river did a great thing when he selflessly gave his own life to save the lives of five other people. But Jesus Christ did an even greater thing: he gave his life to save the spiritual lives of everyone on earth. This lesson will discuss Jesus Christ's role as our Savior.

We Need a Savior

Discussion	Ask class members to review what they remember about the Fall from the previous lesson.

Remind class members that because Adam and Eve ate the fruit of the tree of knowledge of good and evil, both spiritual and physical death came into the world.

• What happens in physical death? (A person's body is separated from his or her spirit.)

• What happens in spiritual death? (A person is separated from Heavenly Father.)

Explain that without a Savior, both physical death and spiritual death would be permanent. After death our bodies and spirits would be separated forever, and we would be unable to live with Heavenly Father again. But just as the Fall was part of Heavenly Father's plan, Heavenly Father also planned for us to have a Savior who would overcome both physical and spiritual death.

Jesus Christ Was Chosen to Be Our Savior

Scripture discussion	Have one or more class members read aloud John 1:1–3, 14 and Moses 4:2 (you may need to explain that "the Word" in John 1 is used as a name for Jesus Christ). Remind class members that Jesus Christ was with Heavenly Father before the earth was created and that he was chosen in the premortal world to create the earth and become our Savior.

• How was Jesus' existence on earth different from everyone else's? Why are these differences important?

Answers may vary, but bring out that Jesus was the Only Begotten Son of Heavenly Father (Heavenly Father was the father of Jesus' physical body as well as his spirit) and that he was the only person to lead a sinless life on earth. Explain that these two qualities—his Godhood and his sinlessness—were necessary to enable Christ to atone for our sins and be our Savior.

• What does the word *atone* mean? (As used in the scriptures, to atone is to "correct or overcome the consequences of sin" and make "at one" people who have been separated [see "Atonement," Bible Dictionary, 617].)

• How does Jesus Christ's Atonement help us become "at one" with Heavenly Father?

Refer to the four pictures shown earlier in the lesson. Explain that eternal law, or justice, requires that whoever violates a law must be punished. Through his suffering in the Garden of Gethsemane and his death on the cross, Jesus Christ took upon himself the punishment for the sins of everyone who ever lived on the earth. Because of this Atonement, we can repent of our sins, be freed from guilt, and be worthy to dwell with Heavenly Father again.

Because of Jesus Christ We Can Be Saved If We Repent

Video presentation

Show the video segment "The Mediator." If the videocassette is not available, read or tell the story in the fourth enrichment activity. Before you start the video or tell the story, you may need to explain that a debtor is someone who borrows or owes money, and a creditor is someone who lends money.

Discussion

After you have shown the video or shared the story, explain that this story is a parable symbolizing our relationship with our Savior.

- Who does the debtor represent? (Each of us.)

- What does the creditor represent? (The laws of justice.)

- Who does the debtor's friend represent? (Jesus Christ.)

Explain that when we agreed to come to earth and receive bodies, we knew that we would sometimes make wrong decisions. Our sins are like the debt of the man in the story. The laws of justice demand that our sins be paid for if we are to return to live with Heavenly Father again. Because Jesus was sinless and the Only Begotten Son of Heavenly Father, he was the only one who could atone for our sins and satisfy justice.

- In the story, the mediator (the debtor's friend) said he would become the debtor's new creditor. The debt would be repaid on his terms. What terms has Christ set for us? In other words, what must we do to receive all the blessings of Christ's Atonement?

Scripture discussion

To help class members find the answer, have three class members each read aloud one of the following scriptures: John 3:16, 2 Nephi 9:21–22, and Doctrine and Covenants 19:16.

Explain that because of Christ's Atonement for us, we are unconditionally saved from physical death. Everyone will be resurrected. But in order to be saved from spiritual death and be with Heavenly Father again, we must believe in Christ, follow and obey him, and repent of our sins.

- What will happen to us if we do not repent of our sins? (See D&C 19:17–18; we will have to suffer for our own sins.)

- What would have happened to the debtor in the story if his friend had not offered to help him? (He would have gone to prison and had all his possessions taken away.) What would happen to us if Jesus Christ had not atoned for us? (See 2 Nephi 9:7–9; we would not be resurrected, and our sins in this life would keep us out of the presence of Heavenly Father forever.)

- How do you feel, knowing that Jesus Christ has paid the price for your sins? (Invite class members to answer this question to themselves if they do not wish to share their feelings with the class.)

Testimony	Testify of the Savior's love for each class member, which he showed by atoning for our sins. Express your gratitude for his Atonement.
	Urge class members to follow Jesus Christ and repent of their sins so they may receive the full blessings of Christ's Atonement.

Enrichment Activities	You may want to use one or more of these activities during the lesson.

1. Bring to class the front page of a major newspaper in your area. Point out that the front page is reserved for the most important events of the day.

   - If a newspaper company released a special issue covering the entire history of the world, what stories do you think would be on the front page?

   Have a class member read the following statement from Elder Neal A. Maxwell of the Quorum of the Twelve Apostles:

   "The wondrous and glorious Atonement was the central act in all of human history" (in Conference Report, Apr. 1985, 93; or *Ensign*, May 1985, 73.)

   - Why was the Atonement the most important event in history?

   - How can knowing about the Atonement help you deal with the bad news and terrible events that are frequently reported in the newspaper?

2. Help class members memorize the third article of faith.

3. Sing or listen to a recording of "I Stand All Amazed" (*Hymns*, no. 193) or "How Great the Wisdom and the Love" (*Hymns*, no. 195).

4. If the videocassette called for in the lesson is not available, tell the following story by Elder Boyd K. Packer (this is the same story presented on the videocassette):

   "Let me tell you a story—a parable.

   "There once was a man who wanted something very much. It seemed more important than anything else in his life. In order for him to have his desire, he incurred a great debt.

   "He had been warned about going into that much debt, and particularly about his creditor. But it seemed so important for him to do what he wanted to do and to have what he wanted right now. He was sure he could pay for it later.

   "So he signed a contract. He would pay it off some time along the way. He didn't worry too much about it, for the due date seemed such a long time away. He had what he wanted now, and that was what seemed important.

   "The creditor was always somewhere in the back of his mind, and he made token payments now and again, thinking somehow that the day of reckoning really would never come.

   "But as it always does, the day came, and the contract fell due. The debt had not been fully paid. His creditor appeared and demanded payment in full. Only then did he realize that his creditor not only had the power to repossess all that he owned, but the power to cast him into prison as well.

"'I cannot pay you, for I have not the power to do so,' he confessed.

"'Then,' said the creditor, 'we will exercise the contract, take your possessions, and you shall go to prison. You agreed to that. It was your choice. You signed the contract, and now it must be enforced.'

"'Can you not extend the time or forgive the debt?' the debtor begged. 'Arrange some way for me to keep what I have and not go to prison. Surely you believe in mercy? Will you not show mercy?'

"The creditor replied, 'Mercy is always so one-sided. It would serve only you. If I show mercy to you, it will leave me unpaid. It is justice I demand. Do you believe in justice?'

"'I believed in justice when I signed the contract,' the debtor said. 'It was on my side then, for I thought it would protect me. I did not need mercy then, nor think I should need it ever. Justice, I thought, would serve both of us equally as well.'

"'It is justice that demands that you pay the contract or suffer the penalty,' the creditor replied. 'That is the law. You have agreed to it and that is the way it must be. Mercy cannot rob justice.'

"There they were: One meting out justice, the other pleading for mercy. Neither could prevail except at the expense of the other.

"'If you do not forgive the debt there will be no mercy,' the debtor pleaded.

"'If I do, there will be no justice,' was the reply.

"Both laws, it seemed, could not be served. They are two eternal ideals that appear to contradict one another. Is there no way for justice to be fully served, and mercy also?

"There is a way! The law of justice *can* be fully satisfied and mercy *can* be fully extended—but it takes someone else. And so it happened this time.

"The debtor had a friend. He came to help. He knew the debtor well. He knew him to be shortsighted. He thought him foolish to have gotten himself into such a predicament. Nevertheless, he wanted to help because he loved him. He stepped between them, faced the creditor, and made this offer.

"'I will pay the debt if you will free the debtor from his contract so that he may keep his possessions and not go to prison.'

"As the creditor was pondering the offer, the mediator added, 'You demanded justice. Though he cannot pay you, I will do so. You will have been justly dealt with and can ask no more. It would not be just.'

"And so the creditor agreed.

"The mediator turned then to the debtor. 'If I pay your debt, will you accept me as your creditor?'

"'Oh yes, yes,' cried the debtor. 'You save me from prison and show mercy to me.'

21

"'Then,' said the benefactor, 'you will pay the debt to me and I will set the terms. It will not be easy, but it will be possible. I will provide a way. You need not go to prison.'

"And so it was that the creditor was paid in full. He had been justly dealt with. No contract had been broken.

"The debtor, in turn, had been extended mercy. Both laws stood fulfilled. Because there was a mediator, justice had claimed its full share, and mercy was fully satisfied" (in Conference Report, Apr. 1977, 79–80; or *Ensign,* May 1977, 54–55).

Mortality: A Time to Learn through Experience

Lesson

5

Purpose

To help class members understand that mortality is a part of God's plan, a time for us to receive a physical body and learn by experience.

Preparation

1. Prayerfully study 2 Peter 1:5–7; 2 Nephi 31:16; Alma 34:32; Doctrine and Covenants 4:2; 88:123; 121:9; 130:18–19.

2. Make a poster of the following quotation (from *The Teachings of Spencer W. Kimball,* ed. Edward L. Kimball [1982], 25):

   "God has given us a plan. He has sent us all to earth to obtain bodies and to gain experience and growth." —President Spencer W. Kimball

   If it is not feasible to make a poster, plan to read the quotation aloud during the lesson.

3. Materials needed:
   a. The plan of salvation chart from lesson 2.
   b. A set of scriptures and a scripture marking pencil for each class member. Continue to encourage class members to bring their own scriptures to class each week.

Note to the teacher

With the many pressures of daily life, it is sometimes easy to lose sight of the significance of mortality. Earth life is a time to learn. We obtain our bodies, tabernacles for our spirits, and then learn to control them. Help class members understand that "this life is the time . . . to prepare to meet God" (Alma 34:32).

Suggested Lesson Development

Earth Life Is a School

Chart and poster discussion

Display the chart of the plan of salvation. Also display the poster containing the quotation from President Kimball, but turn it away from class members so they cannot see the quotation. Referring to the chart, ask:

• What stage of the plan of salvation are we in right now?

Have a class member point out mortality, or earth life.

• Why are we here on earth? Why is mortality an important part of the plan of salvation?

After class members have had a few moments to respond, turn over the poster and have a class member read President Kimball's statement (if you did not make a poster, read the quotation out of the manual). Remind class members that President Kimball was the twelfth President of the Church. Explain that as President Kimball said, two important reasons we have come to earth are to

23

receive a body and to gain experience. As spirits in the pre-earth life we had learned much, but to continue to progress we needed to come to earth and receive bodies.

Quotation

Have a class member read the following statement by President Kimball:

"My brothers and sisters, we're away from home. We're off to school. Our lessons will not be easy. The way we react to them, the way we conquer and accomplish and live will determine our rewards, and they will be permanent and eternal. . . .

"You are sent to this world with a very serious purpose. You are sent to school, for that matter, to begin as a human infant and grow to unbelievable proportions in wisdom, judgment, knowledge, and power" (*The Teachings of Spencer W. Kimball*, 28, 31).

Chalkboard discussion

- What home is President Kimball referring to when he says "we're away from home"? (Our home with our Father in Heaven.)

- What is the school President Kimball is referring to? (Mortality.)

- What have you learned already in your years in this school?

Have class members take turns naming things they have learned, and list their answers in a column on the chalkboard. Continue for two or three minutes or until class members cannot think of any more answers.

Refer again to the poster containing President Kimball's statement. Explain that some of the things we need to learn and some of the experiences we have on earth are directly related to having a body. Our bodies are great blessings to us, but we must learn to control them and use them righteously.

Point out a few physical skills listed on the chalkboard, such as walking and talking.

- How can these skills be used righteously? (We should use our physical abilities in keeping with God's commandments. For example, we should not use our ability to walk to take us into places where we should not be, and we should not use our ability to talk to lie or take the Lord's name in vain.)

Explain that learning to control our bodies and use them righteously also includes learning to control our appetites and desires. Commandments such as the Word of Wisdom and the law of chastity help us use our bodies righteously.

We Must Prepare to Meet God

Chalkboard discussion

Explain that we have much to learn in this earthly school before we will be ready to return home to Heavenly Father. Have class members turn to Alma 34:32, and ask a class member to read it aloud.

- What do you think we need to learn to be prepared to meet God?

List class members' answers on the chalkboard next to the list of what they have already learned. (If class members have difficulty thinking of answers, have them look up 2 Peter 1:5–7 and 2 Nephi 31:16 and use the qualities mentioned in these verses to begin the list.)

Scripture discussion	Explain that the different circumstances and situations we experience in life help us learn different things to prepare us to live with Heavenly Father again. List on the chalkboard the four situations below and the corresponding scripture references. Have class members find and read the scriptures to discover things those situations can teach us. (You may want to divide class members into four groups and have each group look up one scripture.)

For example, being part of a family helps us learn love and unselfishness (note that the answers in parentheses are not the only appropriate answers; class members may think of other things these situations can teach us).

Family: Doctrine and Covenants 88:123 (love and unselfishness)

Church callings: Doctrine and Covenants 4:2 (service)

Friends: Doctrine and Covenants 121:9 (loyalty)

School, Church, and seminary classes: Doctrine and Covenants 130:18–19 (knowledge and understanding)

Have class members look again at the list of things necessary to be prepared to meet God, and have them think of a situation or experience that has helped them learn one of these lessons. (For example, caring for a younger sibling may have helped them learn patience; dealing with a disability may have helped them learn compassion; experiencing disappointment or failure may have helped them learn persistence.) Invite them to tell the other class members about the experience and what they learned.

Whether class members share the experience or not, encourage them to record the experience and what they learned from it in their journals when they get home, if they have not done so already.

Our Vision Is Limited

Story and discussion	Remind class members that our earthly experiences are a part of our eternal life. We have a limited vision of eternity right now, but after we die, we will better understand the importance of mortality as a time to learn.

Ask students to imagine that they are standing inside a lighted room, looking out a window into the night.

• What can you see?

Read or tell the following story told by President Kimball about an experience he had before he became President of the Church:

"While in the city of Honolulu, we stayed in a room which was enclosed in glass on three sides. The light in the room illumined it and we could see the shining glass, the beautiful furniture, ceiling, floor, walls, the vases and other ornaments, everything in the room only. Our vision was limited to the small room and its contents. And then we turned out the lights and went to the window and through that window, which before had been the end of our vision, now we could see clearly over the housetops, over the trees, to the thoroughfares beneath with their many street lights, studded with the lights of automobiles, and beyond that we could see the seashore and the great hotels and Waikiki Beach, the Punchbowl and Old Diamond Head with their craters, and the great ocean with its ships carrying the commerce of the world.

"[This] is like eternity. Here [on earth] we are limited in our visions. With our eyes we can see but a few miles. With our ears we can hear but a few years. We are encased, enclosed, as it were, in a room, but when our light goes out of this life, then we see beyond mortal limitations. . . .

"The walls go down, time ends and distance fades and vanishes as we go into eternity . . . and we immediately emerge into a great world in which there are no earthly limitations comparable to ours as to time, distance, or speed" (*The Teachings of Spencer W. Kimball,* 40–41).

- How can the knowledge that we have of eternal life help us use mortality as a time to learn and gain experience?

Remind class members that President Kimball said that "our lessons [in this life] will not be easy," but point out that the reward we can gain from learning these lessons—exaltation—is worth the effort required.

Testimony

Express your gratitude for the experiences you have had in life and what they have taught you. Testify that Heavenly Father made mortality a time to learn and grow because he loves us.

Encourage class members to look at all their experiences as challenging opportunities to learn and grow.

Enrichment Activities

You may want to use one or more of these activities during the lesson.

1. Teach class members that both good and bad experiences help us learn and grow. Ask class members to think of the worst thing that happened to them in the past week. Then ask them to think of one lesson, however small, that they could learn from that experience.

   Then have class members think of the best thing that happened to them in the past week and what they could learn from that experience. Invite class members to share, if appropriate, their worst or best experience and what they learned from it.

2. With class members, sing or read the words to "Teach Me to Walk in the Light" (*Hymns,* no. 304). Discuss with class members how parents and teachers can help us learn and gain experience.

   Note to the teacher: Singing hymns or Primary songs with your class can help bring the Spirit, and the Spirit will witness to the truths you have taught. (See Teaching— No Greater Call, *137–38.)*

3. Before class, write each phrase from the following list on a separate card. In class, mix the cards up and lay them face down on a table or the floor. Divide class members into teams. Have the teams take turns trying to choose two cards that match (make a complete and accurate statement). If the cards match, the team keeps the cards and takes another turn. If the cards do not

match, the team turns them face down in the same places, and the next team takes a turn. Continue until all the matches have been made.

Matches:

This life is the time	to prepare to meet God.
We have come to earth to receive	a body and gain experience.
Earth life is but a part	of our eternal existence.
Our experiences on earth	help us learn.
Mortality is also called	our second estate.
The plan of salvation was designed by	Heavenly Father.
Heavenly Father chose Jesus Christ	to be our Savior.
Agency is	the power to choose.
The Fall brought about spiritual	and physical death.

4. Ask class members:

• Have you ever watched the Olympics (or another prestigious athletic competition), in person or on television?

Let class members share their experiences for a few moments. Then explain that while it is exciting to watch skillful athletic performances, few spectators realize the years of dedication, discipline, and training that each athlete must experience before he or she is ready for competition. An athlete's performance is a direct result of step-by-step progress toward an ultimate goal.

• How is life like the Olympics? (Answers may include that both require preparation and hard work for success or that both involve persistence in the face of failure.)

• How is life unlike the Olympics? (One possible answer is that in the Olympics very few athletes can receive gold medals, but each of us can receive life's highest reward.)

Explain that like Olympic athletes, we are training to reach an important goal. The "gold medal" we are seeking is exaltation in the celestial kingdom, and we can receive this reward only after showing dedication and discipline in keeping the commandments and covenants God has given us.

Lesson 6

Adversity Can Help Us Grow

Purpose	To encourage class members to see trials and adversity as opportunities for growth.

Preparation	1. Prayerfully study Matthew 7:24–27; 2 Nephi 2:11, 22–23; Doctrine and Covenants 122:7.
	2. Materials needed: A set of scriptures and a scripture marking pencil for each class member. Continue to encourage class members to bring their own scriptures to class each week.
Note to the teacher	*When adversity comes, a young person may sometimes feel that he or she is the only one who has ever had a problem. But all of us chose to come to the earth to be tested and tried, and the adversities we face give us the opportunity to grow and progress. Help class members see that understanding why we experience adversity can help us learn from our trials and disappointments.*

Suggested Lesson Development	**How Do You React to Adversity?**
Story and discussion	Tell or read the following story:

Diane Ellingson loved gymnastics. She worked hard to develop her talent, and she won national (United States) championships while she was in high school and college. She was planning to participate in a national gymnastics tour with several famous gymnasts, but during practice for that tour she came off a vault and landed wrong, breaking her neck. The injury paralyzed her. She would never participate in gymnastics again; she would never even be able to walk again.

• How would you react if something like this happened to you?

Give class members a few moments to respond, then finish the story:

Diane spent five months in the hospital after her accident. During the first few months, she felt despair and frustration. She received a priesthood blessing, which did not promise her that she would be healed but did bring her great peace. Finally she realized, "I can either give up or get on with my life." She learned to use a wheelchair and take care of herself again. After she got out of the hospital, she went back to college, graduated, and became an elementary school teacher. She also gives talks to young people to help them overcome discouragement and adversity. Diane says, "People always think, 'You're so amazing, you're so incredible,' but I'm not. . . . You have to take whatever life gives you and deal with it, even if you might not want to. . . . You just learn and that's what's so great about time and the healing process. You don't have to be miraculous." (See Kendra Kasl Phair, "A Champion Again," *New Era,* Nov. 1988, 21–25; see also Renon Klossner Hulet, "Matters of Balance," *Ensign,* Dec. 1992, 63.)

Why Do We Experience Adversity?

Discussion

Remind class members that a few weeks ago they learned about Adam and Eve (see lesson 3).

- What was life like for Adam and Eve in the Garden of Eden? (They did not experience sorrow, pain, sickness, or death; food grew without their effort.)

- What was life like for Adam and Eve after they were cast out of the Garden of Eden? (They had to work hard to grow food and get other things they needed; they became subject to sorrow, pain, sickness, and death.)

Explain that like Adam and Eve after the Fall, we too must work hard, and we will experience sorrow, pain, sickness, and death. When we chose to receive a body and come to earth, we also chose to face adversity. Although our trials are different, every person on the earth faces some kind of adversity.

- Why must we experience adversity?

Quotation

Read or have a class member read the following statement by Elder Richard G. Scott of the Quorum of the Twelve Apostles:

"Trials, disappointments, sadness, and heartache come to us from two basically different sources. Those who transgress the laws of God will always have those challenges. The other reason for adversity is to accomplish the Lord's own purposes in our life that we may receive the refinement that comes from testing. . . . [Some trials] are evidence that the Lord feels you are prepared to grow more" (in Conference Report, Oct. 1995, 18; or *Ensign*, Nov. 1995, 16).

Chalkboard discussion

Point out that we can avoid the adversity that comes from the first source, disobedience to the commandments of God. We do this by making righteous choices.

- What kinds of adversity can we choose to avoid?

List class members' responses in a column on the chalkboard. Responses may include bad health or addiction because of breaking the Word of Wisdom, family quarrels because of selfishness and greed, guilt or punishment because of breaking the law of the land, or any other adversity brought on by our own poor choices.

Explain that if we are facing adversity that comes from sin, we should work toward repenting of that sin. Repenting of the sin will help remove or reduce the adversity. (You may need to point out that sometimes we face adversity brought on by other people's sins. Because each person is free to choose his or her own actions, this kind of adversity comes under the second category, below.)

- What kinds of adversity might come to us regardless of our own choices?

List class members' responses in a second column on the chalkboard. Responses may include many kinds of disease or disability, injuries or financial losses caused by accidents or weather, and disappointment from not receiving a hoped-for opportunity or blessing.

Explain that while we cannot choose to avoid these kinds of trials, we can determine how we will react to them. If we regard our trials as opportunities to learn and grow, they can become blessings for us.

We Can Learn and Grow through Adversity

Scripture discussion

Explain that Lehi's son Jacob suffered trials and sorrow because of his older brothers (see 2 Nephi 2:1). Lehi explained to Jacob why we need affliction and adversity to learn.

Have class members read and mark (in their own scriptures) 2 Nephi 2:11, 22–23.

- Why must we know misery in order to know joy?

- What are some other opposites we learn about through adversity? (Answers may include sickness and health or sinfulness and righteousness.)

- How have your trials helped you appreciate your blessings?

Chalkboard discussion

Write two headings on the chalkboard: *Trial* and *Lessons to Be Learned*.

Ask class members to suggest some trials people their age might suffer. List these on the chalkboard under the first heading. The list could include doing poorly on a school assignment, breaking an arm or a leg, losing a game, moving away from friends, facing the death of a loved one, or having a long or debilitating disease.

Then discuss with class members lessons that can be learned through each trial. For example, losing a game may teach us humility or give us greater empathy for others who experience disappointment. The death of a loved one may increase our testimony of the plan of salvation. List these lessons on the chalkboard under the second heading, and discuss how each lesson can help us become more like our Father in Heaven and our Savior.

We Can Prepare for Adversity

Quotation and discussion

Have a class member read the following statement by Elder Scott:

"Life never was intended to be easy. Rather, it is a period of proving and growth. It is interwoven with difficulties, challenges, and burdens. . . . Yet these very forces, if squarely faced, provide opportunity for tremendous personal growth and development. The conquering of adversity produces strength of character, forges self-confidence, engenders self-respect, and assures success in righteous endeavor" (in Conference Report, Oct. 1981, 13; or *Ensign,* Nov. 1981, 11).

- How can we conquer adversity? (Use the discussion in the rest of this section to help class members answer this question.)

Scripture discussion

Have class members read and mark Matthew 7:24–27.

- How did the man who built his house upon the rock differ from the man who built his house upon sand?

Point out that both houses had to endure the same storms. The difference was the foundation: the house built on the rock was able to weather the storm, while the house built on sand was not.

- What does the rock represent in this parable? (See Matthew 7:24; the teachings of Jesus Christ.) How can faith in Jesus Christ help us in times of adversity?

Discussion

- Although we do not know what specific kinds of adversity we may experience in the future, what can we do to prepare and strengthen ourselves to face adversity?

List class members' responses on the chalkboard. Make sure the following general principles are brought out in the discussion:

1. Everyone will face adversity. When we chose to come to earth, we knew we would be tried and tested here. Realizing that we were willing to endure adversity can help us prepare for and deal with adversity.

2. The best way to prepare for adversity is to build a house upon the rock—to keep the commandments and live according to the doctrines and principles of the gospel.

3. Sincere prayer helps us endure adversity. Sometimes when we are faced with a trial we don't feel like praying, but if we are in the habit of praying sincerely, it will be easier to pray for strength to overcome the trial.

4. In times of adversity we can obtain help from others, such as our parents and other family members, home teachers, and Church leaders. Establishing good relationships with these people before times of adversity will make it easier to turn to them when we need help.

Testimony

Remind class members that everyone faces adversity. Have a class member read aloud Doctrine and Covenants 122:7 to find out what the Lord told Joseph Smith in Liberty Jail about the adversity and afflictions he was facing.

Testify that the adversity we face can help us learn and grow and can be for our good. You may want to tell about some kind of adversity you have faced and how you grew from the experience.

Encourage class members to treat their trials as opportunities to learn and grow.

Enrichment Activities

You may want to use one or more of these activities during the lesson.

1. Make copies of the crossword puzzle on page 33. Give each class member or pair of class members a copy of the puzzle, and have them look up the scriptures to complete the puzzle. Or put the puzzle on the chalkboard and have the entire class work together to solve it.

   Answers:

   Across: 1-Smith; 3-peace; 4-Liberty; 6-experience; 7-trust; 8-gain.
   Down: 1-small; 2-endure; 3-patient; 5-blessing.

2. Place a lightweight ball (such as a table tennis ball) in the bottom of a large glass jar with a lid. Fill the rest of the jar with uncooked wheat or rice, and put the lid on. Shake the jar up and down. As you do so, the ball will gradually rise to the top of the jar.

   Explain that though the ball started at the bottom of the jar, it rose to the top because it is lighter than the wheat that surrounds it. Similarly, if we keep a positive attitude about our trials, we can rise above them instead of being kept down by them.

3. Explain that when we face adversity, it is helpful to remember that Heavenly Father loves us and knows what is best for us. While we may not understand how a particular trial or experience can be for our good, Heavenly Father does understand, and he will help us understand in his own time.

Read or have a class member read the following story told by Elder Hugh B. Brown, who was a member of the Quorum of the Twelve Apostles:

"I was living up in Canada. I had purchased a farm. . . . I went out one morning and saw a currant bush. It had grown up over six feet high. It was going all to wood. There were no blossoms and no currants. I was raised on a fruit farm . . . and I knew what ought to happen to that currant bush. So I got some pruning shears and went after it, and I cut it down, and pruned it, and clipped it back until there was nothing left but a little clump of stumps. It was just coming daylight, and I thought I saw on top of each of these little stumps what appeared to be a tear, and I thought the currant bush was crying. . . . I looked at it, and smiled, and said, 'What are you crying about?' You know, I thought I heard that currant bush talk, and I thought I heard it say this: 'How could you do this to me? I was making such wonderful growth. I was almost as big as the shade tree and the fruit tree that are inside the fence, and now you have cut me down.' . . . I said, 'Look, little currant bush, I am the gardener here, and I know what I want you to be. I didn't intend you to be a fruit tree or a shade tree. I want you to be a currant bush, and some day, little currant bush, when you are laden with fruit, you are going to say, "Thank you, Mr. Gardener"'" ("The Currant Bush," *New Era,* Jan. 1973, 14).

- How did the gardener show his concern for the currant bush? (He cut it back so that it could produce currants again.)

- How are we like the currant bush? Who is like the gardener?

Explain that Elder Brown followed the story about the currant bush with a similar story from his own life. He had been bitterly disappointed when he was denied a promotion because he was a member of the Church. Years later, he looked back and realized that his life was better than it would have been if he had received the promotion. He was a stronger member of the Church and more the person that Heavenly Father wanted him to be.

Testify that Heavenly Father loves us and knows what is best for each of us. If we strive to live righteously and learn as we endure our trials, these trials will be for our good and help us become the people Heavenly Father wants us to be.

Crossword Puzzle

Complete the crossword puzzle by filling in the blanks in the following statements.

Across

1. The first President of The Church of Jesus Christ of Latter-day Saints was Joseph _____ .

3. D&C 121:7: "My son, _____ be unto thy soul."

4. Joseph received the revelations found in D&C 121 and 122 in _____ Jail.

6. D&C 122:7: ". . . all these things shall give thee _____ ."

7. Proverbs 3:5: "_____ in the Lord."

8. 2 Nephi 2:2: ". . . he shall consecrate thine afflictions for thy _____ ."

Down

1. D&C 121:7: ". . . thine adversity and thine afflictions shall be but a _____ moment."

2. D&C 24:8: ". . . thou shalt have many [afflictions]; but _____ them."

3. D&C 24:8: "Be _____ in afflictions."

5. D&C 103:12: "After much tribulation . . . cometh the _____ ."

Lesson 7

What Happens after Death?

Purpose	To help class members understand that death is a temporary separation of the spirit from the body and that during this period of separation, spirits dwell in a place called the spirit world.

Preparation	1. Prayerfully study 1 Peter 3:18–20; Alma 34:34; 40:11–14; Doctrine and Covenants 88:15–16; 138:29–34, 57. You may also want to study the rest of Doctrine and Covenants 138.
	2. Copy the chart on page 35 onto the chalkboard or a piece of posterboard.
	3. Materials needed: a. A glove (not a mitten) for the object lesson. b. A set of scriptures and a scripture marking pencil for each class member. Continue to encourage class members to bring their own scriptures to class each week.
Note to the teacher	*All of us must one day die, and many of us have loved ones who have passed on and now inhabit the spirit world. Elder Robert D. Hales of the Quorum of the Twelve Apostles said that the spirit world is "a place of paradise and happiness for those who have lived righteous lives. It is not something to fear" (in Conference Report, Oct. 1996, 89; or* Ensign, *Nov. 1996, 66). People who were not able to hear the gospel on earth will receive an opportunity to hear it in the spirit world. Present this lesson with reverence and caution, avoiding speculation and sensational stories.*

Suggested Lesson Development	**Death Is the Separation of the Spirit from the Body**
Note to the teacher	*Class interest and attention are greatly enhanced when class members actively participate. Invite class members to assist you with demonstrations. Let them help with object lessons, hold up charts, or write on the chalkboard. (See* Teaching— No Greater Call, *103–4.)*
Object lesson	Introduce the lesson by using the following object lesson, which is an adaptation of a presentation by Elder Boyd K. Packer of the Quorum of the Twelve Apostles (see Conference Report, Apr. 1973, 79–80; or *Ensign,* July 1973, 51, 53):
	Have a class member come to the front of the class. Hold up a glove and point out that it has no life; it cannot move by itself. Then invite the class member to put the glove on his or her hand.
	• How might this be compared to our body and spirit?
	Explain that in this example the glove represents the physical body and the hand represents the spirit. When the spirit enters the body, the body can live, work, and act. Have the class member move his or her fingers inside the glove. A spirit combined with a physical body makes a person—a living soul.

Have class members read and mark Doctrine and Covenants 88:15–16.

Point out that earth life was not intended to last forever. One day each of us will die; our spirit and body will be separated. Death is part of God's plan. When the spirit and body are separated, the body cannot move. It has died. (Have the class member remove his or her hand from the glove.) But the spirit is still alive. (Have the class member move his or her fingers.)

Explain that as part of his Atonement, Jesus Christ overcame mortal death. Because of this, the separation of the spirit from the body will not be permanent. Each of us will be resurrected. At the time of resurrection, the body and spirit will be united forever in a perfect state. (Have the class member put the glove back on.) Explain that today you will discuss the spirit's condition between the time of death and the time of resurrection. (Have the class member remove the glove and return to his or her seat.)

Chart

Illustrate the steps from premortal life to the spirit world using the chart below. You may want to ask class members to briefly share what they remember from previous lessons about premortal life and earth life.

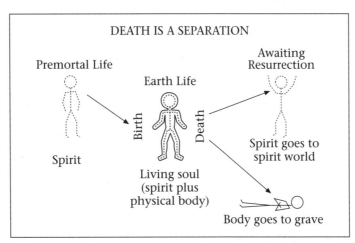

Explain that in mortality the spirit and body are joined together. As shown in the object lesson, when we die the spirit and body are separated. While the body loses its life, the spirit remains alive and dwells in a place called the spirit world.

We Go to the Spirit World between Death and Resurrection

Scripture discussion

Explain that Alma described the conditions of life after death to his son Corianton. Have class members read and mark Alma 40:11.

• Where do we go when we die?

Quotation

Tell class members that President Joseph Fielding Smith referred to Alma 40:11 when he said: "'Taken home to God,' simply means that their mortal existence has come to an end, and they have returned to the world of spirits, where they are assigned to a place according to their works with the just or with the unjust, there to await the resurrection" (*Answers to Gospel Questions,* comp. Joseph Fielding Smith Jr., 5 vols. [1957–66], 2:85).

Our Righteousness on Earth Determines Our Place in the Spirit World

Scripture
discussion

Have class members read and mark Alma 34:34.

• What will our personalities be like when we die?

Help class members see that our spirits will carry to the spirit world the same tendencies, appetites, and desires that we had when we lived on the earth.

Quotation

Have a class member read the following statement by President Brigham Young, second President of the Church:

"Suppose . . . that a man is evil in his heart—wholly given up to wickedness, and in that condition dies, his spirit will enter into the spirit world intent upon evil. On the other hand, if we are striving with all the powers and faculties God has given us to improve upon our talents, to prepare ourselves to dwell in eternal life, and the grave receives our bodies while we are thus engaged, with what disposition will our spirits enter their next state? They will be still striving to do the things of God, only in a much greater degree" (*Discourses of Brigham Young,* sel. John A. Widtsoe [1941], 379).

Scripture
discussion

Have class members read and mark Alma 40:12–14.

Explain that people who have accepted the gospel of Jesus Christ and lived righteously are assigned to a state of happiness known as paradise. People who have rejected the gospel and people who have died without a knowledge of the truth are assigned to a state of darkness called spirit prison, sometimes called hell.

• Why do you think "spirit prison" is an appropriate name for the condition of people who die without having accepted the gospel? (Because the people there are shut off from the peace and joy they would feel if they had received the truth and lived righteously.)

The Righteous Do the Lord's Work in the Spirit World

Scripture
discussion

Explain that during the three days after he was crucified, Jesus Christ visited the righteous in paradise. Have class members read and mark 1 Peter 3:18–20.

• What did Christ do among the spirits in paradise?

Have class members read and mark Doctrine and Covenants 138:29–34.

Explain that Christ appointed messengers to preach to those in spirit prison. Until that time, the spirits in spirit prison were not permitted to have contact with the spirits in paradise.

Quotation

Have someone read the following explanation by Elder Bruce R. McConkie, who was a member of the Quorum of the Twelve Apostles:

"Now that the righteous spirits in paradise have been commissioned to carry the message of salvation to the wicked spirits in hell, there is a certain amount of mingling together of the good and bad spirits. Repentance opens the prison doors to the spirits in hell; it enables those bound with the chains of hell to free themselves from darkness, unbelief, ignorance, and sin. As rapidly as they can overcome these obstacles—gain light, believe truth, acquire intelligence, cast off sin, and break the chains of hell—they can leave the hell that imprisons them and dwell with the righteous in the peace of paradise" (*Mormon Doctrine,* 2nd ed. [1966], 755).

Scripture discussion	• Who preaches to the spirits in prison? What is their message?

Have class members read and mark Doctrine and Covenants 138:57.

• What is the duty of faithful Latter-day Saints who have died?

Point out that many members of the class will be called to serve full-time missions in this life. Since the Church is organized in the spirit world and there are still spirits there who have not heard and accepted the truth, we will also be able to serve missions after death if we have lived righteously.

Testimony

Testify that death is part of the great plan of salvation. As the glove without the hand is lifeless, so the physical body without the spirit is dead. While righteous spirits await their resurrection, they are busy carrying on the work of our Heavenly Father.

Encourage class members to live righteously now so they can enter paradise later and be able to serve the Lord in the spirit world.

Enrichment Activities

You may want to use one or more of these activities during the lesson.

1. If *Family Home Evening Video Supplement 2* (53277) is available, show "Life after Death," a five-minute segment.

2. Divide the class into groups of three or four people. Appoint a leader for each group and give him or her a piece of paper and a pen or pencil. Have the groups pretend that they are in the spirit world and have an opportunity to write one piece of advice to their friends and family members who are still alive. Have the group leaders write down the groups' ideas. After about five minutes, invite the group leaders to read the advice their groups have written.

3. To emphasize the importance of living righteously in mortality, sing with class members "Today, While the Sun Shines" (*Hymns,* no. 229).

   • What does this hymn have to do with a lesson about the spirit world?

   Suggest that class members read the chorus of the hymn again, thinking of the word *today* as a representation of earth life and the word *tomorrow* as a representation of life after death.

   • With this interpretation in mind, what work must we do "today" to prepare for "tomorrow"?

Lesson 8	# The Three Kingdoms of Glory

Purpose	To encourage class members to strive for exaltation in the celestial kingdom by keeping the commandments and exercising faith in Jesus Christ.

Preparation	1. Prayerfully study John 14:2; 1 Corinthians 15:40–42; Revelation 7:9–10; 2 Nephi 25:23; Alma 3:26; Doctrine and Covenants 58:27–28; 76:32–89, 98–106; 82:10; 131:1–4; 137:7–10; 138:29–34; Articles of Faith 1:3.
	2. Make a copy for each class member of the quiz "The Truth about Heaven and Hell," found at the end of the lesson (page 43). If it is not feasible to make copies, bring a blank piece of paper for each class member.
	3. Materials needed: a. A pen or pencil for each class member. b. A set of scriptures and a scripture marking pencil for each class member. Continue to encourage class members to bring their own scriptures to class each week.
Note to the teacher	*The extent of our obedience to the laws and ordinances of the gospel determines the glory we will receive after we are resurrected. Encourage class members to have as their goal exaltation in the highest kingdom, the celestial kingdom, where we can experience a fulness of happiness.*

Suggested Lesson Development	**The Truth about Heaven and Hell**
Quiz	Give each class member a pen or pencil and a copy of the quiz. Have class members mark each statement as "True" or "False." (If you have not made copies of the quiz, give each class member a blank piece of paper and have them write their answers as you read the statements.)
Scripture discussion	After everyone has completed the quiz, discuss each answer until you are sure everyone understands it well. Following are the statements and answers with some suggestions for discussion:

1. After we have been resurrected and judged, each of us will dwell in one of three kingdoms of glory.

True. Just as there are different degrees of righteousness on the earth, there are kingdoms of differing glory in the next life: the celestial kingdom is the highest, followed by the terrestrial and the telestial. To reward many different levels of faithfulness, there will be "many mansions" (see John 14:2).

2. God has already determined which kingdom each of us will inherit, no matter what we do.

False. We are agents unto ourselves (see D&C 58:27–28). This means that we are responsible for the choices we make. We will be judged by our thoughts and actions. Have a class member read the following statement by Elder Russell M. Nelson of the Quorum of the Twelve Apostles:

"Each of you will be judged according to your individual works and the desires of your hearts. . . . Your eventual placement in the celestial, terrestrial, or telestial kingdom will not be determined by chance. The Lord has prescribed unchanging requirements for each. You can know what the scriptures teach and pattern your lives accordingly" (in Conference Report, Oct. 1993, 48; or *Ensign,* Nov. 1993, 35).

3. All you have to do to get to the celestial kingdom is say that you believe in Jesus Christ.

False. We must do more than just say we believe in Jesus Christ; we must follow him. All people, regardless of their level of righteousness, will be saved from death because of the Resurrection of Christ. However, in order to attain the highest degree of glory in the resurrection, we need to "come unto Christ, and be perfected in him" (Moroni 10:32). We come unto Christ by having faith in him, repenting of our sins, being baptized, receiving the gift of the Holy Ghost, receiving other saving priesthood ordinances, obeying the commandments, and keeping the covenants we make with our Heavenly Father. How we live *does* make a difference.

Have class members read, mark, and discuss Alma 3:26.

4. To be damned is to be stopped or held back from blessings we might have received if we had obeyed God's commandments.

True. When we sin, we prevent our own progress. Our Heavenly Father wants to bless us. However, because he is just, he will reward us only when we obey his commandments (see D&C 82:10).

5. Hell is a place of never-ending suffering where sinners go. Most of mankind will be there forever because of their wickedness.

False. Hell, or spirit prison, is a place for people who have rejected the gospel and people who have died without a knowledge of the gospel. The gospel is preached to them there, and those who accept the gospel and repent of their sins will be released and allowed to enter paradise until the Resurrection and Judgment (see D&C 138:29–34). Most of those who do not accept the gospel there will have to suffer for their own sins but will eventually be resurrected and go to a kingdom of glory (see D&C 76:81–85, 98–106).

6. A great multitude of Heavenly Father's children will dwell in the celestial kingdom.

True. See Revelation 7:9–10, in which John describes his vision of the exalted sons and daughters of God.

7. There are three degrees of glory in the celestial kingdom. In order to receive the highest of these degrees, a person must be sealed to his or her spouse in the temple.

True. Have class members read, mark, and discuss Doctrine and Covenants 131:1–4. Then have a class member read the following statement by Elder Dallin H. Oaks of the Quorum of the Twelve Apostles about the highest degree of the celestial kingdom:

"Those who have met the highest requirements for this kingdom, including faithfulness to covenants made in a temple of God and marriage for eternity, will be exalted to the godlike state referred to as the 'fulness' of the Father or eternal life (D&C 76:56, 94; see also D&C 131; 132:19–20). . . . Eternal life is family life with a loving Father in Heaven and with our progenitors [ancestors] and our posterity" (in Conference Report, Apr. 1995, 115; or *Ensign,* May 1995, 86–87).

Be sure to emphasize that temple marriage is not a guarantee of exaltation in the celestial kingdom. Those married in the temple should strive to be exalted together in the celestial kingdom by continually growing in their love for each other and for the Lord.

8. God loves all his children and will give them the greatest reward that they have prepared for through their obedience and their faith in Jesus Christ.

True. Have class members read and mark Doctrine and Covenants 76:89, and point out that even the telestial kingdom, the lowest of the three kingdoms, is a place of indescribable glory.

Note to the teacher	*Class members may ask questions that you are unable to answer. If this happens, tell them that you do not know the answer to the question but will try to find an answer (see* Teaching—No Greater Call, *85). Then follow up on your promise, and be sure to tell class members the answer to the question when you have found it. If in your study you find that an answer to the question has not been revealed, avoid speculation. In such a circumstance, follow up on your promise by telling class members that the answer has not been revealed.*

The Three Kingdoms of Glory

Scripture discussion	Explain that the Apostle Paul taught about the three kingdoms of glory. Have class members read and mark 1 Corinthians 15:40–42 (note that in the Joseph Smith Translation of verse 40, Paul also mentions "bodies telestial").

• How did Paul describe the differences in the glory of the celestial kingdom, the terrestrial kingdom, and the telestial kingdom? (See 1 Corinthians 15:41. He compared the celestial to the sun, the terrestrial to the moon, and the telestial to the stars.) What do these comparisons tell us about the differences between the kingdoms?

Scripture and chalkboard discussion	Explain that through the Prophet Joseph Smith we have received a more detailed definition of the three kingdoms of glory. He and Sidney Rigdon, who later became First Counselor in the First Presidency, were given a vision in which they saw each of the kingdoms of glory. They also received a revelation concerning the people who would go to each of the kingdoms.

Divide class members into three groups. Have the first group read about the telestial kingdom (see Doctrine and Covenants 76:81–83, 98–103). Have the second group read about the terrestrial kingdom (see Doctrine and Covenants 76:71–80). Have the third group read about the celestial kingdom (see Doctrine and Covenants 76:50–70; 137:7–10). Ask the group members to work together to find information about the people who will dwell in each of the kingdoms of glory. Encourage them to mark words or phrases that they think are important. Give them four or five minutes to work together. Then list on the chalkboard the qualifications they have found. Your chart should look something like this (you may abbreviate the chart as necessary):

WHO WILL INHERIT TELESTIAL GLORY? (D&C 76:81–83, 98–103)

Those who:
    a. Reject the gospel (D&C 76:82, 101).
    b. Reject the testimony of Jesus (D&C 76:82–83, 101).
    c. Are liars, sorcerers, adulterers, and whoremongers (D&C 76:103).

WHO WILL INHERIT TERRESTRIAL GLORY? (D&C 76:71–80)

Those who:
    a. Reject the gospel in this life but receive it in the spirit world (D&C 76:71–74).
    b. Are honorable but are blinded by the craftiness of men (D&C 76:75).
    c. Are not valiant in the testimony of Jesus (D&C 76:79).

HOW CAN WE INHERIT CELESTIAL GLORY? (D&C 76:50–70)

We must:
    a. Receive the testimony of Jesus (D&C 76:51).
    b. Be baptized by one with priesthood authority (D&C 76:51).
    c. Keep the commandments (D&C 76:52).
    d. Receive the gift of the Holy Ghost (D&C 76:52–53).
    e. Overcome the world by faith (D&C 76:53).
    f. Be made perfect through the Atonement of Jesus Christ (D&C 76:69).

WHO ELSE WILL INHERIT CELESTIAL GLORY? (D&C 137:7–10)

Those who:
    g. Die without a knowledge of the gospel but "would have received it with all their hearts" (D&C 137:7–9).

And those who:
    h. "Die before they arrive at the years of accountability" (D&C 137:10).

Have class members review Doctrine and Covenants 76:69–70. Emphasize that no one but Jesus Christ will ever live a perfect life. Since we cannot be perfect on our own, we must be "made perfect."

- How can we be made perfect so we can dwell in the celestial kingdom? (See 2 Nephi 25:23; Articles of Faith 1:3.)

Explain that we can be made perfect only through the Atonement of Jesus Christ. As we do all we can to follow the Savior, working diligently to keep the commandments and to live pure lives, we come closer to him and become more like him. When we sin, we can repent sincerely and be forgiven. Because Jesus Christ took our sins upon himself, we can be made clean, pure, and worthy to dwell in the celestial kingdom.

Testimony

Testify that Heavenly Father has prepared great things for us. Express your gratitude for the plan of salvation and for the Atonement of Jesus Christ. Encourage class members to keep the commandments, repent of their sins, and be true to their covenants so they can be "made perfect through Jesus" and inherit a place in the celestial kingdom.

Enrichment Activities

You may want to use one or more of these activities during the lesson.

1. After bearing your testimony, give class members an opportunity to express how they feel about the promised blessings of exaltation in the celestial kingdom. If time permits, invite each person to express one idea he or she has learned or felt more deeply because of this lesson.

2. With class members, sing or read the words to all four verses of "O My Father" (*Hymns,* no. 292). Have class members look for connections between the words of the hymn and the truths they have learned from this lesson. Give close attention to the fourth verse.

3. Have class members memorize 1 Corinthians 2:9. To help them memorize the verse, write the following numbers and phrases on separate strips of paper (adjust the numbers of strips to match the number of class members):

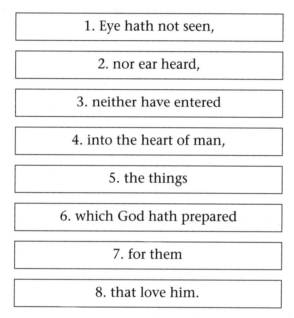

| 1. Eye hath not seen, |
| 2. nor ear heard, |
| 3. neither have entered |
| 4. into the heart of man, |
| 5. the things |
| 6. which God hath prepared |
| 7. for them |
| 8. that love him. |

Give a strip of paper to each class member and have class members read the phrases in order according to the number before each phrase. Then collect the papers and hand them out in a different order. Once again, have class members read the phrases in order according to the number before each phrase. Continue this process until class members can recite the verse without looking at the papers.

Testify to class members that the blessings of the celestial kingdom are wonderful beyond what we can imagine. Encourage class members to seek these blessings.

The Truth about Heaven and Hell

Place a *T* for *True* or an *F* for *False* beside each number.

_____ 1. After we have been resurrected and judged, each of us will dwell in one of three kingdoms of glory.

_____ 2. God has already determined which kingdom each of us will inherit, no matter what we do.

_____ 3. All you have to do to get to the celestial kingdom is say that you believe in Jesus Christ.

_____ 4. To be damned is to be stopped or held back from blessings we might have received if we had obeyed God's commandments.

_____ 5. Hell is a place of never-ending suffering where sinners go. Most of mankind will be there forever because of their wickedness.

_____ 6. A great multitude of Heavenly Father's children will dwell in the celestial kingdom.

_____ 7. There are three degrees of glory in the celestial kingdom. In order to receive the highest of these degrees, a person must be sealed to his or her spouse in the temple.

_____ 8. God loves all his children and will give them the greatest reward that they have prepared for through their obedience and their faith in Jesus Christ.

Lesson 9

The Power of Personal Prayer

Purpose	To assure class members that Heavenly Father hears and answers prayers and to encourage them to establish a regular pattern of sincere personal prayer.

Preparation	1. Prayerfully study Matthew 6:9–13; 2 Nephi 32:8–9; Alma 34:17–28; 3 Nephi 18:15–18.
	2. Materials needed: A set of scriptures and a scripture marking pencil for each class member. Continue to encourage class members to bring their own scriptures to class each week.
Note to the teacher	*Prayer is such a frequent practice in the Church that we often take it for granted. Remind class members that although we should pray daily, prayer is not merely an everyday routine to be taken lightly. It is an opportunity to sincerely thank Heavenly Father for our blessings and ask him for guidance in our lives. Heavenly Father loves to have us pray. He listens to our prayers and answers them.*

Suggested Lesson Development	**Gaining a Testimony of Prayer**
Story	Have someone read the following story, which is from Daniel 6:1–28:

Daniel was a young man of Jerusalem who depended on the Lord to guide him. When his country was invaded, he was among those taken captive by the Babylonian conquerors. The kings of Babylon gained confidence in Daniel because of his great wisdom, and he continued to be in favor among the Persians when they conquered Babylon. Darius, the Persian king who ruled over Babylon, gave Daniel a prominent position in the kingdom's government.

The Persian princes resented having Daniel, a Hebrew captive, rule over them, so they worked out a plan to remove Daniel. Knowing that Daniel prayed faithfully, they wrote a rule that for 30 days anyone making a request to anyone but the king should be cast into a den of lions. They took it to King Darius and tricked him into signing the decree and making it an unchangeable law.

Daniel knew about the new law, but he trusted the Lord and continued to pray as he had done before. The princes then ran to the king, saying, "Daniel . . . regardeth not thee, O king, nor the decree that thou hast signed, but maketh his petition [to his God] three times a day" (Daniel 6:13).

When Darius saw that he had been tricked, he tried to save Daniel. But the law was unchangeable, so Daniel was thrown into a den of lions. The king spent the night fasting. Early the next morning the king went to the den of lions and called out, "O Daniel, servant of the living God, is thy God, whom thou servest continually, able to deliver thee from the lions?" (Daniel 6:20).

Daniel replied, "My God hath sent his angel, and hath shut the lions' mouths, that they have not hurt me" (Daniel 6:22).

Daniel was released immediately. Then King Darius made a law that all the people should respect the God of Daniel. Darius declared: "He is the living God. . . . He delivereth and rescueth, and he worketh signs and wonders in heaven and in earth" (Daniel 6:26–27).

Discussion

- Why do you think Daniel continued to pray, even though he could have died because of it?

Invite class members to think about the following questions without answering them aloud:

- Is prayer as important to you as it was to Daniel? If not, what can you do to make prayer a more important part of your life?

How Do We Pray?

Scripture discussion

Have class members read, mark, and discuss Matthew 6:9 (you may want to use the first enrichment activity to conduct the discussion).

Explain that the Savior gave us the pattern of prayer, giving clear instructions: "After this manner therefore pray ye." Point out that he showed us that we should address all our prayers to Heavenly Father. Also, by saying "hallowed [holy] be thy name," Jesus taught us that we should show reverence for Heavenly Father. (You may also want to explain that we should close our prayers in the name of Jesus Christ. See 2 Nephi 32:9.)

Have class members read and mark Matthew 6:10.

- In his prayer, Jesus said, "Thy will be done in earth, as it is in heaven." What quality did Jesus demonstrate when he said this? (Willingness to accept Heavenly Father's will.) How will our prayers be affected if we develop this quality?

- Why is it sometimes difficult to accept Heavenly Father's will?

Point out that Heavenly Father knows what is best for us. He will answer our prayers according to our needs, not necessarily according to the things we want.

Story and discussion

Share the following story:

Sarah was riding her bicycle when she was hit by a car. She was critically injured, and her parents prayed that Heavenly Father would spare her life. After she had suffered for a week and it appeared that she would not recover, her family members gathered the courage to ask that Heavenly Father's will be done. Within a few hours, Sarah died peacefully.

- Why is it important to accept Heavenly Father's will?

Scripture discussion

Have class members read and mark Matthew 6:11–13. Then discuss the following questions:

- What could Jesus' request to "give us this day our daily bread" teach us about what we should ask for when we pray? (We should pray daily for blessings we need, not for luxuries. Our Heavenly Father, who knows our needs, will bless us accordingly.)

- What can we learn from Jesus' words "forgive us our debts, as we forgive our debtors"? (We should always pray with a repentant attitude. We must forgive others to be able to receive forgiveness ourselves.)

- The Savior prayed, "Lead us not into temptation, but deliver us from evil." (Note that in the Joseph Smith Translation of this verse, the Savior says, "Suffer [allow] us not to be led into temptation." Heavenly Father does not tempt us to sin.) What can we learn from this request that can help us in our personal prayers? (See 3 Nephi 18:15–18; we should ask for guidance and help to avoid falling into sin.) How does Heavenly Father help us avoid falling into sin?

- The Savior closed his prayer by saying, "For thine is the kingdom, and the power, and the glory, for ever." Why is it important that we recognize Heavenly Father's power as we pray?

- We should also express gratitude when we pray. How can we show our gratitude?

Heavenly Father Hears Our Prayers

Story

Have a class member read the following story:

When Jonathan saw that his friend Brian had left some money on a table at school, he took the money and quickly slipped it into his pocket.

Feeling bad about what he had done, Jonathan wanted to return the money. But he was afraid of the consequences. He could be expelled from school, and maybe Brian would never talk to him again.

Jonathan's parents had always taught him to pray for help in difficult situations, but he felt unworthy. He felt that Heavenly Father would not want to hear from someone so sinful.

Discussion and quotation

- Why does our sinfulness sometimes make us feel unworthy to pray? How can we overcome such feelings?

Elder Richard G. Scott of the Quorum of the Twelve Apostles said: "[God] is your Father; pray to him. If your life is in disarray and you feel uncomfortable and unworthy to pray because you are not clean, don't worry. He already knows about all of that. He is waiting for you to kneel in humility and take the first few steps. Pray for strength. Pray for others to be led to support you and guide you and lift you. Pray that the love of the Savior will pour into your heart. Pray that the miracle of the Atonement will bring forgiveness because you are willing to change. I know that those prayers will be answered, for God loves you. His Son gave his life for you. I know they will help you" (in Conference Report, Oct. 1988, 91; or *Ensign*, Nov. 1988, 77).

Scripture discussion

Have class members read and mark 2 Nephi 32:8–9.

- Who prompts people to believe that they are not worthy to pray? Why do you think Satan does not want us to pray?

Story

Ask a class member to read the following story:

Andy never did as well in school as he knew he could. He got nervous when he took tests. Even when he studied and felt confident about his knowledge of the information that would be on a test, he seemed to forget it all as soon as he got the test. He discussed the problem with his father. His father suggested that, after careful study and before taking his tests, he pray for help to recall what he had studied.

Scripture discussion

• Why is it appropriate to pray for help with tests and other things that might not seem important spiritually?

After class members have discussed answers to this question, have them read Alma 34:20–27. Point out that the words "cry unto the Lord" refer to our prayers to Heavenly Father. Note Amulek's counsel to pray for temporal things, such as fields and flocks, in addition to spiritual things.

• After we pray for help, what should we do?

Explain that like Andy in the story, we should not simply wait to be blessed; we should work toward receiving the blessings we have prayed for.

Testify that Heavenly Father always hears our prayers—even about small things and even if we feel unworthy.

Heavenly Father Answers Our Prayers

Story

Have a class member read the following story:

Stacey accepted a request to baby-sit for a family she did not know. She was comfortable while she was caring for the children, but when the children had gone to sleep and Stacey was alone in the house, she began to feel uneasy. The creaks of an unfamiliar house and the sound of fighting neighbors made her too frightened to sleep. Remembering the experience, Stacey later said:

"The thought came to my mind that my father, who was a fireman, might still be awake and that I could call him on his private line at the station. Within seconds my father was on the phone speaking to me with a comforting voice. He suggested that I lie down on the couch and try to rest. I fought his counsel, telling him over and over again that I was too afraid to ever rest in that environment.

"My father calmed my fears with a promise that he would stay on the line and not hang up. I did lie down and rest. However, I awoke with a bolt of fear several times during the following two hours, each time calling, 'Dad, are you there?' And every time my father was there, still holding on the line, never leaving me alone."

Discussion

• How was Stacey's communication with her father like our communication with our Heavenly Father?

Story continued

Share Stacey's comments about the experience:

"I continue to find that life can be scary and uncertain. . . . The lesson in faith and trust [my father] taught me on that night years ago still comforts me. Now, when I need comfort and reassurance, I pray to my Heavenly Father, 'Father, are you there?' And I am comforted, knowing that he loves me and is still on the line, aware of my situation and 'a very present help in trouble' (Ps. 46:1)" (Stacey Child Weeks, "Dad, Are You There?" *Ensign*, June 1996, 53).

Discussion and quotations

• Stacey said that sometimes Heavenly Father answers her prayers by blessing her with comforting, peaceful feelings. What are some other ways that prayers are answered?

The following quotations may help you lead a discussion of this question:

Elder Richard G. Scott taught: "Talk to your Father. He hears every prayer and answers it in His way. When we explain a problem and a proposed solution, sometimes He answers yes, sometimes no. Often He withholds an answer, not for lack of concern, but because He loves us—perfectly. He wants us to apply truths He has given us. For us to grow, we need to trust our ability to make correct decisions. We need to do what we *feel* is right. In time, He will answer. He will not fail us" (in Conference Report, Oct. 1989, 38; or *Ensign*, Nov. 1989, 31).

President Spencer W. Kimball said: "God does notice us, and he watches over us. But it is usually through another person that he meets our needs" ("Small Acts of Service," *Ensign*, Dec. 1974, 5).

• How have you been blessed by answers to your prayers? (You may want to share an experience you have had with prayer.)

Testimony

Bear your testimony of prayer, and encourage class members to establish a regular pattern of sincere personal prayer.

Enrichment Activities

You may want to use one or more of these activities during the lesson.

1. Write the following scripture references on separate strips of paper and put them in a bowl. Have class members take turns choosing a strip of paper from the bowl, reading the passage of scripture cited on the strip of paper and explaining what that passage teaches us about how we should pray. (You may want to use this activity with the section of the lesson called "How Do We Pray?")

Matthew 6:9	Matthew 6:10	Matthew 6:11
Matthew 6:12	Matthew 6:13	2 Nephi 32:9
3 Nephi 18:15–18		

2. Ask class members to list things they usually ask for when saying a prayer in Sunday School class. Have one class member write the responses on the chalkboard. Then discuss the responses. The following questions may help you lead the discussion:

• Do we view an invitation to pray as a burden or a privilege?

• Do we express gratitude for things that we are truly grateful for, or do we just say the same things that everyone else says?

- Heavenly Father often answers prayers in behalf of others by inspiring us to serve. When we ask Heavenly Father to bless others, are we willing to help those people? (For example, when we ask him to bless absent class members to come to church next week, do we know who is absent? Are we willing to help them come to church?)

- We often ask Heavenly Father to bless us with his Spirit. After saying such prayers, do we act and speak in a way that will invite the influence of the Holy Ghost?

Have class members read and mark Moroni 7:9.

- What do you think it means to pray "with real intent of heart"? (To be sincere in thanking Heavenly Father and asking him to bless you and others.)

Encourage class members to evaluate their personal prayers by silently asking themselves, "Do I pray with real intent?"

3. Sing or read with class members "Did You Think to Pray?" (*Hymns,* no. 140).

4. If *Family Home Evening Video Supplement 2* (53277) is available, show "Heavenly Father Answers Prayers," a three-minute segment.

Lesson 10

Fasting—Hungry or Full?

Purpose	To instill in class members a desire to seek spiritual growth through fasting and prayer.

Preparation

1. Prayerfully study Doctrine and Covenants 59:13–14 and the scriptures listed below (in the second preparation item), which give reasons why we fast.

2. Write each of the scripture references below on a separate piece of paper, and then put the papers in a bowl or other container.

   Doctrine and Covenants 88:76
   Luke 2:37
   Alma 45:1
   Mosiah 27:22–23
   Alma 5:46
   Alma 17:3
   Alma 6:6
   Isaiah 58:6–7
   Joel 2:12

3. Materials needed: A set of scriptures and a scripture marking pencil for each class member. Continue to encourage class members to bring their own scriptures to class each week.

Note to the teacher

Rather than being spiritually uplifted through fasting, many people merely experience hunger. Help class members see that we can become spiritually "full" by preparing, praying, and fasting with a purpose. When we abstain from food and take spiritual nourishment during the fast, the Lord blesses us with his Spirit.

Suggested Lesson Development

Fasting Is More than Not Eating

Discussion

Ask class members to imagine themselves in the following situation:

You are about to prepare your breakfast one Sunday morning when your mother (or father) comes in and reminds you that it is fast Sunday.

• What are your first thoughts? Are you happy that it is fast Sunday?

Point out that many people think of fasting as just not eating. The only feeling they experience while fasting is hunger. But with proper preparation and observance of the fast, fasting can be a joyful and spiritually uplifting experience.

When and Why We Fast

Scripture activity

Remind class members that one Sunday a month we go without food and drink for two consecutive meals. We also attend fast and testimony meeting, and we (or our parents) make a donation called a fast offering to the bishop to help care for those in need. In addition to the regular fast Sunday, we can also fast any time we feel the need for extra spiritual help, although we do not need to make a fast offering on those occasions.

- Why do we fast?

Have a class member take a piece of paper from the bowl and write on the chalkboard the scripture reference given on the paper. Have all class members find the indicated passage in their scriptures. Then have the class member who chose the paper read the scripture passage aloud and tell what reason it gives for fasting. List the reason on the chalkboard next to the reference. Repeat, giving other class members an opportunity to choose a paper, until all the papers have been used.

Your completed list may look like this:

WHY DO WE FAST?

Doctrine and Covenants 88:76—To obey God's commandment.

Luke 2:37—To serve God.

Alma 45:1—To worship God and show gratitude to him.

Mosiah 27:22–23—To receive special blessings, such as healing.

Alma 5:46—To gain a testimony.

Alma 17:3—To gain the spirit of prophecy and revelation and the ability to teach.

Alma 6:6—For the conversion of people who are not yet members of the Church.

Isaiah 58:6–7—To feed the hungry and clothe the naked.

Joel 2:12—To draw closer to God.

Discussion

Discuss briefly how fasting can help us do each of these things.

Proper Observance of the Fast

Scripture discussion

Have class members read and mark Doctrine and Covenants 59:13–14.

- What do these verses compare fasting to? Do you ever feel joyful when you are fasting?

- What can we do to make fasting joyful?

Accept class members' answers, then continue the discussion on the following two ways to make fasting joyful: preparation and prayer.

Discussion	*Preparation*

Write *Preparation* on the chalkboard. Explain that we must plan ahead and look forward to a fast to be able to enjoy it to the fullest.

- What can we do to prepare to fast?

Answers may include praying before beginning our fast, settling our other concerns so we can concentrate on our fast, and deciding to make the fast a meaningful spiritual experience.

Explain that one of the most important ways of preparing to fast is choosing a purpose for fasting.

- What difference can it make when we fast with a purpose? (Having a purpose can make fasting more personal and meaningful. We may find it easier to fast when we are fasting for a specific reason.)

Point out that class members have already discussed some purposes for fasting, and briefly review the list on the chalkboard. Help class members understand that they can fast whenever they need spiritual strength or special blessings for themselves or others. For example, they can fast when they are taking on a new responsibility, such as a Church calling, or when a family member or friend is sick.

Invite class members to tell about purposes for which they have fasted.

Prayer

Write *Prayer* on the chalkboard. Have class members turn again to the scriptures they used to discover reasons for fasting.

- Which of these scriptures include prayer with fasting?

- Why is it important that we pray when we fast?

Explain that some purposes for which we may want to pray as we fast include to ask for strength in fasting, to discuss our purpose for fasting with Heavenly Father, and to thank Heavenly Father for the opportunity to fast and receive the spiritual growth that can come with it.

Invite class members to share experiences they have had with fasting and prayer.

Note to the teacher	*Help class members form a positive attitude toward fasting and prayer. Fasting and prayer can become two of the most valuable spiritual tools they will ever acquire. Your testimony and your positive attitude will be two of the most important gifts you give class members this year. (See* Teaching—No Greater Call, *171.)*

Spiritual Fulfillment through Fasting

Discussion and quotation	Point out that because we are going without food, we may feel physically weak when we fast. However, in other ways fasting can make us stronger.

- What kind of strength do we receive from fasting?

Read or have a class member read the following statement made by Bishop John H. Vandenberg when he was Presiding Bishop:

"Fasting and prayer equip a person with a much greater degree of strength and power than would otherwise be his if he were left to his own devices. Fasting and prayer can bring an individual to a point of humility and faith where the Lord can give him the extra strength and power needed to complete a task or to solve a problem" ("The Presiding Bishop Talks to Youth About: Fasting," *Improvement Era,* Feb. 1969, 71).

Testimony

Bear testimony of the spiritual strength and blessings that can be received through fasting and prayer.

Encourage class members to remember preparation and prayer next time they fast, so that they can receive spiritual fulfillment and not just go hungry.

Enrichment Activities

You may want to use one or more of these activities during the lesson.

1. Bring to class a large bowl, enough rocks to fill the bowl, and enough apples to fill the bowl. (You may replace the bowl with any other container and the rocks and apples with two other items.)

   Put all the rocks in the bowl. Then ask two class members to fill the bowl with the apples. They will see that they can only fill the bowl with the apples if they first take the rocks out of the bowl.

   Have class members read and mark Alma 22:15. Explain that this verse contains the words of a king who repented for rebelling against the Lord. The king offered to give up his kingdom and all his possessions in order to receive the Spirit of God (the Holy Ghost).

   • What did the king really need to give up to feel the Spirit? (See Alma 22:18.)

   Point out that just as the rocks needed to come out of the bowl before the bowl could be filled with apples, the wickedness in the king needed to leave before the king could be filled with the Holy Ghost.

   • What do we need to do to be filled with the Holy Ghost? (We need to rid ourselves of unrighteous thoughts and actions.) How can sincere fasting be one way to "empty" ourselves of unrighteousness so we can be filled with the Holy Ghost?

   Explain that even though our stomachs are empty when we fast, we can be filled with the Holy Ghost. Being hungry for food when we fast is not wrong, especially if it reminds us to "hunger and thirst after righteousness, [so we can] be filled with the Holy Ghost" (3 Nephi 12:6).

2. If *Family Home Evening Video Supplement* (53276) is available, show "The Law of the Fast," a four-minute segment.

3. Copy the handout at the end of this lesson and cut it into strips as indicated.

Write the following names on the chalkboard:

Ahasuerus = king

Esther = queen

Mordecai = Esther's cousin

Haman = wicked prime minister

Pass out the story strips at random. Have class members try to put the strips into the correct sequence of events, placing them on a table or the floor. When they have finished, briefly review the story, emphasizing Esther's request that the other Jews fast with her before she went in to the king to plead for the lives of her people (see Esther 3–8).

• How do you think it helped Queen Esther to have her people fast with her?

• How might it help you to have your family or friends fast with you?

Esther, a Jewish woman, was Queen of Persia and Media. She was afraid for her people because they were condemned to die. The wicked prime minister Haman had

deceitfully convinced King Ahasuerus that the Jews in his kingdom were wicked and should be put to death. The king did not know his wife was a Jew. Haman persuaded the king to kill all Jews because a Jew named Mordecai refused to

bow down to him. Mordecai was Esther's cousin and had raised her from the time her parents had died. He asked

Queen Esther to persuade her husband, King Ahasuerus, to reverse his decision to put the Jews to death. Even for the queen, however, it was dangerous to

speak to the king. Anyone approaching the king without having been summoned would be put to death unless the king indicated his approval by

lowering his scepter. Knowing this, Queen Esther said to Mordecai, "Go, gather together all the Jews that are present in Shushan, and

fast ye for me, and neither eat nor drink three days, night or day: I also and my maidens will fast likewise, and so will I go in unto the king, which is not according to the law: and if I perish, I

perish" (Esther 4:16). After three days of fasting, Esther summoned her courage and faith in the Lord and entered the king's throne room. When the king saw Esther, he smiled and lowered his scepter toward her. Esther asked the king to

attend a banquet. At the banquet she asked him to spare her life and the lives of her people. When the king realized how Haman had deceived him into condemning the Jews to death, he sentenced Haman to be

hanged. Mordecai was made prime minister in Haman's place, and the king made a decree allowing the Jews to defend themselves against those who wanted to hurt or kill them. To this day Jewish people all over the world celebrate this event and honor Queen Esther.

Lesson 11

Faith in Jesus Christ

Purpose	To teach class members that faith in Jesus Christ is essential to salvation and to encourage them to increase their faith in him.

Preparation

1. Prayerfully study Genesis 22:2–3, 9–13; 2 Kings 5:1–3, 10–14; John 14:6, 12; Romans 10:17; Hebrews 11; 1 Nephi 17:7–8, 17–18; 2 Nephi 9:23; Mosiah 3:17; Alma 32:21; Articles of Faith 1:4.

2. Additional reading: Bible Dictionary, "Faith," 669.

3. Make a poster of Alma 32:21, replacing words with blanks as indicated below (if you are unable to make a poster, write the words and blanks on the chalkboard before class begins):

   " _____ is not to have a perfect knowledge of things; therefore if ye have _____ ye _____ for things which are _____ _____ , which are _____ " (Alma 32: ____).

4. Materials needed:
   a. A marker to fill in the blanks on the poster.
   b. A picture of Jesus Christ (picture 2 in the picture section of the manual; 62572; Gospel Art Picture Kit 240).
   c. A set of scriptures and a scripture marking pencil for each class member. Continue to encourage class members to bring their own scriptures to class each week.

Note to the teacher

Faith in Jesus Christ is the first principle of the gospel. It is a principle of power, motivating us to act on true principles even when we cannot see immediate results for our actions. The role of the Savior is at the core of the gospel, so faith in him is essential. Help class members understand how they can increase their faith in Jesus Christ.

Suggested Lesson Development

What Is Faith?

Poster and discussion

Display the poster (or refer to the words and blanks on the chalkboard). Without telling class members the topic of the lesson, tell them that the Prophet Joseph Smith taught that the word that goes in the first two blanks of this statement is "the moving cause of all action" and a "principle of power" (*Lectures on Faith,* 1:10, 15).

• Which principle do you think Joseph Smith was referring to?

When class members have guessed (or you have told them) the principle is faith, write *faith* in the first two blanks on the poster.

Help class members use their scriptures to find the verse on the poster. Invite a class member to fill in the remaining blanks on the poster, or invite five class members to each fill in one of the blanks.

- What is faith?

Help class members understand that faith is a trust or confidence in someone or something, even though that person or thing is not seen. Faith is more than just a belief that something is real and true; it is a feeling that motivates us to do something based on our belief.

- Why do you think Joseph Smith called faith a "principle of power" and "the moving cause of all action"?

Discuss some ways faith is a necessary "moving cause" of ordinary actions. For example, farmers plant seeds because they have faith that the seeds, if properly cared for, will grow. Students study for a test because they have faith that studying will help them do well on the test. People buy bus tickets because they have faith that the bus will take them where they want to go. Allow class members to come up with some examples of their own.

Point out the last phrase of the scripture on the poster. Remind class members that faith must be based on truth. Farmers who hope for crops to grow but who do not plant seeds first are not exhibiting real faith. People who buy tickets on a northbound bus while hoping to travel south are not showing faith.

Faith in Jesus Christ Is Essential to Exaltation

Note to the teacher

Teachers must live by the principles they teach. Elder Bruce R. McConkie said: "We must be doers of the word and not hearers only. It is more than lip service; it is not simply confessing with the mouth the divine Sonship of the Savior. It is obedience and conformity and personal righteousness" (in Conference Report, Oct. 1974, 46; or Ensign, *Nov. 1974, 35). Your daily actions should demonstrate to class members your own faith in Jesus Christ. (See* Teaching—No Greater Call, *9.)*

Scripture discussion

Have class members recite the fourth article of faith. (If no one in the class has it memorized, have class members find it in the scriptures and read it aloud. The Articles of Faith are located at the end of the Pearl of Great Price.)

- What two things does this scripture teach us about faith? (That it is the first principle of the gospel and that it must be centered in Jesus Christ.)

Emphasize that this article of faith teaches us that "faith in the Lord Jesus Christ," rather than faith in general, is the first principle of the gospel. (Display the picture of Jesus Christ.) We can have faith in other things, such as seeds growing and busses getting to their destinations, but faith in Jesus Christ is the only faith that will lead us to exaltation (see 2 Nephi 9:23; Mosiah 3:17).

Quotation

Have a class member read aloud the following statement from Elder Richard G. Scott of the Quorum of the Twelve Apostles:

"The need to *exercise faith in Jesus Christ* is absolutely essential. It is the foundation of the plan of salvation" (in Conference Report, Oct. 1993, 119; or *Ensign*, Nov. 1993, 87; italics in original).

• Why do you think faith in Jesus Christ is the first principle of the gospel?

To help answer this question, review with class members Jesus Christ's role in the plan of salvation:

1. In the premortal world, he was chosen to be our Savior and Redeemer.

2. He came to earth and lived a sinless life, setting a perfect example for us.

3. He atoned for our sins.

Teach class members that only through faith in Jesus Christ and his Atonement can we return to dwell with him and with our Heavenly Father. Since Jesus Christ makes exaltation possible, we must have faith that through his Atonement we will be resurrected and can be forgiven of the sins we have committed. Point out that faith in Jesus Christ is the first principle of the gospel because it is the basis for understanding and accepting other principles and ordinances of the gospel. For example, if we do not have faith in Jesus Christ, we will not understand why we need to be baptized in his name.

Faith in the Savior Brings Great Blessings

Scripture discussion

Remind class members that faith is a principle of power. Many great blessings have come to people because of this power. Have class members turn to Hebrews 11 and quickly look through the chapter for blessings that resulted from faith. Ask them to report the results, and list their responses on the chalkboard. The list may include the following:

1. Enoch was translated (taken from the earth without dying; see verse 5).

2. Noah and his family were saved from the flood (see verse 7).

3. Sarah conceived Isaac in her old age (see verse 11).

4. The walls of Jericho fell (see verse 30).

Ask the following question about each example on the chalkboard:

• How did the person (or people) who received this blessing demonstrate faith? (For example, Noah built an ark as the Lord had commanded.)

Point out that because of their faith, these people obeyed the Lord's instructions. They were then blessed for their obedience.

Story

Tell the following story:

Randall Ellsworth was a missionary in Guatemala when that country suffered a terrible earthquake. Eighteen thousand people were killed. Elder Ellsworth survived, but he was severely injured and his legs were paralyzed. He received some medical treatment in Guatemala and then was sent back to his home in the United States. Those who knew how severe his injuries were thought he would never walk again, but Randall Ellsworth had faith that the Lord would not only help him walk again but would also help him finish his mission.

Randall and his family and friends continued praying, and Randall worked hard at regaining strength in his legs. He went to physical therapy twice as often as the doctors asked him to. Eventually he was able to walk again, with the help of two canes, and the Missionary Department approved his return to Guatemala to finish his mission. When Randall heard that he would be able to finish his mission in Guatemala, the first thing he did was say a prayer thanking Heavenly Father for this great blessing.

Randall Ellsworth returned to Guatemala, and one day he was talking with his mission president. "You have been the recipient of a miracle," the president said. "Your faith has been rewarded. If you have the necessary confidence, if you have abiding faith, if you have supreme courage, place those two canes on my desk and walk." Slowly Elder Ellsworth placed his canes on the desk and took a few steps. It was not easy for him to walk at first, but he never used the canes again. He finished his mission and later graduated from medical school. (See Thomas S. Monson, in Conference Report, Oct. 1986, 53–54; or *Ensign,* Nov. 1986, 41–42. See also Thomas S. Monson, "Which Road Will You Travel?" *Ensign,* Mar. 1991, 4–5.)

Discussion

- How was faith involved in this healing? How did Randall Ellsworth and his friends and family members demonstrate their faith?

Point out that exercising faith does not always result in miracles. Part of having faith is accepting God's will, even when it is not what we want. Remind class members of Diane Ellingson, whose story was told in lesson 6. Diane initially thought that because she had faith, she would be healed. When she realized it was not God's will that she be healed, her faith in Jesus Christ gave her comfort and the strength to succeed in life despite her difficulties. (See Kendra Kasl Phair, "A Champion Again," *New Era,* Nov. 1988, 21–25.)

- How have you or your family members been blessed because of faith in Jesus Christ? (You may want to share an example from your own life.)

We Can Increase Our Faith in Jesus Christ

Scripture discussion

As you discuss the following scripture passages, remind class members that faith is demonstrated by obeying the Lord's commandments (you may need to point out that showing faith in Jesus Christ includes showing faith in his chosen servants, the prophets).

Have class members read 1 Nephi 17:7–8, 17–18.

- Did Laman and Lemuel exhibit faith?

Next read 2 Kings 5:1–3, 10–14.

- Did Naaman exhibit faith?

Point out that Naaman initially showed a lack of faith by refusing to do what the prophet Elisha had instructed him to do. But he did eventually act on faith by bathing in the Jordan River, and he was healed as Elisha had promised.

Next read Genesis 22:2–3, 9–12.

- Did Abraham exhibit faith?

Point out that Abraham set out to obey the Lord immediately and without question, even though the Lord commanded him to do a very difficult thing.

Because the Lord was pleased with Abraham's obedience, he provided a ram to be sacrificed instead of Isaac (see Genesis 22:13).

- Which of these people should we strive to be like? How can we develop faith as strong as Abraham's?

Scripture discussion

Have class members read and mark Romans 10:17.

- Where can we hear or find the word of God? (Answers may include in the scriptures, the words of latter-day prophets, Church magazines, and Church meetings.)

- How does studying the word of God increase our faith?

- What are some additional ways to increase our faith in Jesus Christ? (Answers may include prayer, fasting, and serving others.)

Explain that increasing our faith in Jesus Christ is similar to developing any other characteristic or skill. If we want to improve our ability to play soccer, compose music, or cook, we must study and practice and consciously try to better our ability. The same holds true for increasing our faith in the Savior. Our faith in Jesus Christ increases as we put it into practice by following his example (see John 14:12).

Testimony

Testify that faith in Jesus Christ is essential to our salvation. You may want to tell class members how your faith in Jesus Christ has affected your life.

Encourage class members to increase their faith in Jesus Christ through study, prayer, and obedience to his commandments.

Enrichment Activities

You may want to use one or more of these activities during the lesson.

1. Explain that faith begins small, like a seed, but with proper nourishment and care it will grow to be very great. Provide paper and crayons or colored markers, and let class members creatively describe the present status of their faith in terms of a growing plant. Encourage class members to take their drawings home and put them in their journals.

2. Discuss with class members the following statement from President Ezra Taft Benson, thirteenth President of the Church:

"Faith in [Jesus Christ] is more than mere acknowledgment that He lives. It is more than professing belief.

"Faith in Jesus Christ consists of complete reliance on Him. As God, He has infinite power, intelligence, and love. There is no human problem beyond His capacity to solve. Because He descended below all things (see D&C 122:8), He knows how to help us rise above our daily difficulties.

"Faith in Him means believing that even though we do not understand all things, He does. We, therefore, must look to Him 'in every thought; doubt not, fear not' (D&C 6:36.)" (in Conference Report, Oct. 1983, 7; or *Ensign,* Nov. 1983, 8).

- How can your faith in Jesus Christ help you with your daily problems and difficulties?

3. Have one class member leave the room (or close his or her eyes) for a moment. Hide a small object somewhere in the classroom. Have the class member come back in (or open his or her eyes).

   The class members who saw where you hid the object are to help the other class member find it. They may do this only by saying "faith" as the person approaches the hidden object or "doubt" as the person moves away from the object. Point out that this game illustrates the idea that faith is believing in things one cannot see. The class member who left the room believes the hidden object exists and is willing to put effort toward finding it, even though he or she has not actually seen the object.

4. Sing with class members or play a recording of "Faith" (*Children's Songbook*, 96) or "I Know That My Redeemer Lives" (*Hymns*, no. 136).

Lesson 12

Repentance Is a Blessing

Purpose	To create in class members a desire to repent of their sins.

Preparation	1. Prayerfully study Mosiah 26:30; Alma 36:19–21; Doctrine and Covenants 1:32; 19:16; 58:42–43; Moses 6:57.
	2. Additional reading: Address given at the October 1995 general conference by President Boyd K. Packer (in Conference Report, Oct. 1995, 21–25; or *Ensign,* Nov. 1995, 18–21); address given at the April 1995 general conference by Elder Richard G. Scott (in Conference Report, Apr. 1995, 100–104; or *Ensign,* May 1995, 75–78).
	3. Prepare a label that says *Repentance* and attach it to the chalkboard eraser you will be using during the lesson.
	4. Materials needed: a. The picture Jesus Praying in Gethsemane (picture 4 in the picture section of the manual; 62175; Gospel Art Picture Kit 227). b. A set of scriptures and a scripture marking pencil for each class member. Continue to encourage class members to bring their own scriptures to class each week.
Note to the teacher	*Heavenly Father has lovingly included repentance in the gospel plan and promised to receive all who forsake their sins and come to him with a broken heart and contrite spirit. Be sure to leave class members with hope and encouragement following this lesson. Repentance is necessary for everyone. It is a great blessing that allows us to be forgiven and cleansed of our sins so we can achieve exaltation.*

Suggested Lesson Development	**Repentance Allows Us to Become Clean Again**
Story	Tell or have a class member tell the following story:
	Once a young girl was asked what she was thankful for. She replied, "Erasers." When asked to explain, she said, "I make lots of mistakes doing math problems. Without an eraser I can't undo my mistakes and write the correct answers on my paper."
Chalkboard discussion	On the chalkboard write in large letters *SINS*.
	• Have you ever done something wrong and wished you had a giant eraser to undo your action? (This is a general question. Do not ask class members to name the actions they are thinking of.)
	Using the eraser labeled *Repentance,* erase the word *SINS* from the chalkboard. Make sure class members can see the label as you erase.

Explain that repentance is the process Heavenly Father has given us for "erasing" our sins. Heavenly Father wants us to return to live with him after this life, but no unclean, or sinful, person can live with him (see Moses 6:57). Heavenly Father knows that everyone will make mistakes and commit sins while on the earth, so he has given us a way to become clean again after we have sinned. This is repentance.

Picture presentation

Display the picture of Jesus praying in Gethsemane. Explain that because Jesus Christ paid for all our sins with his suffering, when we repent we can be forgiven and can become clean again (see D&C 19:16).

We All Must Repent

Story and discussion

Read or tell the following story:

At the age of fifty-seven, Charlie was living in Leavenworth, Kansas—in prison. He had been in many of the United States' high security institutions for most of his life. He had grown up with crime. His father and mother were alcoholics and convicts. When he was thirteen, the flu epidemic killed all the members of his family. After the funerals, Charlie hopped on a freight train and began a nomadic life across the United States. His life included crime, beginning with car theft, then burglary, and finally armed robbery. By the age of fifty-seven Charlie had spent thirty-five years in prison.

• Do you think there is any hope for a person like this?

Continue the story:

Charlie finally realized he was living a dead-end existence. He later described how he felt at that time:

"I slowly came to realize I did not like myself. How could I change? If I kept up my criminal acts, I would die in a prison cell and be buried in some unmarked plot on prison property."

• What did Charlie need to do to change his life?

Charlie began studying religion. He eventually read the Book of Mormon and realized that The Church of Jesus Christ of Latter-day Saints was the true Church. He wrote to Church headquarters and asked for more information about the Church. He was unable to be baptized because he was in prison, but he studied the books and other materials he received from the Missionary Department.

As Charlie gained a testimony of Jesus Christ and the gospel plan, he made a complete change in his behavior. He would learn a principle of the gospel, then live it, and become strengthened; then he would learn another principle, live it, and become strengthened; then learn another principle, live it, and become strengthened further. As Charlie learned about the things that Heavenly Father and Jesus wanted him to do, he started doing those things and stopped doing wrong things.

Charlie eventually had a chance for parole (to be let out of prison under strict supervision). He decided that he would start a new life. He met with the stake president in the area, who was so impressed with Charlie that he went to the parole officer and guaranteed that he would get Charlie a job and a place to live if Charlie were released on parole.

Charlie was released from prison, and the stake president found a job and an apartment for him. The missionaries taught Charlie the gospel discussions. When his parole was finished, Charlie was baptized. Two and a half years later he came to Church headquarters to meet the person who had answered his first letter and to attend general conference. Charlie, who was now the high priests group leader in his ward, testified of the truthfulness of the gospel. He was a completely new man.

Discussion

- In what way was Charlie a new man?

Point out that as Charlie learned the gospel, he repented of the things he had done wrong. Repentance enabled him to change from being a criminal to being a member of the Church with a responsible calling and a strong testimony of the gospel.

- Why is repentance important?

Explain that sins can slow or stop our spiritual development and move us away from Heavenly Father and Jesus Christ. Repentance allows us to turn back to Heavenly Father and Jesus and begin to grow spiritually again. Although we may not commit big sins like Charlie's, all of us commit sins, so we all need to repent.

Repentance Requires Effort

Quotation

Have a class member read Charlie's comments about repentance:

"Because of . . . agency, I had to make the first move in changing my lifestyle. Repentance is definitely a change of mind. Repentance begins by a desire to scrap all your past by reading, studying, and pondering God's word. Repentance is reaching out from the midst of my pains and negativeness and turning them to joy and positiveness."

Chalkboard discussion

Explain that there is a process that helps us turn the pain and guilt of sin into joy through repentance. Charlie mentioned the first step in this process when he said, "Repentance begins by a desire to scrap all your past."

Write on the chalkboard:

1. Recognize your sin and desire to change.

- Why is recognition that you have sinned the first step in repentance? Why is it important to feel sorrow for what you have done wrong and desire to do better?

To find the next two steps, have class members read and mark Doctrine and Covenants 58:43.

Write on the chalkboard:

2. Confess your sin.

3. Forsake your sin.

• Why is it necessary to confess your sin? To whom should you confess?

Explain that all sins must be confessed to the Lord. If we have sinned against another person (for example, if you lied to your mother), we should also confess to that person. Serious sins must also be confessed to the bishop or branch president. Confession shows that we are sincere about wanting to repent.

• What does it mean to forsake your sin?

Explain that to forsake means to give up. If we forsake a sin, we resolve never to do that wrong thing again.

• Why is forsaking your sin an important part of repentance?

Write on the chalkboard:

4. Make restitution.

Explain that to make restitution means to make right, as much as is possible, what we have done wrong. Give class members examples of a few specific actions for which restitution can be made and ask them to tell how those wrongs could be made right. For example, if we have stolen something, we return it or pay for it. If we have lied, we tell the truth. If we have damaged something, we repair or replace it.

You may want to point out that sometimes a wrong action cannot be made right, no matter what we do. For example, if we have said untrue things about a person we can apologize and tell the truth, but we may not be able to undo the damage done to the person's reputation. If we have stolen or damaged something, we may be able to replace the object but not exactly as it was. In this kind of situation, Jesus Christ, through his Atonement and mercy, will take responsibility for setting things right. But this happens only after we have done all we can.

Write on the chalkboard:

5. Keep the commandments.

Explain that the last step in repentance is striving to keep all the commandments of God (see D&C 1:32). Repentance is a process that we will have to use throughout our lives, but as we become more perfect in keeping the commandments, we will do less for which we need to repent.

Read Charlie's testimony to the class:

"I know the extent [of the] damage done by my years of rebellion. But I also know that repentance and endurance based on faith is the way to my personal salvation. When I am called from this mortal life, I hope and pray, that since [I found the gospel], in the words of Paul [in] 2 Timothy 4:7, I can say, 'I have fought a good fight,' I did the best I could with my Church callings, and I kept my faith and love for the Lord and Heavenly Father."

Point out that once Charlie had repented of his sins, he endured to the end—he spent the rest of his life trying to live the way Heavenly Father and Jesus Christ wanted him to live.

Heavenly Father and Jesus Christ Will Forgive Us When We Repent

Scripture discussion

Explain that repentance can be a long and difficult process. But the effort required to repent is more than repaid by the blessings we receive when we do repent.

- What blessings come to us when we repent?

Have class members find and mark Mosiah 26:30 and Doctrine and Covenants 58:42. Have two class members each read one of these verses aloud.

- What does the Lord promise to do when we repent of our sins?

- What does it mean that the Lord "will remember [our sins] no more"? (He will not consider them when we are judged. When we have sincerely and completely repented, to the Lord it is as if we had never sinned.)

Have class members find and mark Alma 36:19–21. Have a class member read the verses aloud.

- According to these verses, how will we feel when we have repented and have been forgiven?

Explain that sin brings us guilt and pain, but repentance brings us joy. Tell class members that it is better not to sin and thus avoid the pain of sin and the effort of repentance, but when we do sin, we can repent and again feel the joy of being clean.

Quotation

Have a person read the following statement by Elder Spencer W. Kimball when he was a member of the Quorum of the Twelve Apostles:

"What relief! What comfort! What joy! Those laden with transgressions and sorrows and sin may be forgiven and cleansed and purified if they will return to their Lord, learn of him, and keep his commandments" (*The Miracle of Forgiveness* [1969], 368).

Testimony

Testify of the joy and gratitude you feel for the principle of repentance, which enables us to be forgiven of our sins. Express your gratitude for Christ's Atonement, which makes repentance possible.

Encourage class members to sincerely repent of their sins and strive to live righteously. Remind them of the joy and relief that can come through repentance.

Enrichment Activities

You may want to use one or more of these activities during the lesson.

1. If *Book of Mormon Video Presentations* (53911) is available, show "Becoming Children of Christ," an eleven-minute segment. Discuss how repentance helps us put off the natural man (see Mosiah 3:19) and become children of Christ.

2. Sing or say the words to "Come unto Jesus" (*Hymns*, no. 117). Discuss how the words to this song relate to repentance.

3. Emphasize to class members that while repentance and forgiveness are wonderful gifts, it is better to avoid sin. We should *never* deliberately sin

with the thought, "I will just repent later." Read or have a class member read the following illustration of this idea, by Elder Hugh W. Pinnock of the Seventy:

"Live the commandments. Never feed the foxes! What does that mean? *Breaking commandments is like feeding foxes.* In England where we live, my wife and I had heard that foxes were right in town. We wanted to see a fox. A neighbor told us that if we left food for the foxes we probably would see one. Our butcher gave us some bones. Each night we would place some bones out in the backyard. Soon a fox came to eat. Then a few more. Now we have at least five foxes racing through our flower garden, digging up the lawn, and leaving a shambles every night. . . .

"What started out as a curiosity is now a problem, and sin is much the same. An indiscretion can begin a process that can make a mess of a whole life. Remember, if you don't start feeding the foxes, they will never tear up your yard. If you avoid making the seemingly small and harmless mistakes, your life will be free of many larger problems later on" (in Conference Report, Oct. 1993, 57–58; or *Ensign*, Nov. 1993, 41).

Point out that the Pinnocks were eventually able to get the foxes out of their yard, but not without much effort and not before the foxes had caused great damage to the yard. Repentance can bring us forgiveness and make us clean again, but not without much effort and not before we have experienced the pain and damage caused by sin.

4. For the following object lesson, bring to class a clear bottle or bowl of water, a few drops of red food coloring, and a few drops of liquid bleach. (You may want to practice this object lesson at home before presenting it in class.)

Have class members read and mark Isaiah 1:18.

- Why do you think the prophet Isaiah used the colors scarlet and crimson in describing sins? (The color red represents blood, which implies serious sin. Isaiah is saying that we can repent even if we have committed serious sins.)

- In contrast, why did he use the phrase *white as snow* to show God's forgiveness? (To represent purity. Through repentance we can become pure and clean again.)

Show the class the container of water. Explain that the clean, clear water represents a person free from sin. Add a few drops of red food coloring to the water. Have class members observe the coloring as it gradually discolors all the water. Explain that sin discolors our lives like the food coloring discolored the water.

Add a few drops of the liquid bleach to the container and gently stir or swirl until the water is clear again.

- What gospel principles does the bleach represent? (Repentance and forgiveness.)

Explain that as the bleach makes the water clear again, sincere repentance enables us to be forgiven and become clean again after we have sinned.

Baptism: Taking upon Ourselves the Name of Christ

Purpose	To review the symbolism of baptism and inspire in class members a commitment to keep their baptismal covenants.

Preparation	1. Prayerfully study John 3:3–5; Romans 6:3–6; 2 Nephi 31; Mosiah 18:8–10; Doctrine and Covenants 20:37, 71, 77; 49:13–14.
	2. Write the numbers 1 through 5 on separate strips of paper. Fold the strips of paper and place them in a bowl or other container (see the activity on page 71).
	3. Materials needed:
	a. The pictures Boy Being Baptized (62018); Burial of Jesus (62180; Gospel Art Picture Kit 231); The Resurrected Jesus Christ (picture 9 in the picture section of the manual; 62187; Gospel Art Picture Kit 239); and Alma Baptizes in the Waters of Mormon (picture 5 in the picture section of the manual; 62332; Gospel Art Picture Kit 309).
	b. A set of scriptures and a scripture marking pencil for each class member. Continue to encourage class members to bring their own scriptures to class each week.

Note to the teacher	*Baptism is one of the first steps we take to come to Christ. Understanding the symbolism of baptism helps us understand the eternal nature of the covenants and blessings that come because of baptism. Through continued obedience, we can overcome spiritual death and return to the presence of our Father in Heaven. Since this is made possible by the Atonement of Jesus Christ, we take Jesus' name upon us when we are baptized and promise to remember him in all that we do.*
	As you teach this lesson, be sensitive to the feelings of class members who have not yet been baptized.

Suggested Lesson Development	**The Purposes of Baptism**
Discussion	Show the picture of a boy being baptized.
	• What do you remember about your baptism?
	Allow class members to talk about their baptisms. You may want to share some memories of your own baptism.
Scripture discussion	• Why were you baptized?
	Be sure the following purposes of baptism are discussed (you may want to have class members read and mark the accompanying scriptures):

1. To receive remission, or forgiveness, of sins (see D&C 49:13).

2. To show willingness to keep Heavenly Father's commandments (see 2 Nephi 31:14).

3. To become members of the Church (see D&C 20:71).

4. To begin on the path to eternal life (see 2 Nephi 31:17–20).

5. To be able to receive the gift of the Holy Ghost (see D&C 49:14).

- Why did Jesus, who did not sin, need to be baptized?

Have class members read 2 Nephi 31:6–9, marking words and phrases that answer this question. Help class members see that like us, Jesus needed to be baptized to show obedience to Heavenly Father. Jesus also was baptized to set an example for us.

Baptism Brings a Spiritual Rebirth

Scripture discussion

Explain that the Apostle Paul talked about baptism as a symbol. A symbol is an object or action that represents something else. Have class members read and mark Romans 6:3.

Show the picture of the burial of Jesus.

- What do you think it means to be "baptized into [Christ's] death"? (See Romans 6:3.)

Explain that the word *baptism* means "to immerse" (see Bible Dictionary, "Baptism," 618). The act of immersion—being momentarily buried under water—represents the death and burial of a person's sinfulness. The Atonement of Jesus Christ makes it possible for us to repent of our sins and be forgiven.

Have class members read and mark Romans 6:4–5.

Show the picture of the resurrected Jesus Christ.

- How is baptism "in the likeness of [Christ's] resurrection"?

Explain that the act of coming out from under the water represents a birth into a new life, just as the resurrected Jesus Christ rose from the tomb.

Explain that in a conversation with a man named Nicodemus, Jesus talked about this aspect of baptism. Have class members read and mark John 3:3–5.

- How does a person become born of water? (By being baptized.)

- How does a person become born of the Spirit? (By receiving the Holy Ghost after baptism. Tell class members that you will discuss the gift of the Holy Ghost in next week's lesson.)

Story

Read the following testimony related by a convert as he bore his testimony in a Church meeting:

"I came from a broken home. We had no religion, and I was not taught any particular moral values. My life was meaningless, empty, and full of conflict.

I committed many sins. Then the gospel came into my life. I accepted the Savior wholeheartedly. I began to believe in Him and to turn away from my former ways. I was baptized, and I received the marvelous gift of the Holy Ghost. Brothers and Sisters, for years and years I felt as if I were 'dead' *inside,* and now for the first time in life, I feel 'alive'" (in *My Errand from the Lord* [Melchizedek Priesthood study guide, 1976], 161).

We Made Covenants at Baptism

Scripture discussion

Explain that section 20 of the Doctrine and Covenants contains a revelation given to Joseph Smith on the day that The Church of Jesus Christ of Latter-day Saints was organized. Joseph Smith was given instructions for the people who wanted to be baptized as members of the Church. Have class members read and mark Doctrine and Covenants 20:37. Explain that this verse contains the baptismal covenant. A covenant is an agreement between us and the Lord in which we promise to obey his commandments and he promises to bless us according to our obedience.

- What do people have to covenant to do in order to be baptized? (List the following requirements on the chalkboard as they are mentioned.)

1. Humble themselves before God.

2. Repent of their sins.

3. Be willing to take upon themselves the name of Jesus Christ.

4. Be willing to serve the Lord.

5. Show by their works that they have received the Spirit of Christ.

Scripture discussion

- What does it mean to take upon ourselves the name of Christ?

Point out that we take upon ourselves Jesus' name when we follow his example. Explain that to learn about how we can do this, you are going to discuss some teachings of Alma, a prophet in the Book of Mormon.

Display the picture of Alma baptizing in the waters of Mormon. Explain that Alma was converted through the teachings of Abinadi and then taught the gospel to others. To help the people prepare to be baptized, he reviewed things they would be expected to do as members of the Church.

Have class members read and mark Mosiah 18:8–10. Write on the chalkboard *"Come into the fold of God, and . . . be called his people."*

- What things must we be willing to do to be able to "come into the fold of God, and . . . be called his people"?

Write the following on the chalkboard as the items are mentioned:

1. "Bear one another's burdens."

2. "Mourn with those that mourn."

3. "Comfort those that stand in need of comfort."

4. "Stand as witnesses of God at all times and in all things, and in all places."

- In what ways can we bear one another's burdens? How have you seen people do this? How have other people helped bear your burdens?

- Why is it sometimes helpful to "mourn with those that mourn"? What are some things we can do to comfort those who need comfort? How have other people helped you during difficult times?

- What does it mean to stand as a witness of God?

Activity

Ask a class member to choose one of the strips of paper you have prepared and read the number written on it. Then read the corresponding situation below and ask class members to describe how they could stand as witnesses of God in that situation. Repeat the activity until every situation has been discussed.

Situation 1

You are playing basketball with a group of friends. One of your friends misses an easy shot and in frustration takes the Lord's name in vain.

Situation 2

A friend who is not a member of the Church comes to your home and notices a copy of the Book of Mormon on a table.

Situation 3

You are at an activity for the young men and young women in your ward. A new bishop has just been called, and several people your age are talking about him. "I can't believe they called *him*," one of them says.

Situation 4

You are at home by yourself. You know that your parents will not be home for a few hours. There is a movie on television that you have wanted to see. You know that it has a few offensive scenes and some profanity, but many of your friends have told you that it is an exciting movie.

Situation 5

You have been planning for months to go to the temple with the young men and young women in your ward to perform baptisms for the dead. A friend who is not a member of the Church invites you to a party that same evening. You say that you can't go to the party, and your friend asks what you will be doing that evening.

Scripture discussion

- How do the four promises in Mosiah 18:8–10 relate to our promise to take upon ourselves the name of Jesus Christ?

- Why do you think we have been talking about baptism even though most (or all) of us have already been baptized?

Have a class member read Doctrine and Covenants 20:77, which contains the prayer on the sacramental bread. Point out the similarities between this prayer and the baptismal covenant in Doctrine and Covenants 20:37. Explain that the baptismal covenant is so important that we renew it each week when we take the sacrament. Baptism is more than just being immersed in the water. The covenants we make and the blessings we can receive are eternal.

Testimony	Bear testimony of the joy we experience when we keep our baptismal covenants. Encourage class members to remember their baptismal covenants and be true to them.

Enrichment Activities

You may want to use one or more of these activities during the lesson.

1. Give each class member a copy of the handout "Break the Code," on the next page. (Be sure to erase the chalkboard before starting this activity.)

   Have class members try to break the code of the messages on the handout. Allow two or three minutes. If no one has broken the code by then, tell class members that each letter in the code represents the letter that comes just before it in the alphabet. Give them a few more minutes to decode the messages on the handout. The correct messages are listed below:

Message 1:	BEAR ONE ANOTHER'S BURDENS
Message 2:	MOURN WITH THOSE THAT MOURN
Message 3:	COMFORT THOSE THAT STAND IN NEED
Message 4:	STAND AS WITNESSES OF GOD

2. Bring to class two objects that are somewhat heavy but that any member of the class could hold with one hand. Ask for two volunteers to come to the front of the class. Give each of them one of the objects. Have them hold the objects in front of them by placing their right hand under the objects. As they do this, explain that in this activity the objects represent burdens, or personal difficulties that may come to us. Their right hand represents a person trying to bear burdens alone.

   • What are some burdens we sometimes carry? How do those burdens weigh us down?

   The objects will start to feel heavy. Have the volunteers face each other, and invite each volunteer to place his or her left hand securely under the object the other person is holding without letting go of his or her own object. After the volunteers have felt the weight lifted from their right arms, have them give the objects back to you and return to their seats. Ask the following questions:

   • How did this exercise show what it is like to bear one another's burdens?

   Point out that although the burdens were not taken away, they were made lighter when the two class members worked together. In the same way, we can sometimes help others bear their burdens even when we have burdens ourselves. As we help each other, our own burdens will be made lighter.

3. With class members, sing or read the words to "When I Am Baptized" (*Children's Songbook*, 103).

4. If *Family Home Evening Video Supplement* (53276) is available, you may want to show "Baptism—A Promise to Follow Jesus," a nine-minute segment. Although the presentation is suited more for Primary children, the principle taught is true and important for all members of the Church.

Break the Code

The following messages are written in code. They are quotations from key scriptures used in this lesson. Break the code to find the key messages.

Message 1

C F B S   P O F   B O P U I F S ' T

_ _ _ _   _ _ _   _ _ _ _ _ _ _ _

C V S E F O T

_ _ _ _ _ _ _

Message 2

N P V S O   X J U I   U I P T F

_ _ _ _ _   _ _ _ _   _ _ _ _ _

U I B U   N P V S O

_ _ _ _   _ _ _ _ _

Message 3

D P N G P S U   U I P T F   U I B U

_ _ _ _ _ _ _   _ _ _ _ _   _ _ _ _

T U B O E   J O   O F F E

_ _ _ _ _   _ _   _ _ _ _

Message 4

T U B O E   B T   X J U O F T T F T

_ _ _ _ _   _ _   _ _ _ _ _ _ _ _ _

P G   H P E

_ _   _ _ _

Lesson 14

The Gift of the Holy Ghost

Purpose	To teach class members to recognize and follow the promptings of the Holy Ghost.

Preparation	1. Prayerfully study John 14:26; 15:26; 16:13; 1 John 5:7; 2 Nephi 32:5; Moroni 10:5; Doctrine and Covenants 6:23; 8:2; 11:12–13; 42:17; 75:27; 76:53; 84:46; 130:22; Articles of Faith 1:1.
	2. Additional reading: Bible Dictionary, "Holy Ghost," 704.
	3. Number four pieces of paper from 1 to 4, and write on each one the corresponding portion of the quotation found on page 78.
	4. Materials needed: A set of scriptures and a scripture marking pencil for each class member. Continue to encourage class members to bring their own scriptures to class each week.
Note to the teacher	*One of the choicest blessings we will ever receive comes to each of us shortly after baptism, when bearers of the Melchizedek Priesthood place their hands on our head and say, "Receive the Holy Ghost." We are then entitled to guidance from the Holy Ghost as long as we remain worthy. All of us face daily decisions—some small, some monumental—involving eternal blessings. The Holy Ghost can impress on our hearts and minds the direction the Lord would have us go. Help class members understand that this gift from Heavenly Father is one of our greatest resources.*
	As you teach this lesson, be sensitive to the feelings of class members who have not yet been baptized and confirmed.

Suggested Lesson Development	**Being Born of the Spirit**
Scripture discussion	Write on the chalkboard *We must be born of _____ and of _____ _____ to enter the kingdom of God.* Remind class members that you discussed being born again in the previous lesson, and ask them to fill in the blanks in the statement. (If they need help in doing so, have them find and read John 3:5.)

• How do we become born of water? (By being baptized.)

• How do we become born of the Spirit? (By receiving the gift of the Holy Ghost after baptism.)

Explain that before Jesus was crucified, he promised his Apostles that after he died Heavenly Father would send a Comforter to be with them (see John 14:26; 15:26; 16:13). This Comforter, who is the Holy Ghost, would testify of Jesus Christ. He would also comfort the Apostles and help them know what to do when Jesus was gone. Tell class members that this lesson will help them understand how they, like Jesus' Apostles, can be blessed and strengthened by the power of the Holy Ghost.

Receiving the Gift of the Holy Ghost

Note to the teacher

Ask questions that encourage thought and discussion rather than questions that can be answered with a single word or statement. Pause for a few moments after asking a question so that class members have time to think about their answers. (See Teaching—No Greater Call, *106.)*

Discussion

- Who is the Holy Ghost?

Have class members share what they know about the Holy Ghost. If class members do not mention the following points, bring them up yourself:

1. The Holy Ghost is the third member of the Godhead. (See 1 John 5:7; Articles of Faith 1:1.)

2. He is a personage of Spirit. He is a person, but he does not have a body of flesh and bones as Heavenly Father and Jesus Christ do. (See D&C 130:22.)

3. He is also known as the Comforter, the Spirit, the Spirit of God, or the Holy Spirit. (See D&C 75:27; 84:46; 76:53.)

Scripture activity

Assign each class member or pair of class members to look up and read one of the following scriptures: John 14:26; 2 Nephi 32:5; Moroni 10:5; Doctrine and Covenants 11:12; Doctrine and Covenants 42:17.

Then have class members read their assigned scriptures aloud and tell what each scripture says about what the Holy Ghost does. List the responses on the chalkboard.

- What must we do to have the Holy Ghost help us with all these things? (We must receive the gift of the Holy Ghost through the laying on of hands after we are baptized, and then we must live worthy of that gift.)

Teacher presentation

Explain that a person can be influenced by the Holy Ghost before baptism. The Holy Ghost helps people know that Jesus Christ is our Savior and Redeemer and that the gospel is true. But the gift of the Holy Ghost can only be received after baptism. The gift of the Holy Ghost is the privilege and right to have the companionship of the Holy Ghost at all times. This gift is given through the laying on of hands by those who have proper Melchizedek Priesthood authority, and it remains in effect as long as we are trying to live righteously. The Holy Ghost can bring us comfort, help us choose between right and wrong, and direct us in what Heavenly Father and Jesus Christ want us to do. (You may want to mention also that answers to our prayers often come through promptings from the Holy Ghost.)

Recognizing the Promptings of the Holy Ghost

Story and discussion

Explain that if we are worthy to receive help from the Holy Ghost and willing to listen to him, he will always help us. Sometimes, however, it takes experience and practice to learn how to recognize the promptings of the Holy Ghost.

Read or tell the following account by Elder Boyd K. Packer of the Quorum of the Twelve Apostles:

"One of our sons has always been interested in radio. When he was a little fellow, his Christmas present was a very elementary radio construction set.

"As he grew, and as we could afford it, and as he could earn it, he received more sophisticated equipment.

"There have been many times over the years, some very recently, when I have sat with him as he talked with someone in a distant part of the world.

"I could hear static and interference and catch a word or two, or sometimes several voices at once.

"Yet he can understand, for he has trained himself to tune out the interference.

"It is difficult to separate from the confusion of life that quiet voice of inspiration. Unless you attune yourself, you will miss it. . . . You can train yourself to hear what you want to hear, to see and feel what you desire, but it takes some conditioning.

"There are so many of us who go through life and seldom, if ever, hear that voice of inspiration, because 'the natural man receiveth not the things of the Spirit of God: for they are foolishness unto him: neither can he know them, because they are spiritually discerned' (1 Cor. 2:14)" (in Conference Report, Oct. 1979, 27–28; or *Ensign,* Nov. 1979, 19–20).

- How are the promptings of the Holy Ghost like the radio signal in this story? (Answers may include that we must pay close attention to hear the promptings of the Holy Ghost; other things can cause interference and distract us from listening to the Holy Ghost; as we gain experience in listening to the Holy Ghost, we are better able to hear and understand him.)

Chalkboard and scripture discussion

Point out that although we talk about "hearing" or "listening to" the Holy Ghost, he rarely speaks to us in an audible voice, like another person speaks to us. His promptings usually come in other ways.

Explain that the scriptures teach us several ways in which promptings from the Holy Ghost may come. Write *D&C 6:23* on the chalkboard, and have class members read and mark this verse.

- What is one way the Holy Ghost communicates with us?

Write *Peace* on the chalkboard following *D&C 6:23.* Explain that if we feel peaceful about a question or decision, that is usually the Holy Ghost telling us that what we have decided is right.

Write *D&C 8:2* on the chalkboard, and have class members read and mark this verse.

- What does this scripture tell us about how the Holy Ghost communicates with us?

Write *Knowledge in our minds and hearts* on the chalkboard following *D&C 8:2.* Explain that sometimes the Holy Ghost gives us thoughts or feelings that we could not receive from any other source. For example, we may know that a friend needs encouragement, even though he or she appears happy and has not said anything about feeling discouraged. This knowledge is an example of communication from the Holy Ghost. A knowledge that the gospel is true also comes this way.

Write *D&C 11:13* on the chalkboard, and have class members read and mark this verse.

- What does this scripture tell us about how the Holy Ghost communicates with us?

Write *Enlightenment and joy* on the chalkboard following *D&C 11:13*. Explain that the Holy Ghost can enlighten our minds by helping us understand things, such as the meaning of a passage of scripture we have read. He can also give us feelings of joy to help us know we are doing what is right.

Following the Promptings of the Holy Ghost

Discussion

- What should we do when we receive promptings from the Holy Ghost?

Point out that we should follow the promptings we receive from the Holy Ghost, even if it is sometimes difficult to do so.

- Why does it sometimes take courage to follow the promptings of the Holy Ghost?

Quotation

Have a class member read the following statement from Elder F. Enzio Busche of the Seventy:

"It takes courage and commitment to follow the promptings of the Spirit because they may frighten us as they lead us to walk along new paths, some-times paths that no one has walked before, paths of the second mile, of acting totally differently from how worldly people act. For instance, we may be prompted to smile when someone offends us, to give love where others give hate, to say thank you where others would not find anything to be thankful for, to accept jobs that others would be too proud to do, to apologize where others would defend themselves, and to do all the seemingly crazy things that the Spirit prompts a righteous, honest, listening heart to do" ("The Only Real Treasure," *New Era,* Dec. 1979, 5).

Explain that promptings from the Holy Ghost tell us things Heavenly Father wants us to know or do. The blessings we receive from following these promptings outweigh any difficulty or inconvenience we may experience from doing so.

Quotation and discussion

Read the following comments from a man who was a convert to the Church. Do not reveal the man's identity until after the questions have been discussed.

"I cannot help but think back to the day when I, as an investigator of the Church, was confronted with the missionaries' challenge to prepare for my baptism. This step seemed to be too big for me to take, but . . . I already had a testimony burning within me of the truthfulness of this work. . . .

"So I accepted the challenge for baptism, with a fearful heart, but I told the missionaries that I would do it only on two conditions: First, that I would never be called to any Church position, and second, that I would never have to give a talk."

- Why did it take courage for this man to join the Church? (Joining the Church would require him to make changes in his life.)

- Why did he decide to be baptized? (The Holy Ghost had helped him gain a testimony of the gospel.)

- What might have happened to this convert if he had followed the promptings of the Holy Ghost to be baptized, then rejected later promptings by refusing to accept a calling or give a talk?

Explain to class members that this man did follow the guidance of the Holy Ghost after baptism as well as before. He is Elder F. Enzio Busche of the First Quorum of the Seventy, the same man who made the statement that was read aloud by a class member a few minutes ago. Elder Busche told about his baptism in general conference, concluding with the following remarks:

"Without the loving influence and the power and security of the Holy Ghost, which I received by the laying on of hands after baptism to help me, I could not have done anything in my various Church assignments" (in Conference Report, Apr. 1980, 37; or *Ensign*, May 1980, 27).

Quotation

Give the four papers containing the quotation below to four class members. Explain that after the death of the Prophet Joseph Smith, Brigham Young had a dream in which Joseph Smith appeared to him and gave him some instructions. (See *Manuscript History of Brigham Young, 1846–1847,* comp. Elden J. Watson [1971], 529–30.) Have the four class members share those instructions with the class by reading their papers in numerical order.

1. *"Tell the people to be humble and faithful, and be sure to keep the spirit of the Lord and it will lead them right. Be careful and not turn away the small still voice; it will teach you what to do and where to go. . . .*

2. *"Tell the brethren to keep their hearts open to conviction, so that when the Holy Ghost comes to them, their hearts will be ready to receive it. They can tell the Spirit of the Lord from all other spirits; it will whisper peace and joy to their souls; it will take malice, hatred, strife and all evil from their hearts; and their whole desire will be to do good, bring forth righteousness and build up the kingdom of God.*

3. *"Tell the brethren if they will follow the spirit of the Lord they will go right.*

4. *"Be sure to tell the people to keep the Spirit of the Lord."*

Testimony

Testify of the value of the gift of the Holy Ghost in your life, and express your gratitude that Heavenly Father has given this gift to help us. As appropriate, you may want to tell class members about a time when you were prompted by the Holy Ghost.

Encourage class members to learn to listen to the promptings of the Holy Ghost and to follow those promptings when they receive them.

Enrichment Activities

You may want to use one or more of these activities during the lesson.

1. Tell in your own words the following account from the journal of Wilford Woodruff, who later became the fourth President of the Church:

"When I got back to Winter Quarters from [a mission to England], President Young said to me, 'Brother Woodruff, I want you to take your wife and children and go to Boston, and stay there until you can gather every Saint of God in New England and Canada and send them up to Zion.' I did as he told me. It took me two years to gather up everybody, and I brought up the rear with a company. When I got into Pittsburg with this company it was dusk, and I saw a steamer just preparing to go out. I walked right up to the captain and asked him if he was ready to go out. He said he was. 'How many passengers have you?' 'Two hundred and fifty.' 'Can you take another hundred?' 'I can.' 'Then,' said I, 'I would like to go aboard with you.' The words were hardly out of my mouth when the Holy Ghost said to me, 'Don't you, nor your company go aboard that steamer.' . . . I turned and told the captain that I had made up my mind not to go at present. That steamer started out. It was a dark night, and before the steamer had gone far she took fire, and all on board were lost. We should probably have shared the same fate, had it not been for that monitor within me" (*Collected Discourses Delivered by President Wilford Woodruff, His Two Counselors, the Twelve Apostles, and Others,* comp. Brian H. Stuy, 5 vols. [1987–92], 5:239).

Invite class members to share, as appropriate, experiences when they or someone they know has been made safe because of a prompting from the Holy Ghost.

2. Bring to class a treat, such as a piece of candy, or a useful item, such as a pencil. Present this item to a class member, saying it is a gift from you. Then tell the class member to put the item in a pocket or under a chair and not pay any more attention to it. After the class member has done so, ask him or her:

   • How much use is this gift to you right now? Are you glad you were given this gift? Have you really received this gift?

   • What would you rather do with this gift?

Explain that the gift of the Holy Ghost is given to all members of the Church when they are confirmed after baptism. This is a very valuable gift from our Father in Heaven. But often we do the spiritual equivalent of sticking our gift in a pocket or under a chair, ignoring it. For this gift to be useful and valuable to us, we must truly "receive the Holy Ghost" by seeking and listening to his promptings.

3. If *Family Home Evening Video Supplement* (53276) is available, show "Following the Spirit," a six-minute segment.

4. Sing with class members "The Still Small Voice" (*Children's Songbook,* 106) or "Listen, Listen" (*Children's Songbook,* 107).

Lesson
15

Recognizing Personal Revelation

Purpose	To teach class members to better understand, receive, and act on personal revelation.

Preparation	1. Prayerfully study Doctrine and Covenants 6:14–15; 9:7–9; Articles of Faith 1:9.
	2. Familiarize yourself with the following scriptures describing ways revelation can come: Genesis 41:1–36; Luke 1:26–38; 1 Nephi 4:1–18; 8; 16:10; Doctrine and Covenants 6:22–23; Moses 1:8; Joseph Smith—History 1:30, 33, 59, 62.
	3. Additional reading: Bible Dictionary, "Revelation," 762.
	4. You may want to invite the bishop or another guest (with the bishopric's approval) to tell about how personal revelation has affected his or her life. (This comes at the end of the lesson; the guest does not need to be present the entire class time).
	5. Materials needed: A set of scriptures and a scripture marking pencil for each class member. Continue to encourage class members to bring their own scriptures to class each week.
Note to the teacher	*The First Presidency has said, "The Church of Jesus Christ of Latter-day Saints owes its origin, its existence, and its hope for the future to the principles of continuous revelation" (Church News, 10 Jan. 1970, 12). The prophet receives revelation for the Church as a whole, but each individual can receive revelation for his or her own personal needs. Help class members be aware of the importance of personal revelation in their lives.*

Suggested Lesson Development	**Revelation Is God's Way of Communicating with His Children**
Activity	Write the letter *R* on the chalkboard and ask class members what gospel-oriented word it stands for. If class members do not guess *Revelation* right away, add letters one at a time until class members guess the right word.
Discussion	• What is revelation? (God's way of communicating with his children on earth.)
	Help class members find "Revelation" in the Bible Dictionary (page 762). Ask a class member to read the following excerpt from that section, and suggest that class members mark the excerpt in their own scriptures.
	"Divine revelation is one of the grandest concepts and principles of the gospel of Jesus Christ, for without it, man could not know of the things of God and could not be saved with any degree of salvation in the eternities. Continuous revelation from God to his saints, through the Holy Ghost . . . makes possible daily guidance along true paths and leads the faithful soul to complete and eternal salvation in the celestial kingdom."

- Some churches believe that revelation has stopped, that God no longer communicates with his children on earth. Why is it important to know that revelation continues today?

Every Worthy Church Member Has the Right to Receive Personal Revelation

Quotation
and discussion

- Who can receive revelation? (You may want to list class members' responses on the chalkboard.)

Have someone read the following statement from Elder Boyd K. Packer:

"Revelation is not confined to the prophet. It is shared by the General Authorities.

" . . . Fathers and mothers also may receive inspiration, revelation . . . to help guide their families. And of course each of us, if we will live for it, may be the recipient of spiritual communications for our own personal guidance" (in Conference Report, Apr. 1974, 135; or *Ensign,* May 1974, 93).

Explain that every worthy Church member has the right to receive revelation, but each of us is given revelation based on our responsibilities and stewardship.

- Who has the right to receive revelation for the whole Church? (The prophet.)

- For the ward? (The bishop.)

- For the ward Primary? (The ward Primary president.)

- For your family? (Your father and mother.)

- For you individually? (You.)

Emphasize that each class member, if he or she is trying to live righteously, has the right and privilege to receive personal revelation.

Revelation Comes in Many Different Ways

Chalkboard
discussion

Explain that the revelations of God come in a variety of ways.

- What are some of the methods God uses to communicate with his children?

List class members' responses on the chalkboard. As class members mention a method, ask if they can think of an incident in the scriptures or Church history when this method of revelation was used. (Spend only a few minutes on this discussion.)

Answers may include:

1. Heavenly messengers (Moroni's appearance to Joseph Smith; the angel Gabriel's appearance to Mary, the mother of Jesus).

2. Visions and dreams (Moses' vision of the earth's creation; Lehi's dream; Joseph's interpretation of Pharaoh's dream; Brigham Young's dream of Joseph Smith, discussed in lesson 14).

3. Sacred instruments (Lehi's use of the Liahona for direction; Joseph Smith's use of the Urim and Thummim to translate the Book of Mormon).

4. Inspiration (Oliver Cowdery receiving peace and a testimony through the Holy Ghost; Nephi determining how to obtain the brass plates from Laban).

- Which method of revelation will most members of the Church likely experience? (Inspiration.)

Teacher presentation

Remind class members that inspiration comes through the Holy Ghost, and it can come by way of feelings, thoughts, or words. Review from lesson 14 the ways the Holy Ghost may inspire us (see pages 76–77).

Explain that personal revelation can also come to us through the scriptures or another person. The Holy Ghost may prompt us to read a certain verse of scripture, or he may inspire a parent, teacher, or Church leader to tell us what we need to hear. (For example, when Joseph Smith needed to know which church to join, he was prompted to pray when he read James 1:5 in the Bible.) Priesthood blessings can also be valuable sources of personal revelation.

Note to the teacher

Many class members have received and recognized inspiration from the Holy Ghost. Some, however, may not have received it or may not have recognized it as inspiration. As appropriate, encourage class members who are familiar with the promptings of the Holy Ghost to share their experiences with other class members.

You may want to point out to class members that Satan tries to imitate the promptings of the Holy Ghost. See the third enrichment activity for information you can share on how to distinguish between genuine personal revelation and counterfeit promptings from Satan.

Stories and discussion

Tell in your own words the following stories. Discuss with class members how the person in each story received personal revelation through inspiration.

Story 1

In 1921 Elders David O. McKay (who later became the ninth President of the Church) and Hugh J. Cannon visited missions around the world. While in Hawaii, they visited the Kilauea volcano, the largest active volcano in the world, with some of the missionaries. They discovered a natural balcony just inside the volcano, and Elder McKay and several of the missionaries climbed down to stand on it. On this balcony they were out of the chilly wind and had a marvelous view of the inside of the volcano. After a while, Elder McKay said, "Brethren, I feel impressed that we should get out of here." Almost immediately after they climbed back to the rim, the balcony on which they had been standing crumbled and fell into the molten lava below. (See *Cherished Experiences from the Writings of President David O. McKay,* comp. Clare Middlemiss, rev. ed. [1976], 51–53.)

Story 2

A young elder of the Church in the armed services was stationed in Australia during World War II. He became acquainted with a family living on a nearby farm and spent a good deal of time with them while off duty. The family members became interested in the gospel and desired to learn more about it. The elder had attended seminary, priesthood meetings, and Church classes as a boy but felt unqualified to teach this family the gospel. He decided, however, to do his best and pray for help. He later explained that in his attempt to teach the family he quoted many scriptures that he had long forgotten.

Story 3

When Annie was born she was so tiny that her mother's wedding ring would fit over her wrist. When Annie's mother died, she left the ring to Annie. One day Annie wore the ring, which she loved dearly, while she was doing her housework. When the work was all done, she discovered that the ring was gone. She frantically searched the house, but it was nowhere to be found. Finally she knelt down and asked Heavenly Father to help her. She felt she should look in the bedroom. She looked everywhere in there, but could not find the ring. Disappointed, she went into another room, but again she felt she should look in the bedroom. As she went through the bedroom door, there, beneath the bed, she saw the ring.

We Can Ask for Personal Revelation

Scripture discussion

Explain that sometimes inspiration or revelation simply comes to us, as it did to Elder McKay in the story above. More often, however, we must ask for the revelation we need, as the people in the other two stories did.

• How did Annie and the young elder in the military ask for personal revelation? (Through prayer.)

Explain that when Joseph Smith and Oliver Cowdery were working on the translation of the Book of Mormon, the Lord taught Oliver how to seek and receive the revelation he needed to translate. We can use the same pattern to seek personal revelation.

Read with class members Doctrine and Covenants 9:7–9, and discuss the steps for receiving revelation given in these verses. Explain that we should ask Heavenly Father if a decision is right rather than ask him to make the decision for us.

Point out that we will not necessarily receive our inspiration the same way Oliver Cowdery did. We may have a feeling of peace rather than a burning in the bosom, or we may feel uncomfortable about a wrong decision rather than forgetting it.

Chalkboard discussion

• What are some specific areas in which people your age may want to seek personal revelation? (If it is appropriate for your class, you may want to substitute the first enrichment activity for this chalkboard discussion.)

Write class members' answers on the chalkboard. Answers may include:

Resisting temptation.
Understanding the scriptures.
Enduring sickness and trials.
Overcoming discouragement.
Keeping safe.
Choosing friends.
Receiving a testimony.
Preparing for a mission.
Filling Church callings.
Dealing with family members.

Have a class member read the following statement by President Lorenzo Snow, fifth President of the Church:

"The spirit of God . . . will reveal to [people], even in the simplest of matters, what they shall do, by making suggestions to them. We should try to learn the nature of this spirit, that we may understand its suggestions, and then we will always be able to do right. This is the grand privilege of every Latter-day Saint. We know that it is our right to have the manifestations of the spirit every day of our lives" (in Conference Report, Apr. 1899, 52).

Emphasize to class members that they can seek the Lord's guidance on any subject.

We Must Act on Revelation We Receive

Explain to class members that once we receive revelation or inspiration about something we should do, we must act. Read or have class members read the following stories, and discuss what would have happened if the person in each story had not acted on the inspiration.

Story 1

"We were riding horses at my uncle's ranch. Dad said my younger brother and sister and I could ride into the field where my uncle was working. We had just started when my brother and sister both said they didn't want to go. I started across the field, when it seemed someone said, 'Go back.' At first I just kept going, but the voice came again. It was a very quiet voice. I stopped the horse. Just then the horse saw a large snake and started to rear back. I was able to turn him around and calm him down, but if we had been going fast when he reared back I would have been thrown off and hurt."

- What might have happened if this person had ignored the voice that said, "Go back"?

Story 2

"I was with some friends. One girl was not a member of the Church, and I got the idea that I should tell her what our church believed. Just thinking about it frightened me. I thought I couldn't, but something seemed to say to me, 'Yes, you can. Go ahead.' I told her I'd like to tell her about our church. She said, 'All right,' so I did. I didn't feel frightened. Soon she was asking questions, and all the girls were telling her about the Church. We talked for a long time. I was glad I received the courage to ask her."

- What might have happened if this girl had not followed the inspiration to tell her friend about the Church?

Point out that in this case, the girl would not have been hurt by ignoring her inspiration, but her friend would not have learned about the Church at that time. Also point out that if we do not act on inspiration we receive, it becomes harder to receive inspiration the next time we need it. The more we seek and act on personal revelation, the more in tune we are to receive it.

Have the invited guest tell about how personal revelation has affected his or her life. If you did not invite a guest, tell about how personal revelation has affected your life, or bear testimony of the importance of personal revelation in our lives.

Encourage class members to prayerfully seek personal revelation when they need guidance in their lives.

Enrichment Activities	You may want to use one or more of these activities during the lesson.

1. Write on separate pieces of paper situations where class members may need personal revelation (prepare at least one piece of paper for each class member). Put these pieces of paper into a bowl, basket, or jar and bring them to class. Also bring a thin-necked bottle, such as a soda pop bottle.

   Have class members arrange their chairs in a circle. Put the bottle on the floor in the middle of the circle, and spin it. When the bottle stops spinning, the class member to whom it is pointing chooses a piece of paper and tells how personal revelation could help if he or she was in that situation.

   When the class member has answered, he or she spins the bottle, and another class member has a turn to choose a piece of paper (if the bottle points to a class member who has already had a turn, spin it again).

   Possible situations:

   > You are tempted to use harmful drugs.
   > Your mother is sick with cancer.
   > You have no close friends.
   > You feel you lack a testimony.
   > Your father has lost his job.
   > You want to understand the scriptures better.
   > You want to know how to begin preparing for a mission.
   > You do not get along with your older brother.

2. If *Book of Mormon Video Presentations* (53911) is available, show "I Will Prepare the Way," a seven-minute segment. Discuss why the young woman in the segment needed personal revelation and how she received it.

3. Explain to class members that sometimes Satan can give us strong feelings that we may confuse with revelation from God. President Boyd K. Packer of the Quorum of the Twelve Apostles teaches us how we can recognize a feeling from Satan. Have a class member read the following statement from President Packer:

   "There can be counterfeit revelations, promptings from the devil. . . . As long as you live, in one way or another the adversary will try to lead you astray. . . . If ever you receive a prompting to do something that makes you *feel* uneasy, something you know in your *mind* to be wrong and contrary to the principles of righteousness, do not respond to it!" (in Conference Report, Oct. 1994, 78–79; or *Ensign*, Nov. 1994, 61; italics in original).

   You may want to point out that in a situation like this, it is the feeling of uneasiness that is the actual revelation. This uneasiness is the Holy Ghost warning us that what we are considering is wrong.

   Emphasize to class members that God will never give them personal revelation that contradicts what has already been revealed in the scriptures.

Hold to the Rod

Purpose	To increase class members' appreciation for the scriptures and their desire to study and apply them.

Preparation	1. Prayerfully study 1 Nephi 8; 15:23–24; 19:23; 2 Nephi 4:15–16; Doctrine and Covenants 1:38; 18:34–36; 68:3–4.
	2. Write on a separate card each of the five situations described in the lesson on page 89 (or five similar situations more applicable to members of your class). Include on each card the description of the situation and the question that follows it, but do not include the scripture references that follow the question.
	3. Familiarize yourself with the following scriptures that may be used in the situation activity: Exodus 20:15; Psalms 31:1; 37:8; Matthew 6:33; Luke 15:11–32; 1 Thessalonians 5:22; 1 Timothy 4:12; 1 Nephi 3:7; 2 Nephi 2:27; 9:18; Mosiah 13:20; Alma 27:27; Doctrine and Covenants 4:2; 10:5; 88:119; Articles of Faith 1:13.
	4. Prepare for each class member a copy of a calendar grid like the one at the end of the lesson (page 92).
	5. Materials needed: a. A pen or pencil for each class member. b. The picture Lehi's Dream of the Tree of Life (picture 6 in the picture section of the manual; 62620). c. A set of scriptures and a scripture marking pencil for each class member. Continue to encourage class members to bring their own scriptures to class each week.
Note to the teacher	*When we read the scriptures, it is as though we are hearing the Lord speak directly to us (see D&C 18:35–36). Help class members understand that sincere scripture study not only gives us the key to understanding eternal principles but also gives us strength to meet today's challenges by providing inspiration and answers to our problems. Elder Dallin H. Oaks of the Quorum of the Twelve Apostles said: "Because we believe that scripture reading can help us receive revelation, we are encouraged to read the scriptures again and again. By this means, we obtain access to what our Heavenly Father would have us know and do in our personal lives today. That is one reason Latter-day Saints believe in daily scripture study" ("Scripture Reading and Revelation," Ensign, Jan. 1995, 8).*

Suggested Lesson Development	**"My Soul Delighteth in the Scriptures"**
Quotation	Have a class member read the following statement by President Harold B. Lee, eleventh President of the Church:
	"If there is any one thing most needed in this time of tumult and frustration, when men and women and youth and young adults are desperately seeking

for answers to the problems which afflict mankind, it is an 'iron rod' as a safe guide along the straight path on the way to eternal life" (*Stand Ye in Holy Places* [1974], 351).

<table>
<tr><td>Scripture discussion</td><td>

• What could be the "iron rod" to which President Lee referred?

Acknowledge all answers, and then explain that President Lee referred to the iron rod that the prophet Lehi saw in a dream. Display the picture of Lehi's dream and briefly summarize 1 Nephi 8. Then have class members read 1 Nephi 15:23–24.

• In what ways can the word of God be compared to an iron rod?

• Where can we find the word of God?

List class members' responses on the chalkboard. If they name only the standard works, have them read Doctrine and Covenants 1:38, and add "teachings of latter-day prophets" to the list. Explain that the scriptures (including the teachings of latter-day prophets, which are considered scripture) contain the word of God to his people (see also D&C 18:34–36; 68:3–4).

</td></tr>
<tr><td>Story and discussion</td><td>

Have a class member read the following story told by President Spencer W. Kimball about some Latter-day Saints who went to war:

"Some of our men were taken prisoner and kept in nearly total isolation. Permitted no access to the scriptures, they later told how they hungered for the words of truth, more than for food, more than for freedom itself. What they would have given for a mere fragment of the Bible or Book of Mormon that lay so idly on our shelves! They learned by hard experience something of Nephi's feelings when he said:

"'For my soul delighteth in the scriptures, and my heart pondereth them, and writeth them for the learning and the profit of my children.

"'Behold, my soul delighteth in the things of the Lord; and my heart pondereth continually upon the things which I have seen and heard.' (2 Nephi 4:15–16)" ("How Rare a Possession—the Scriptures!" *Ensign,* Sept. 1976, 4).

• Why were the scriptures so important to these men?

Ask class members to consider the answers to the next questions silently:

• How important are the scriptures to you? Do you "delight" in the scriptures?

</td></tr>
</table>

"I Did Liken All Scriptures unto Us"

<table>
<tr><td>Scripture discussion</td><td>

• Why is it important to read and study the scriptures? (Answers may include because they testify of Christ; because God has commanded us to do so; because they teach us the gospel; because they can help us gain or increase our testimony; because they can help us find solutions to our problems.)

Remind class members of the previous lesson on personal revelation. Explain that we can receive personal revelation through reading and studying the scriptures. The scriptures contain counsel from the Lord that applies to us as well as to the people who first received and recorded that counsel.

</td></tr>
</table>

Have class members read and mark 1 Nephi 19:23. Have one class member read the verse aloud.

- What does it mean to "liken all scriptures" unto ourselves?

Story and discussion

Read or tell the following story:

Jessi Ramsey was the only teenage girl in the tiny branch of the Church in Sand Point, Alaska. She often felt alone and wondered if she really believed the gospel. She said, "For a while, I'd read the Book of Mormon and never seemed to get anywhere. Satan seemed to be doing all he could to keep me from gaining a testimony."

Then she had a particularly bad day at school. She had forgotten her lunch, argued with a friend, and been hit by a hockey puck. When she came home, she went to her room to cry.

She explained: "As my tears ceased, I noticed I had left my triple combination on my desk. As I walked over to put it away, it fell open to a page marked by a card. The verses marked in ink caught my eye. I read in Doctrine and Covenants 18:10–11: 'Remember the worth of souls is great in the sight of God; For, behold, the Lord your Redeemer suffered death in the flesh; wherefore he suffered the pain of all men, that all men might repent and come unto him.'

"Suddenly I realized that Christ loved me and I wanted to know him better. I had expected my testimony to be handed to me. I assumed it would be easy. I know now that I have to search, ponder, and pray. . . . If I have faith, my Savior will help me. . . .

"That night I decided to start reading the Book of Mormon again. This time, I was committed to finishing it" (Jessi Ramsey, "No Girl Is an Island," *New Era*, Mar. 1994, 9).

- How did Jessi "liken [the] scriptures unto [herself]"? How did this help her?

- When have you felt that a scripture you read specifically applied to you? How have the scriptures helped you make a decision or solve a problem?

Give class members a few moments to think about these questions before answering. You may want to share an experience of your own.

Scripture activity

Point out that in the previous story, Jessi found the scripture that helped her just by opening her scriptures. Usually, however, we find answers to questions and solutions to problems by studying and seeking out specific scriptures. (You may want to teach class members how to use the Topical Guide before beginning the following activity. See the first enrichment activity for more information.)

Divide the class into small groups, and give each group a card describing one of the following situations (or another situation applicable to class members). Have the members of each group search the scriptures for verses that could help the person described on their card. (There are many possibilities for each situation. Give class members time to search their scriptures on their own. However, if a group is having trouble finding verses, direct the group to the references listed with the appropriate situation.)

When each group has found at least one applicable scripture, have group members share with the rest of the class the situation on their card and the scriptures they found. Have them explain how those scriptures could help a person in the situation described.

Situation 1

Kent is the only member of the Church in his school. Most of his classmates respect and admire him for living Church standards, but a few students ridicule and harass him.

- What scriptures could help Kent deal with the ridicule and harassment he receives? (Psalm 31:1; 2 Nephi 9:18; D&C 10:5)

Situation 2

Karla has a sister who has become less active. Her parents have spent countless hours trying to love her sister back into the Church. Lately Karla has been tempted to stop going to church so she can get some of the attention her sister is receiving.

- What scriptures might help Karla control these negative thoughts? (Psalm 37:8; Luke 15:11–32; Mosiah 13:20)

Situation 3

During the last few weeks, Heather has had many responsibilities and pressures. She doesn't seem to have enough time in each day to accomplish everything she needs to do. She finally made a decision not to take on any new responsibilities. Now her bishop has called her to be president of her Beehive class.

- What scriptures might be helpful to Heather? (Matthew 6:33; 1 Nephi 3:7; D&C 4:2; 88:119)

Situation 4

Clark's friends are planning a party. Part of the entertainment at the party will be a videotape that does not meet the standards of the Church or Clark's family.

- What scriptures might help Clark make a decision about this party? (1 Thessalonians 5:22; 1 Timothy 4:12; 2 Nephi 2:27)

Situation 5

Jamie and a friend went shopping. After they left the store, the friend showed Jamie several pencils she had taken. She told Jamie that it was easy to hide them when the store clerk wasn't looking and that because the pencils were inexpensive, she was not hurting anyone by taking them. She dared Jamie to take something next time they went into the store.

- What scriptures might help Jamie decide what to do? (Exodus 20:15; Alma 27:27; Articles of Faith 1:13)

"Study My Word"

Chalkboard
discussion

- Why is it important to study the scriptures every day, not just when we need a specific answer or solution?

- Why do we sometimes have difficulty studying the scriptures every day?

List class members' answers in a column on the chalkboard.

- What can we do to make scripture study easier and more meaningful for us?

List class members' responses in a second column on the chalkboard and briefly discuss each one. Accept all answers, but focus on those that correspond with the difficulties listed in the first column. For example, if we have difficulty studying the scriptures because we are too sleepy, we can find another time of day to read.

Calendar activity

Give each class member a pen or pencil and a copy of the calendar grid. Have class members fill in the dates on the calendar, beginning with today.

Encourage class members to read something in the scriptures—even a single verse—every day for one month. Tell them to keep track of their reading by coloring or placing a check mark in the box for each day they read the scriptures. Have them decide right now when and where they will read and write this information on the back of the calendar.

Testimony

Bear testimony of the importance of the scriptures, both to the Church as a whole and to us personally. You may want to share a personal experience in which the scriptures helped you.

Encourage class members to study the scriptures daily and to turn to them for answers to personal questions or solutions to problems.

**Enrichment
Activities**

You may want to use one or more of these activities during the lesson.

1. Teach class members how to use the study aids in the LDS scriptures, such as footnotes, the Topical Guide, and the Bible Dictionary. (Learning to use the Topical Guide can be especially helpful for youth just learning to study the scriptures.) To help you prepare, you may want to watch "How to Use the LDS Scripture Study Aids," an eleven-minute segment of *Family Home Evening Video Supplement* (53276). This segment is too long to use in class, but it can help you prepare to teach class members how to use these study aids.

2. Bring to class several pictures cut from a magazine or newspaper. Show the pictures to class members and have them find scriptures that could serve as captions to the pictures. You could do this by giving a different picture to each class member and having class members work on their own, or you could show the same picture to all class members and have them find an appropriate scripture together.

Some examples of pictures and scriptures that could accompany them include:

a. a candle or light bulb—Matthew 5:14 ("Ye are the light of the world")
b. the stars at night—Moses 1:33 ("And worlds without number have I created")
c. a farmyard—3 Nephi 15:24 ("Ye are my sheep") or 3 Nephi 10:4 ("I have gathered you as a hen gathereth her chickens under her wings")
d. a meadow scene—Psalm 23:2 ("He maketh me to lie down in green pastures")
e. a baby—Matthew 18:3 ("Except ye be converted, and become as little children, ye shall not enter into the kingdom of heaven")

3. Blindfold a class member and ask him or her to walk in a straight line across the room (be sure to move chairs and other obstacles out of the way). Then have two class members improvise an "iron rod" by stretching a rope or string across the room and holding it taut. Ask the blindfolded class member to again walk in a straight line across the room, this time holding on to the rope or string. Let the class member take the blindfold off, and have him or her tell the class which walk across the room was easier—the one with the "iron rod" or the one without. (If the class member found it was easy to cross the room without the rope or string, ask how far he or she could walk in a straight line without it.)

Explain that going through life without the scriptures would be like trying to walk a straight line without the rope to guide you. The scriptures help us stay on the path of righteousness.

4. With class members, sing or read the words to "The Iron Rod" (*Hymns,* no. 274).

5. If *Family Home Evening Video Supplement* (53276) is available, show "Using the Scriptures," an eight-minute segment. Ask class members to note, as they watch the segment, reasons these Church leaders give for studying the scriptures (you may want to give class members paper and pencils to write down the reasons they hear). After the video, discuss these reasons.

Sunday	Monday	Tuesday	Wednesday	Thursday	Friday	Saturday

We Thank Thee, O God, for a Prophet

Purpose	To inspire class members to listen to, follow, and sustain the prophet.

Preparation	1. Prayerfully study Amos 3:7; Matthew 16:19; Ephesians 2:19–20; 1 Nephi 22:2; Mosiah 8:17; Doctrine and Covenants 1:14, 38; 21:4–6; 58:18; 68:3.
	2. Make a copy of the crossword puzzle found at the end of the lesson (page 97) for each class member. If it is not feasible to make copies, draw the puzzle on a poster or on the chalkboard.
	3. Materials needed:
	a. A pen or pencil for each class member.
	b. A picture of the current President of the Church.
	c. Several copies of recent conference issues of the *Ensign* or the International Magazines for the activity on page 94. (Conference issues are published in May and November for the *Ensign* and July and January for the International Magazines.)
	d. Hymnbooks for class members to use in singing the hymn at the end of the lesson (see page 96).
	e. A set of scriptures and a scripture marking pencil for each class member. Continue to encourage class members to bring their own scriptures to class each week.
Note to the teacher	*The Lord in his love and wisdom has called prophets to guide us and help us meet the challenges of our time. It is a blessing to know that the counsel we receive from the prophet is the same as if it came directly from the Lord. Emphasize to class members the importance of having a living prophet today. We sustain all the members of the First Presidency and the Quorum of the Twelve Apostles as prophets, but this lesson focuses on the President of the Church, the Lord's spokesman on the earth.*

Suggested Lesson Development	**Messages Come from the Lord through the Prophet**
Story and discussion	Read or tell the following story:
	Many years ago, before there was a temple on the island of Tahiti, 30 Tahitian members of the Church had planned for a long time to make a trip to the Hawaii Temple. They had worked hard to repair a boat and to save the money necessary for their journey. They had also requested and received permission for the journey from their government and from President David O. McKay, who was President of the Church at that time.
	Shortly before the voyage was to begin, the Church members who would be making the trip were asked to gather at the mission home for a meeting. There they were informed that a special message had arrived that day from President McKay. He was asking them not to make the trip to Hawaii.

- How would you feel if you had made all these preparations and then you were counseled not to go?

- Would your feelings be different knowing that the prophet of God had asked you to stop the voyage? Why or why not?

Share the conclusion of the story:

The Church members did not understand why they could not make the trip, but they had testimonies that President McKay was a prophet, so they followed his counsel.

A few days later the skipper of the boat the Saints had planned to use received a call from the harbor where the boat was kept. He was told to come quickly because his boat was sinking. When he examined his boat, he found that the repairmen who had been hired earlier had painted over some rotten wood and rusty pipe, which had then broken, causing the boat to sink. If the Church members had begun the trip, the boat would have sunk while they were on their way to Hawaii.

The Church members had accepted the prophet's counsel without knowing why it was given, but now they understood why they had been advised not to make the journey. They were thankful that they had followed the prophet's counsel. (See R. Lanier and JoAnn M. Britsch, "A Prophet's Warning," *New Era,* Mar. 1976, 12–14.)

Activity

Display a picture of the current President of the Church.

Hand out copies of the *Ensign* (or the International Magazines) containing recent conference addresses. You may separate class members into small groups and give a copy to each group, or you may give a copy to each class member. Have class members find talks by the current President of the Church and look for specific things he has counseled us to do.

- What counsel has the Lord recently given us through the prophet?

List class members' responses on the chalkboard. Testify that just as the people in the story were protected because they followed President David O. McKay, we will be blessed when we follow the counsel of the prophet.

We Can Know That the Prophet Represents God

Story and discussion

- Why is it important to have a testimony that the Lord speaks through the prophet?

Have someone read the following story told by Elder Boyd K. Packer:

"I left the office one Friday afternoon . . . [and] waited for the elevator to come down from the fifth floor.

"As the elevator doors quietly opened, there stood President Joseph Fielding Smith. There was a moment of surprise in seeing him, since his office is on a lower floor.

"As I saw him framed in the doorway, there fell upon me a powerful witness—there stands the prophet of God. That sweet voice of Spirit . . . affirmed to me that this was the prophet of God.

"I need not try to define that experience to Latter-day Saints. That kind of witness is characteristic of this church. It is not something reserved to those in high office. It is a witness, not only available but vital, to every member" (in Conference Report, Apr. 1971, 122–23; or *Ensign*, June 1971, 87).

- How did Elder Packer know that President Smith was the prophet of God?

Emphasize that Elder Packer's testimony was confirmed by the Holy Ghost, not by the sight of President Smith. As appropriate, tell class members about how you have received the witness of the Holy Ghost that the President of the Church is God's prophet. Invite class members to tell how they gained a testimony of the prophet.

Chalkboard discussion

- What can we do to receive a witness from the Holy Ghost that the President of the Church is a prophet of God?

List class members' responses on the chalkboard. Some possible responses include praying, fasting, reading the prophet's messages, watching or listening to general conference, and following the prophet's counsel.

The Scriptures Teach Us to Follow the Prophet

Scripture activity

Give each class member a pen or pencil and a copy of the crossword puzzle. (If you did not make copies of the puzzle, draw it on the chalkboard or on a poster, read the questions aloud, and have class members work together to complete the puzzle.) Encourage class members to mark the scripture passages as they read them. Allow enough time for everyone to complete the puzzle. After the class members have finished, read and discuss each completed statement. Below are the completed statements:

Across

1. God reveals his secrets to his servants the <u>prophets</u>. (See Amos 3:7.)

6. The prophet holds the <u>keys</u> of the kingdom of heaven. (See Matthew 16:19.)

7. Those who do not heed the words of the prophets will be <u>cut off</u>. (See D&C 1:14.)

9. We should receive the counsel of the prophet with all patience and <u>faith</u>. (See D&C 21:4–5.)

Down

2. The prophet speaks as prompted by the <u>Holy Ghost</u>. (See D&C 68:3.)

3. We sustain the President of the Church as a prophet, seer, and revelator. A seer knows about the past and about things to <u>come</u>. (See Mosiah 8:17.)

4. The Lord's voice and the voice of the prophet to the Church are the <u>same</u>. (See D&C 1:38.)

5. The organization of the Church is built on the foundation of the apostles and prophets, with <u>Jesus Christ</u> as the chief cornerstone. (See Ephesians 2:19–20.)

8. The <u>laws</u> of the kingdom (the Church) are given by prophets. (See D&C 58:18.)

"We Thank Thee, O God, for a Prophet"

Hymn

Explain that William Fowler, a British convert baptized in 1849, was so moved by the thought of a prophet of God living among the people that he wrote the words to the hymn "We Thank Thee, O God, for a Prophet" (*Hymns,* no. 19).

Distribute hymnbooks and have class members sing or read the words to this hymn.

- Why are you thankful to be led by a prophet?

Testimony

Share with class members your testimony of the current President of the Church. Encourage them to follow his counsel.

Enrichment Activities

You may want to use one or more of these activities during the lesson.

1. Ask class members to raise their hands if they can recite the ninth article of faith. Invite those who raise their hands to recite it. If no one volunteers to repeat the article of faith, help class members review and memorize it by doing the following exercise:

   Write the article of faith on the chalkboard and have class members repeat it several times. Each time they repeat it, erase one of the key words. Do this until they can repeat the entire article of faith from memory.

   - Why is it important to believe that God "will yet reveal many great and important things pertaining to the Kingdom of God"?

   - To whom does God reveal his will concerning the Church, or his kingdom? (The President of the Church.)

2. Display the picture Latter-day Prophets (62575; Gospel Art Picture Kit 506). Use a piece of paper to cover the names under the first row of pictures, and see how many of the prophets class members can identify. Then do the same with each of the other rows of pictures.

   To help class members learn the names of the latter-day prophets, you may want to use the song "Latter-day Prophets" (*Children's Songbook,* 134).

Crossword Puzzle

Complete the crossword puzzle by filling in the blanks in the following statements.

Across

1. God reveals his secrets to his servants the _____ . (See Amos 3:7.)

6. The prophet holds the _____ of the kingdom of heaven. (See Matthew 16:19.)

7. Those who do not heed the words of the prophets will be _____ _____ . (See D&C 1:14.)

9. We should receive the counsel of the prophet with all patience and _____ . (See D&C 21:4–5.)

Down

2. The prophet speaks as prompted by the _____ _____ . (See D&C 68:3.)

3. We sustain the President of the Church as a prophet, seer, and revelator. A seer knows about the past and about things to _____ . (See Mosiah 8:17.)

4. The Lord's voice and the voice of the prophet to the Church are the _____ . (See D&C 1:38.)

5. The organization of the Church is built on the foundation of the apostles and prophets, with _____ _____ as the chief cornerstone. (See Ephesians 2:19–20.)

8. The _____ of the kingdom (the Church) are given by prophets. (See D&C 58:18.)

Lesson 18

Membership in The Church of Jesus Christ of Latter-day Saints

Purpose	To help class members gain a greater appreciation for membership in The Church of Jesus Christ of Latter-day Saints and to encourage them to participate in the Church's mission, which is to invite all to "come unto Christ" (Moroni 10:32).

Preparation

1. Prayerfully study John 3:3–5; Acts 2:38; 2 Nephi 2:6–8; 3 Nephi 27:13–20; Doctrine and Covenants 1:30; 123:12; 128:15; 131:1–4; Articles of Faith 1:4.

2. For each class member, prepare a set of the following wordstrips:

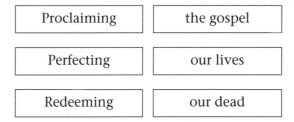

Proclaiming	the gospel
Perfecting	our lives
Redeeming	our dead

Place each set of wordstrips in a separate envelope, withholding one wordstrip from each set. Then place each wordstrip you have withheld into one of the other envelopes. Ensure that each envelope lacks one wordstrip but has two of another wordstrip (see the activity on page 100).

3. Materials needed: A set of scriptures and a scripture marking pencil for each class member. Continue to encourage class members to bring their own scriptures to class each week.

Note to the teacher

The Church of Jesus Christ of Latter-day Saints is the kingdom of God on the earth. As members of the Church, we learn the gospel, receive saving ordinances, and make covenants related to those ordinances. Remind class members that the Church provides us with opportunities to grow and to serve with fellowship, support, and inspiration. The mission of this divinely revealed organization is to invite all people to "come unto Christ, and be perfected in him" (Moroni 10:32).

Suggested Lesson Development

The True Church of Jesus Christ

Discussion

• Often in testimony meetings Latter-day Saints say that they know the Church is true. What does this mean?

After class members have discussed this question, read the following statement:

"The church is the organized body of believers who have taken upon themselves the name of Jesus Christ by baptism and confirmation. To be the true church it must be the Lord's church, and must have his laws, his name, and be governed by him through representatives whom he has appointed" (Bible Dictionary, "Church," 645).

Testify that although other churches teach some truths and do many good things, The Church of Jesus Christ of Latter-day Saints is the only *true* church on the earth because it is the only church that has the complete gospel of Jesus Christ and the priesthood authority to perform ordinances in the name of Jesus Christ. It is Jesus' Church. It has his name and his law, and it is led by his appointed representatives. Express your gratitude for Joseph Smith, the prophet through whom the Lord restored the true Church.

Scripture

Tell class members that Jesus Christ himself testified that The Church of Jesus Christ of Latter-day Saints is true. Have class members read and mark Doctrine and Covenants 1:30.

The Church Strengthens and Unites Us

Story and discussion

Show the drawing of flying geese found at the end of the lesson (page 104).

- Some birds, like geese, migrate to different climates for summer and winter. Why do you think geese fly together in a V-formation when they migrate?

Relate the following in your own words:

Scientists have studied why geese fly in a V-formation when they migrate, and they have found that flying this way is easier on the birds than flying alone. The first bird must fly against the full strength of the wind, but each succeeding bird in the formation has less air resistance to push against. Since the birds take turns being the leader (and having the hardest flight), they can fly longer without getting tired. The geese also honk to encourage each other to keep going.

When a goose gets sick or wounded and has to land, two other geese land with it. They stay with the injured bird until it dies or gains enough strength to fly again. Then they catch up with their flock. (Adapted from Harvey O. Bennett's address to Phi Theta Kappa, 5 May 1990. Used by permission of the Los Angeles County Office of Education.)

- How is the V-formation of the geese like the organization of The Church of Jesus Christ of Latter-day Saints? How are we, as members of the Church, like the individual geese that fly in the formation?

The Mission of the Church

Teacher presentation

Explain that the Church is the organization through which the Lord accomplishes his purposes. Through the Church, truth is taught and people are united in love and in their desire to serve the Lord.

Quotations and chalkboard discussion

- How does the Church help us receive the blessings of the plan of salvation?

After class members have had a chance to share some of their ideas, read the following statement by President Ezra Taft Benson, thirteenth President of the Church:

"The mission of the Church is glorious—to invite all of us to come unto Christ through proclaiming the gospel, perfecting our lives, and redeeming our dead" (in Conference Report, Apr. 1988, 98; or *Ensign*, May 1988, 85).

Write on the chalkboard *Proclaiming the Gospel.*

- Why is it important to preach the gospel? (See 2 Nephi 2:6–8; D&C 123:12.)

You may want to invite class members whose family members have served or are serving full-time missions to talk about the blessings that come through proclaiming the gospel.

- How can we help proclaim the gospel even though we are not full-time missionaries?

Write on the chalkboard *Perfecting Our Lives.*

- What are some of the ordinances we need to gain exaltation? (For some examples, see John 3:3–5; Acts 2:38; D&C 131:1–4.)

- What are the basic principles of the gospel? (See 3 Nephi 27:13–20; Articles of Faith 1:4.)

- How do priesthood ordinances, covenants, and instruction in gospel principles help us progress toward perfection?

Testify that The Church of Jesus Christ of Latter-day Saints is the only church where we can receive priesthood ordinances, make covenants with the Lord, and be instructed in the fulness of the gospel.

Write on the chalkboard *Redeeming Our Dead.*

- How do we help redeem the dead? (By doing work in the temple, such as being baptized for the dead, and by doing work in family history to find the names of ancestors who need to receive ordinances through temple work.)

- Why is it important to do temple work for the dead? (See D&C 128:15.)

- How can doing temple work for the dead help us grow spiritually?

To conclude the discussion, read the following statement by President Gordon B. Hinckley, fifteenth President of the Church:

"We are all in this great endeavor together. We are here to assist our Father in His work and His glory, 'to bring to pass the immortality and eternal life of man' (Moses 1:39). Your obligation is as serious in your sphere of responsibility as is my obligation in my sphere. No calling in this church is small or of little consequence. All of us in the pursuit of our duty touch the lives of others" (in Conference Report, Apr. 1995, 94; or *Ensign,* May 1995, 71).

- How does it make you feel to know that you can "assist [Heavenly] Father in His work and His glory"? How might this knowledge change the way we serve in the Church?

Activity

Erase the words you have written on the chalkboard, and tell class members that you are going to test their memories. Give each of them one of the envelopes you have prepared. Then have each of them organize their wordstrips to display the mission of the Church. Class members will soon find that they cannot fulfill that assignment with the wordstrips they have in their envelopes. When they have discovered this, tell them that they will have to work together. Invite them to share their wordstrips with each other until each person can display the mission of the Church. When they have completed the exercise, ask the following questions:

- How is this exercise like membership in the Church? (We need to work together to fulfill the mission of the Church. We need each other's help.)

- What can we do to work together more effectively to fulfill the mission of the Church?

Being True to the Church

Story

Share the following experience of a young Latter-day Saint doctor:

"I did not realize how much the Church had done for me until I left my home and went to study at a large medical university. I feared I could not keep up with the other students. There were only four Mormons in the entire class, but we all soon found out that we had an advantage over most of the others because of the opportunities the Church had given us. We were not afraid to stand in front of our classes and give reports. We could work well with our classmates and teachers because we had taken part in Church activities that had given us these skills. We did well in our studies because we had learned that help is always near, through prayer.

"We discovered, too, how much we meant to each other. We were suddenly among people with many different beliefs and ways of life, and it was important to us to have friends who believed as we did, friends who knew the way our Father in Heaven wants us to live. We did not want to follow the temptations of the world, and we needed each other.

"I am so grateful for all the Church has done for me as a person, when I didn't even know that it was happening" (in *Walk in His Ways: Basic Manual for Children, Part A* [1982], 76).

Discussion

- How has the Church helped you?

- How can we show that membership in the Church is important to us?

Quotation

Ask class members to think about what their words and actions say about their feelings about the Church. Then read the following statement by President Joseph F. Smith, sixth President of the Church:

"My standing in the Church is worth more to me than this life—ten thousand times. For in this I have life everlasting" (quoted by Joseph Fielding Smith, in *The Progress of Man* [1964], 450).

Testimony

After reading President Smith's testimony, bear your own testimony about the importance of the Church in your life.

Encourage class members to look for ways they can participate in the mission of the Church, and encourage them to show by their words and actions that they are thankful to be members of the true Church of Jesus Christ.

You may want to use one or more of these activities during the lesson.

1. Drop a pebble into a bucket of water. Help class members see that the pebble, though small, creates ripples in the water that extend out to the edges of the bucket.

   • How is this like our membership in The Church of Jesus Christ of Latter-day Saints? (Just as the pebble affects the water all around it, we can affect many people around us by serving faithfully in the Church.)

2. If *Doctrine and Covenants and Church History Video Presentations* (53912) is available, show "Organization of the Church," an eight-minute segment.

3. Tell class members that the establishment of the Church on the earth in the last days was prophesied by an Old Testament prophet. Then read or tell the following story, which is from Daniel 2:

   King Nebuchadnezzar of Babylon had a dream and was troubled because he did not know its meaning. When his magicians and sorcerers could not relate the dream or interpret it, the king was angry and commanded that they be killed. But then Daniel, a captive Hebrew who had found favor with the king, stated that if the king would give him time, he would reveal and interpret the dream.

   Daniel went to his house and asked God for help, and God revealed to him the dream and its interpretation. Later, in the presence of King Nebuchadnezzar, Daniel said that God could reveal secrets and make dreams known and understood. He said that the king had dreamed of a great image. The head of the image was gold, the breast and arms were silver, the belly and thighs were brass, and the legs were iron. The feet were made of a mixture of iron and clay. A stone cut out of a mountain without hands hit the image at the feet, breaking it to pieces. Daniel said, "The stone that smote the image became a great mountain, and filled the whole earth" (Daniel 2:35).

   Daniel also gave the interpretation of the dream. The head of gold represented King Nebuchadnezzar and his powerful kingdom. Lesser kingdoms that were to follow and that would eventually become weak were represented by the other parts of the image. But in the last days "the God of heaven [would] set up a kingdom, which [would] never be destroyed" (Daniel 2:44). That kingdom—The Church of Jesus Christ of Latter-day Saints—was represented in the dream by the stone (see D&C 65:2).

   Have class members read and mark Daniel 2:44–45.

   Display the picture Daniel Interprets Nebuchadnezzar's Dream (62531; Gospel Art Picture Kit 115), and discuss the parts of the picture.

   • Which kingdom will consume all other kingdoms? (See Daniel 2:44; D&C 65:2).

   • How long will that kingdom stand? (See Daniel 2:44.)

- How is Daniel's prophecy being fulfilled today? How are we a part of the fulfillment of the prophecy?

Read the following statement by President Gordon B. Hinckley:

"The little stone which was cut out of the mountain without hands is rolling forth to fill the earth (see D&C 65:2). What a wonderful thing it is to be a part of this growing kingdom of our Lord. There are no political boundaries separating the hearts of the children of God, regardless of where they may live. We are all of one great family. We are sons and daughters of God. We are engaged in the service of His Beloved Son. He is our Redeemer and our Savior, and a testimony of this truth burns within our hearts. Each is entitled to such a testimony of this work. It is an individual knowledge of great fundamental truths that binds us together into what we call the church and kingdom of God" (in Conference Report, Oct. 1995, 3; or *Ensign,* Nov. 1995, 4–5).

Patriarchal Blessings

Purpose	To teach class members basic principles about preparing for and receiving a patriarchal blessing.

Preparation	1. Prayerfully study 1 Nephi 16:10, 16, 28–29; 18:11–12, 20–21.

2. Make five cards, each containing one of the following words: *WHAT, WHO, WHY, WHEN, HOW.* On the back of each card, write the corresponding question or questions below:

   WHAT: What is a patriarchal blessing?

   WHO: Who can receive a patriarchal blessing? Who gives a patriarchal blessing?

   WHY: Why should a person seek a patriarchal blessing?

   WHEN: When can a person receive a patriarchal blessing?

   HOW: How can a person prepare to receive a patriarchal blessing?

   Stick these cards to the bottom of five chairs for class members to find during the lesson, or pass them out to five class members as they come into class.

3. Materials needed:
   a. The picture The Liahona (picture 7 in the picture section of the manual; 62041; Gospel Art Picture Kit 302).
   b. A set of scriptures and a scripture marking pencil for each class member. Continue to encourage class members to bring their own scriptures to class each week.

Note to the teacher

We are all children of God, and he desires to guide us so that we can return to him. One guide he makes available to us is a patriarchal blessing. A patriarchal blessing can help a person understand what the Lord expects of him or her and can motivate the person to live for the promised blessings. Help class members realize that each of them is promised a patriarchal blessing, and encourage them to live worthily so they can receive it when the time is right.

If any class members have already received a patriarchal blessing, encourage them to tell about their experiences (information such as who the patriarch in your stake is, why they decided to seek a patriarchal blessing, or how they prepared for the blessing) as appropriate during the lesson.

Suggested Lesson Development	**A Patriarchal Blessing Is like a Personal Liahona**
Picture discussion	Display the picture of the Liahona and ask class members to tell you about it. If they do not know the answers to the following questions, help them find the answers in the scriptures listed.

- Who is the man kneeling in the picture? (The prophet Lehi.) What is he holding? (The Liahona.)

- What was the Liahona? (See 1 Nephi 16:10.) What did it do? (See 1 Nephi 16:16.)

- What was required for the Liahona to work properly? (See 1 Nephi 16:28–29.)

Help class members understand that the Liahona was a kind of compass given by the Lord to Lehi and his family when they were in the wilderness. It showed them the way they should go, but only when they were faithful and obedient.

- Would you like to have a personalized compass, like the Liahona, to show you which way you should go in life?

Quotation

Read or have a class member read the following statement from President Thomas S. Monson of the First Presidency:

"The same Lord who provided a Liahona to Lehi provides for you and for me today a rare and valuable gift to give direction to our lives, to mark the hazards to our safety, and to chart the way, even safe passage—not to a promised land, but to our heavenly home. The gift to which I refer is known as your patriarchal blessing. Every worthy member of the Church is entitled to receive such a precious and priceless personal treasure" (in Conference Report, Oct. 1986, 81; or *Ensign*, Nov. 1986, 65).

Teacher presentation

Write on the chalkboard *A Patriarchal Blessing: Your Personal Liahona.*

Explain that a patriarchal blessing is similar to the Liahona in several ways. Write the following on the chalkboard below the heading:

Gift from Heavenly Father.

Works according to faith.

Leads you in the right direction.

Explain that in this lesson class members will learn what a patriarchal blessing is, how they can receive one, and how it can be a guide to them as they make decisions throughout their lives.

Patriarchal Blessings Contain God's Counsel to Us

Card 1 discussion

If you put the five cards under chairs, have class members look under their chairs and remove any card they find.

Ask the class member who has the card labeled "WHAT" to read the question on the back of the card:

- What is a patriarchal blessing?

Ask class members to tell all they know about what a patriarchal blessing is. Make sure the following points are covered (have a class member read aloud the quotation from President Monson at the appropriate time in the discussion):

1. A patriarchal blessing is an inspired blessing declaring a person's lineage (the tribe of Israel to which he or she belongs) and giving insight about his or her life.

2. It may include promises of blessings the person may receive, warnings about particular temptations or weaknesses, or counsel about how the person should live.

3. It is given once in a person's lifetime by a stake patriarch.

4. It is recorded, and a copy is given to the person receiving the blessing. A copy is also kept in the archives of the Church.

5. It is a sacred and personal document that should be read and studied often but should not be shared casually with others.

Quotation   President Monson said: "Your patriarchal blessing is yours and yours alone. It may be brief or lengthy, simple or profound. Length and language do not a patriarchal blessing make. It is the Spirit that conveys the true meaning. Your blessing is not to be folded neatly and tucked away. It is not to be framed or published. Rather, it is to be read. It is to be loved. It is to be followed. Your patriarchal blessing will see you through the darkest night. It will guide you through life's dangers" (in Conference Report, Oct. 1986, 82–83; or *Ensign*, Nov. 1986, 66).

Card 2 discussion   Ask the class member who has the card labeled "WHO" to read the questions on the back of the card:

• Who can receive a patriarchal blessing? Who gives a patriarchal blessing?

If class members do not know, explain that any worthy member of the Church can receive a patriarchal blessing when he or she is old enough to understand the opportunities and responsibilities that accompany it. Patriarchal blessings are given by stake patriarchs, priesthood holders who have been ordained to the office of patriarch. (These and subsequent questions may be discussed very briefly if they were mentioned during the discussion of what a patriarchal blessing is; they should be discussed in more detail if they were not previously mentioned.)

• What is the name of our stake patriarch? What are his duties as a patriarch?

Quotation   Have a class member read the following statement from President Joseph F. Smith, sixth President of the Church:

"It is [a stake patriarch's] business and right to bestow blessings upon the people, to make promises unto them in the name of the Lord, . . . by the inspiration of the Holy Spirit, to comfort them in the hours of sorrow and trouble, to strengthen their faith by the promises that shall be made to them through the Spirit of God" (*Gospel Doctrine,* 5th ed. [1939], 181).

Card 3 discussion   Ask the class member who has the card labeled "WHY" to read the question on the back of the card:

• Why should a person seek a patriarchal blessing? (To know God's will, promises, and warnings for him or her.)

Quotation   Have a class member read the following statement from Elder John A. Widtsoe, who was a member of the Quorum of the Twelve Apostles:

"Those who seek patriarchal blessings should ask for them with faith in the reality of the power of the Priesthood. They should seek them with an earnest, prayerful desire to become, through the blessings, more completely happy in their lives, and more perfectly serviceable in the work of the Lord" (*Evidences and Reconciliations*, arr. G. Homer Durham, 3 vols. in 1 [1960], 323).

- How can a patriarchal blessing help us become happier?

- How can a patriarchal blessing help us be more diligent servants of the Lord?

Card 4 discussion Ask the class member who has the card labeled "WHEN" to read the question on the back of the card:

- When can a person receive a patriarchal blessing?

Explain that a patriarchal blessing is given when a person is mature enough spiritually to appreciate the significance of the blessing and desires to receive it. People often receive a patriarchal blessing during their teenage years, when they are old enough to understand the importance of the blessing yet young enough to use it as a guide in making important decisions in life. Encourage class members to counsel with their parents regarding when it would be appropriate for them to receive a patriarchal blessing.

Fulfillment of a Patriarchal Blessing Is Conditional on Righteousness

Discussion Remind class members that the usefulness of the Liahona was dependent on the faith and righteousness of Lehi and his family.

- What happened when some of Lehi's family members were unrighteous? (See 1 Nephi 18:11–12, 20–21.)

Point out that patriarchal blessings are similarly conditional on faith and righteousness. We can receive the promised blessings only when we follow the counsel and commandments we are given by the Lord and his servants.

Explain that it is also important to realize that the promises made in a patriarchal blessing may not all be fulfilled during our earth life. If we are righteous, however, we will eventually receive all the blessings promised us.

Quotation Have a class member read the following statement by Elder Widtsoe:

"Men [and women] have stumbled at times because promised blessings have not occurred in this life. They have failed to remember that, in the gospel, life with all its activities continues forever and that the labors of earth may be continued in heaven" (*Evidences and Reconciliations*, 323).

Discussion Point out that a patriarchal blessing will not answer every question about our lives. Patriarchal blessings vary widely in length and detail; some are very long and some are quite short. Through the patriarch, Heavenly Father will tell each of us what He knows we need to know. The length or detail of a patriarchal blessing is in no way an indication of the recipient's worthiness or Heavenly Father's love for him or her.

- Why do you think Heavenly Father doesn't tell us everything about our lives through our patriarchal blessings?

We Can Prepare to Receive a Patriarchal Blessing

Card 5 discussion

Ask the class member who has the card labeled "HOW" to read the question on the back of the card:

• How can a person prepare to receive a patriarchal blessing?

Explain that the best way class members can prepare now to receive a patriarchal blessing is to continue striving to live righteously. When each class member decides, in counsel with his or her parents, that the time is right to receive a patriarchal blessing, he or she will meet with the bishop to obtain a recommend for the blessing. After the recommend is obtained, an appointment is made with the stake patriarch. Parents and one or two close family members or friends may accompany a person receiving a patriarchal blessing, but large groups should not be invited.

A person who will be receiving a patriarchal blessing may want to spend some time in prayer and fasting before receiving the blessing, although it is not necessary for a person to be fasting at the actual time he or she receives the blessing. Sunday dress is recommended for all those attending the blessing. Everything done in connection with the blessing should invite the Holy Ghost.

Testimony

Testify that a patriarchal blessing contains promises and counsel from Heavenly Father. Emphasize that once we have received a patriarchal blessing, we must study it often, follow the counsel it gives, and live worthy of receiving the blessings it promises. If you have received your own patriarchal blessing, you may want to tell class members how you feel about it or how it has helped you (avoid sharing specific revelations given in your blessing).

Encourage class members to be faithful and obedient so that they will be worthy to receive their patriarchal blessing when the time comes.

Enrichment Activities

You may want to use one or more of these activities during the lesson.

1. A patriarchal blessing may be considered personal scripture. Make for each class member a card containing the quotation below. As you pass out the cards during class, have one class member read the quotation aloud. Encourage class members to keep the card in their scriptures.

   "Receive a patriarchal blessing. Study it carefully and regard it as personal scripture to you—for that is what it is. A patriarchal blessing is the inspired and prophetic statement of your life's mission together with blessings, cautions, and admonitions as the patriarch may be prompted to give. . . . Receive your patriarchal blessing under the influence of fasting and prayer, and then read it regularly that you may know God's will for you" (Ezra Taft Benson, in Conference Report, Apr. 1986, 56; or *Ensign*, May 1986, 43–44).

2. Tell the following story in your own words:

   "My whole life I had heard about the importance of getting a patriarchal blessing. . . . To me, it was kind of frightening. What if I didn't hear anything I wanted to hear? What if there were no great promises for me? I worried about being prepared enough.

"I decided that I needed to have faith and that all would be well. I prayed many times, was interviewed by my bishop, and set up an appointment with the stake patriarch to receive my blessing. Then I waited, while trying to prepare spiritually for this important date.

"On the day I was to receive my blessing, I fasted all day. I thought I would have this super spiritual day, but Satan was working on me and I had a bad day at school. I was a wreck. I came home after school and paced the floor. I thought back . . . to when a man and a woman in our ward whom I admire told us how to prepare, suggesting that we pray for specific things we want to know.

"I went to my room, knelt beside my bed, and prayed that Heavenly Father would tell me what he knew was best for me to hear. I asked that he take away my fears and calm my worried heart.

"Everything turned out fine. In fact, it was a personal miracle. It seemed that the patriarch knew me so completely, even better than I knew myself. I knew he was speaking for Heavenly Father, and when he spoke, I felt the assurance that Heavenly Father did know me. He heard my prayers. . . .

"Now I know why Church leaders are always emphasizing the value of a patriarchal blessing. When we learn the worth of something and pay the price to obtain it, we begin to better understand its value. For me, my blessing and the experience of receiving it was one of the best experiences of my life. I know that my patriarchal blessing will continue to guide me to fulfill its promises" (Rebecca Rose, "My Miracle," *New Era*, June 1995, 54).

3. If *Family Home Evening Video Supplement 2* (53277) is available, show "The Blessings of the Priesthood," a seven-minute segment. In this segment Sister Ardeth G. Kapp, former General President of the Young Women, discusses many blessings of the priesthood. You may want to set the videocassette in advance so that you can show only the one-minute portion in which Sister Kapp speaks about patriarchal blessings.

I Can Know for Myself

Lesson

20

Purpose	To help class members strengthen their testimonies of Jesus Christ and his gospel.

Preparation	1. Prayerfully study Matthew 16:13–17; Alma 32:27–43; Moroni 10:5.
	2. If *Family Home Evening Video Supplement 2* (53277) is available, prepare to show "What Think Ye of Christ?" a five-minute segment.
	3. Materials needed:
	a. A picture of Jesus Christ (picture 2 in the picture section of the manual; 62572; Gospel Art Picture Kit 240).
	b. A set of scriptures and a scripture marking pencil for each class member. Continue to encourage class members to bring their own scriptures to class each week.
Note to the teacher	*A testimony is a personal conviction of gospel truths, based on knowledge revealed by the Holy Ghost. Most Church members have a testimony of some principle of the gospel, and on this foundation a more complete testimony can be built. A testimony motivates us to live righteously, and righteous living causes a testimony to grow. A testimony of the Savior and his gospel is essential to our exaltation.*
	As you prepare the lesson, think of experiences that have strengthened your testimony. Share these as appropriate throughout the lesson presentation.

Suggested Lesson Development	**The Essentials of a Testimony of the Gospel**
Quotation and discussion	Display the picture of Jesus Christ throughout the lesson.

• When you hear the word *testimony,* what do you think of?

After class members have had time to respond to this question, explain that a testimony is really quite simple. Then have a class member read the following statement by Elder Bruce R. McConkie, who was a member of the Quorum of the Twelve Apostles. Ask class members to listen for the three main elements of a testimony.

"A testimony in our day consists of three things: It consists of the knowledge that Jesus is the Lord, that he is the Son of the living God who was crucified for the sins of the world; it consists of the fact that Joseph Smith was a prophet of God called to restore the gospel truths and be the revealer of the knowledge of Christ for our day; and it consists of knowing that The Church of Jesus Christ of Latter-day Saints is the only true and living Church upon the face of the whole earth, the one place where salvation is found, the organization which administers the gospel and therefore administers salvation to the sons of men" ("Gaining a Testimony of Jesus Christ," *Ensign,* Dec. 1980, 15).

111

- What three things does a testimony consist of? Why do you think a testimony must consist of these three things? How does a testimony of these three things serve as a foundation for a testimony of other gospel truths?

Explain that this lesson will show how to obtain and strengthen a testimony.

Obtaining a Testimony

Scripture discussion

- Why is it important that we know *for ourselves* that Jesus is our Savior, that Joseph Smith was called to be a prophet, and that The Church of Jesus Christ of Latter-day Saints is the only true church on the earth?

Point out that we cannot depend on the testimonies of other people. We can be taught and inspired by them, but ultimately we can only gain a strong testimony when we feel the witness of the Holy Ghost ourselves.

Have class members read and mark Matthew 16:13–17.

- Of what truth did Peter testify? How did Peter gain a personal knowledge of this truth? (See Matthew 16:17. Heavenly Father revealed it to him.) How does Heavenly Father reveal truth? (See Moroni 10:5.)

- Peter had walked with Jesus and witnessed the miracles Jesus performed. Why did he need revelation through the Holy Ghost in addition to these experiences?

Quotations

Read or have a class member read the following statement by Elder Dallin H. Oaks:

"The original Apostles were eyewitnesses to the ministry and resurrection of the Savior (see Acts 10:39–41). . . .

"[But] an eyewitness was not enough. Even the witness and testimony of the original Apostles had to be rooted in the testimony of the Holy Ghost. [President Joseph Fielding Smith] has told us that the witness of the Holy Ghost makes an impression on our soul that is more significant than 'a visitation of an angel'" (in Conference Report, Oct. 1990, 36; or *Ensign,* Nov. 1990, 30).

Point out that each of us can obtain a testimony of Jesus Christ and his gospel. Then read the following statement by President Gordon B. Hinckley:

"Every Latter-day Saint has the responsibility to know for himself or herself with a certainty beyond doubt that Jesus is the resurrected, living Son of the living God" (in Conference Report, Apr. 1983, 110; or *Ensign,* May 1983, 80).

Video presentation

Show the video segment "What Think Ye of Christ?" Ask class members to think about their personal testimonies of the Savior as they watch the presentation. Invite them to ask themselves the following question:

- Is my testimony of Jesus Christ strong enough that I will follow him, no matter what other people do and say?

Scripture discussion

Explain that the prophet Alma described how we can gain a testimony. In his example, he showed how we can gain a testimony that the word of God is good.

Have class members read and mark Alma 32:27–28.

- In Alma's example, what does the seed represent? (The word of God.) How can we plant this seed in our hearts?

- What do you think it means to experiment on the word of God?

Have class members read and mark Alma 32:30, 33.

- What do you think it means to have the word of God swell and grow in our hearts? How does this help us know that the word is good?

Explain that this refers to the confirmation we receive when we learn the truth. When we receive such a confirmation, we may feel comforted or uplifted. We may feel a desire to serve the Lord and others.

Chalkboard discussion

Point out that we can use the counsel in Alma 32 to obtain a testimony of specific aspects of the gospel, such as the truthfulness of the Book of Mormon or the blessings of paying tithing.

Write on the chalkboard *I know that* . . . Complete the sentence by bearing your testimony about one or two specific gospel principles. Do it with sincerity and conviction. Give a brief explanation of how you obtained that knowledge. Then invite class members to do the same.

Strengthening Our Testimonies

Scripture discussion

Have class members read and mark Alma 32:37, 41.

- When the word of God has grown in our hearts, how can we nourish it?

Explain that as we work diligently and exercise faith and patience, we can develop testimonies of individual doctrines and principles of the gospel. Our testimonies can grow to include more gospel truths as we progress spiritually. Continued righteous living helps nourish the portion of our testimonies that we have already obtained. Point out that many of the ways the Lord has provided for us to experiment on his word and strengthen our testimonies have been discussed in previous lessons. Faith, repentance, the gift of the Holy Ghost, prayer, fasting, personal revelation, patriarchal blessings, scripture study, following the prophet, and Church service will help us strengthen our testimony.

Our Testimonies Strengthen Us

Story

Point out that as we strengthen our testimonies, our testimonies give us strength. Share the following story told by Elder John B. Dickson of the Seventy:

"I am reminded of a little village called Panacaxtlan, situated where the coastal plains meet the mountains of central Mexico. The village is situated in a lush, green, humid area known as the Huesteca, and the inhabitants are sons and daughters of Lehi. In 1979, . . . missionaries began proselyting in the Huesteca. Fifty-two people joined the Church in Panacaxtlan. . . .

"A short time later, a meeting was called in Panacaxtlan at which Church members were given the following options: denounce the Church, leave the village, or be killed (not an idle threat).

"The members, particularly the women, said they knew the Church to be true and would not denounce it. They also indicated they had worked just as hard as the rest of the community to secure their homesteads, and they would not leave. Boldly stepping forward, they told their taunters if they were going to kill them, to get on with it. The moment grew tense as machetes were raised, then finally lowered while the Latter-day Saints stood up for that which the Spirit had testified to them to be true.

"These Saints eventually learned, as most of us do, that it is harder to live the gospel day by day than to die for it in an instant, but their early commitment came because the Spirit had touched their hearts and changed their lives. Their conversion process had taken place as the Book of Mormon helped build their faith in Jesus Christ, the Son of God" ("The Incomparable Gifts," *Ensign,* Feb. 1995, 7).

Discussion

- What gave the Saints in Panacaxtlan the courage to stand up for the Church?

- Of what gospel truths do you think they had a testimony?

- In this situation, why was it important for them to know for themselves that the gospel was true?

- How can we follow the example of the Saints in Panacaxtlan? (We can stand up for the gospel and the Church in whatever situation we may encounter.)

Quotation

Read the following statement by President Gordon B. Hinckley:

"None of us ever need hesitate to speak up for this Church, for its doctrine, for its people, for its divine organization and divinely given responsibility. It is true. It is the work of God" (in Conference Report, Oct. 1996, 72; or *Ensign,* Nov. 1996, 51).

Discussion

Point out that most members of the Church will not be asked to die in defense of their beliefs. However, we are all asked to "live the gospel day by day" ("The Incomparable Gifts," 7). Then ask the following questions:

- As we strive to "live the gospel day by day," what are some of the difficulties we face? Why do we need to have a testimony to be able to live the gospel despite these difficulties?

Testimony

Bear your testimony simply and sincerely. Tell class members how your testimony of the gospel has influenced your life.

Encourage class members to strive to strengthen their testimonies of the gospel.

Enrichment Activities

You may want to use one or more of these activities during the lesson.

1. Bring to class the following items: a glass jar with a lid, 1/2 cup warm water, one tablespoon granulated sugar, and two tablespoons dry yeast.

   At the beginning of the lesson, explain that the things you will put in the glass jar represent a person's efforts to gain a testimony. The water represents hearing the testimonies of others. Ask a class member to pour the water into the jar and observe the reaction. Explain that although there is no reaction, the jar is more full than it was before. Point out that the testimonies of others can help us begin to gain a testimony, but we still need a testimony of our own.

Tell class members that the sugar represents the person's desire to gain a testimony. Invite another class member to add the sugar to the water and observe the reaction. Explain that although there is very little reaction, the mixture of the water and the sugar are important for the third ingredient to cause a reaction.

Explain that the yeast represents the influence of the Holy Ghost. Ask a third class member to add the yeast to the water and sugar and stir or shake the mixture. At first there will be no noticeable reaction. Invite class members to observe what happens to the mixture as the lesson proceeds.

After about fifteen minutes, when the yeast, water, and sugar have worked together to nearly fill the jar, ask the following questions:

- How do the testimonies of others, our own desire to gain a testimony, and the influence of the Spirit combine to help us gain a strong testimony?

- Why do you think I chose the yeast—and not the water or the sugar— to represent the influence of the Holy Ghost? (The yeast prompted the growth. While the water and sugar were both necessary, they did nothing together until the yeast was added.)

You may want to point out that although the combination of water, sugar, and yeast causes a reaction, it must be combined with other ingredients— such as flour, salt, and milk—in order to make bread. Likewise, a testimony must be combined with such things as service, scripture study, and prayer to truly enrich our lives.

2. As you discuss Alma 32:27–41, display a small pot of soil, and place a seed into the soil. Next to this pot display a potted plant that has sprouted. Have class members read Alma 32:27–28.

Emphasize that a testimony grows a little at a time, like a seed in the earth. If we keep praying, showing love to friends and family members, and doing our duty in the Church, we can grow stronger in our knowledge that the gospel is true.

3. Read the following statement by Elder Robert D. Hales of the Quorum of the Twelve Apostles about one way to strengthen our testimony:

"Share your testimony. . . . Let others know that you know. Bear your testimony in fast meeting. Tell your family; tell your friends. You will find when you share your testimony it becomes stronger, and there are many others around you who also want to embrace the truth" (in Conference Report, Oct. 1994, 27; or *Ensign,* Nov. 1994, 22).

Encourage class members to bear their testimonies in an upcoming fast and testimony meeting, in family home evening, or, as directed by the Spirit, as part of this lesson. Avoid offering rewards to class members who bear their testimonies. Also avoid making people feel unnecessary guilt for not bearing their testimonies.

In Remembrance

Purpose	To help class members understand the meaning of the sacrament and to encourage them to partake of the sacrament worthily.

Preparation	1. Prayerfully study 1 Corinthians 11:28–30; 3 Nephi 18:1–11; 20:8–9; Doctrine and Covenants 20:37, 75, 77, 79; 27:1–4.
	2. Materials needed: a. The pictures Blessing the Sacrament (62343; Gospel Art Picture Kit 603); Passing the Sacrament (62021; Gospel Art Picture Kit 604); and Jesus Praying in Gethsemane (picture 4 in the picture section of the manual; 62175; Gospel Art Picture Kit 227). b. A set of scriptures and a scripture marking pencil for each class member. Continue to encourage class members to bring their own scriptures to class each week.
Note to the teacher	*The sacrament is one of the most important and sacred ordinances of the Church. In partaking of the sacrament we remember our Savior and recommit ourselves to the promises we made at baptism. We take the sacrament so often that sometimes we may forget its significance. Encourage class members to guard against this by preparing always to be worthy to partake of the sacrament and receive the constant companionship of the Spirit.*

Suggested Lesson Development	**We Must Remember the Importance of the Sacrament**
Discussion	Write *In Remembrance* on the chalkboard, and tell class members that it is the title of the lesson.
	• What do you think the topic of the lesson is?
	Allow class members a few guesses about the topic of the lesson. If after a few tries they have not given the correct answer, tell them that the lesson is about the sacrament.
	Display the pictures Blessing the Sacrament and Passing the Sacrament.
Quotation and discussion	State that many of us have partaken of the sacrament hundreds of times in our lives. When something is repeated this often we sometimes forget its importance.
	Read the following statement by Elder Jeffrey R. Holland of the Quorum of the Twelve Apostles:
	"With so very much at stake, [the sacrament] should be taken more seriously than it sometimes is. It should be a powerful, reverent, reflective moment. It

should encourage spiritual feelings and impressions. As such it should not be rushed. It is not something to 'get over' so that the real purpose of a sacrament meeting can be pursued. This *is* the real purpose of the meeting. And everything that is said or sung or prayed in those services should be consistent with the grandeur of this sacred ordinance" (in Conference Report, Oct. 1995, 89; or *Ensign,* Nov. 1995, 68).

- Why is the sacrament more important than the announcements, talks, and hymns at sacrament meeting?

- Why do we partake of the sacrament each week?

Write class members' responses on the chalkboard.

Have class members think back to the last time they partook of the sacrament. Ask them to think silently about the answers to the following questions:

- What are some of the things you thought about the last time you partook of the sacrament? Did those thoughts help you draw nearer to the Savior, or did they distract you from the real purpose of the sacrament?

We Partake of the Sacrament to Remember the Savior's Atonement

Scripture discussion

- Why would a lesson about the sacrament be called "In Remembrance"?

Have class members read and mark Doctrine and Covenants 20:77, 79.

- What does the sacramental bread represent? What does the sacramental water represent? Why is it important to remember the body and blood of the Savior?

Note to the teacher

If class members ask questions about the use of the word wine *in verse 77, explain that when Joseph Smith received the revelation found in section 20, wine was used in the sacramental service. Later the Lord revealed to Joseph Smith that water should be used (see D&C 27:1–4).*

Quotation

Display the picture Jesus Praying in Gethsemane.

Testify that Heavenly Father loved us enough to send his Son to atone for our sins. Share the following statement by Elder Melvin J. Ballard, who was a member of the Quorum of the Twelve Apostles, to show how the sacrament reminds us of that love and to show why we should remember the Savior's Atonement when we partake of the sacrament:

"It is written in the scriptures that God so loved the world that he gave his Only Begotten Son to die for the world, that whosoever believeth on him . . . and keepeth his commandments, shall be saved. But this [sacrifice] did not cost us very much—freely given are all these glorious privileges. . . .

" . . . While we give nothing, perhaps, for this atonement and this sacrifice, nevertheless, it has cost someone something, and I love to contemplate what it cost our Father in heaven to give us the gift of his beloved Son, . . . who so loved the world that he laid his life down to redeem the world, to save us and to feed us spiritually while we walk in this life, and prepare us to go and dwell with him in the eternal worlds. . . .

"Our Father in heaven . . . loved his Son Jesus Christ, . . . for [he] had with him his Son, our Redeemer, in the eternal worlds, faithful and true for ages. . . . God heard the cry of his Son in that moment of great grief and agony, in the garden when . . . he cried out: 'Father, if thou be willing, remove this cup from me.' . . .

" . . . He saw that Son condemned, he saw him drag the cross through the streets of Jerusalem and faint under its load. . . . He saw [Jesus'] body stretched out upon the wooden cross, he saw the cruel nails driven through hands and feet, and the blows that broke the skin, tore the flesh . . . and let out the life's blood of his Son. . . .

"In that hour I think I can see our dear Father, . . . his great heart almost breaking for the love that he had for his Son. Oh, in that moment when he might have saved his Son, I thank him and praise him that he did not fail us, for he had not only the love of his Son in mind, but he had love for us, and I rejoice that he did not interfere, and that his love for us made it possible for him to endure to look upon the sufferings of his Son and give him finally to us, our Savior and our Redeemer. . . .

" . . . My brethren and sisters, . . . if I only knew how essential it was . . . that I should receive the spiritual life that comes from that Son, I am sure I would always be present at the sacrament table to do honor to the gift that has come unto us" ("The Sacramental Covenant," *Improvement Era,* Oct. 1919, 1028–31).

We Partake of the Sacrament to Renew Our Covenants

Discussion

- People often say that when we partake of the sacrament we "renew our covenants." What does this mean?

Make sure class members understand that *renew* means to make new again and that covenants are promises between us and our Heavenly Father. Explain that the sacrament gives us the chance to renew the covenants we made when we were baptized.

Chalkboard and scripture discussion

- According to Doctrine and Covenants 20:77, 79, what promises do we make when we partake of the sacrament?

Erase the chalkboard. On the left-hand side, list the promises class members mention. Answers should include the following:

We promise to:

1. Take upon ourselves the name of Jesus Christ.

2. Always remember him.

3. Keep his commandments.

Refer to lesson 13, in which you discussed the baptismal covenant, and have class members review Doctrine and Covenants 20:37.

- What aspects of this verse are like the promises on the chalkboard?

1. Take upon ourselves the name of Jesus Christ: "Willing to take upon them the name of Jesus Christ."

2. Always remember him: "Having a determination to serve him to the end."

3. Keep his commandments: "Truly manifest by their works that they have received of the Spirit of Christ."

- What is promised to us if we keep the covenants we have made? (See D&C 20:77.)

On the right-hand side of the chalkboard, write *Always have his Spirit to be with us.*

Referring to the list on the chalkboard, ask the following questions:

- How will our lives change if we remember Jesus in everything we do?

- Why is obedience to the commandments necessary for us to have the Holy Ghost with us? Why do we need his constant companionship?

We Must Partake of the Sacrament Worthily

Scripture discussion

Tell class members that when Jesus visited the Nephites after his Resurrection, he taught them about the sacrament. Have class members read 3 Nephi 18:1–11 and mark words they think are important.

- Which words did you mark? Why are those words important?

- How many times is the word *filled* used in these eleven verses? (Four times.) In what way do you think those who partook of the sacrament were filled? (See 3 Nephi 20:8–9. They were filled with the Spirit.) How can we prepare to be filled spiritually when we partake of the sacrament? How can we make partaking of the sacrament each week a more meaningful experience?

- Why did Jesus call the disciples "blessed" after they had partaken of the sacrament? (See 3 Nephi 18:10.)

Point out that he called them blessed because by taking the sacrament they had witnessed that they were willing to keep the commandments. We make the same commitment when we partake of the sacrament, and we will also be blessed for keeping that commitment.

Explain that the Apostle Paul talked about the importance of partaking of the sacrament worthily. Point out that being worthy to partake of the sacrament does not mean being perfect. To partake of the sacrament worthily, we must be doing our very best to keep the covenants we have made—to take upon ourselves the name of Jesus Christ, always remember him, and keep the commandments.

Have class members read and mark 1 Corinthians 11:28–30.

- What are the consequences of partaking of the sacrament unworthily? In what ways might partaking of the sacrament unworthily make us "weak and sickly"?

- What did Paul say we should do to ensure that we partake of the sacrament worthily? How can we "examine [ourselves]" spiritually?

Quotation

Read the following statement that Elder M. Russell Ballard of the Quorum of the Twelve Apostles made to the youth of the Church:

"My dear young friends, I encourage you to take time each week to be by yourself, away from television and the crowd. Have your scriptures with you, and as you read, ponder, and pray, take an honest look at your life. Evaluate where you stand with the promises you have made with Heavenly Father. If you have a problem, talk it over with the Lord in earnest and humble prayer. Counsel with your parents; they will help you. Your bishop and your Young Men and Young Women adult leaders will help. They love you and want you to be at peace with yourself so you can partake of the sacrament worthily each week. When all is said and done, however, only you know if you are living true to your covenants made with God" (in Conference Report, Apr. 1993, 7; or *Ensign,* May 1993, 8).

Testimony

Remind class members that the sacrament gives us the chance to review and remake the covenants we made at baptism. Bear your testimony of the Atonement of Jesus Christ, and express your gratitude for the sacrament.

Encourage class members to partake of the sacrament worthily and to think about the Savior while partaking of the sacrament.

Enrichment Activities

You may want to use one or more of these activities during the lesson.

1. Sing or read the words to a sacrament hymn (*Hymns,* nos. 169–196).

   - Why do you think we sing only certain hymns before the sacrament? What is special about sacrament hymns?

   - What is the purpose of singing sacrament hymns? (To answer this question, you may want to refer back to the statement by Elder Holland in the first section of the lesson.)

2. Invite a deacon in the class to share what it means to him to pass the sacrament. Then discuss the following questions (you may want to arrange for a small group of class members to have a panel discussion on these questions):

   - What can young men do to show reverence and respect as they pass the sacrament?

   - What can young women do to make partaking of the sacrament an uplifting experience for themselves and others?

3. Read the following quotation:

   "While very young . . . I recall telling a dear Sunday School teacher that I was not going to sacrament meeting any more because it was boring and dry. [The teacher] looked at me and said, 'Don't you ever let me hear you say that again! God has invited you to that meeting to partake of the emblems of Jesus Christ's suffering and of his gift to you. You are very privileged to be invited. If you take the right spirit with you to meeting, you will always bring something good away with you'" (LaRue C. Longden, "God Has Invited You," in Leon R. Hartshorn, comp., *Remarkable Stories from the Lives of Latter-day Saint Women,* 2 vols. [1973–75], 1:97–98).

- How would sacrament meeting be different if we remembered the words of this Sunday School teacher? How would *we* be different if we remembered these words?

Lesson
22

Striving for Perfection

Purpose

To help class members understand that perfection is not an instant event but a goal we must strive for throughout our lives.

Preparation

1. Prayerfully study Matthew 5:48; 24:13; Luke 13:32; 3 Nephi 12:48; 27:27; Moroni 10:32; Articles of Faith 1:4.

2. Additional reading: Address given by Elder Russell M. Nelson in the October 1995 general conference (in Conference Report, Oct. 1995, 115–18; or *Ensign*, Nov. 1995, 86–88).

3. Materials needed: A set of scriptures and a scripture marking pencil for each class member. Continue to encourage class members to bring their own scriptures to class each week.

Note to the teacher

Many people find the commandment "be ye perfect" to be overwhelming. Youth especially can get discouraged easily when they make mistakes. They may feel that perfection is unattainable and thus not worth working toward. We all need to realize that perfection in this life is not expected or even possible. What is expected is that we try each day to be better than we were the day before. Help class members understand that they will someday reach perfection if they strive for it as best they can from day to day.

Suggested Lesson Development

Perfection Is Our Goal

Chalkboard activity

Write the following scrambled letters on the chalkboard (you may want to use the first enrichment activity in place of this chalkboard activity):

N R E T O I E P C F

Ask class members to unscramble the letters to discover the subject of today's lesson. Give only a few minutes for this activity. When class members have guessed the word or time has run out, write the unscrambled letters on the chalkboard:

PERFECTION

Scripture discussion

Have class members find and mark Matthew 5:48. Have a class member read the verse aloud.

• What does it mean to you to be perfect?

• How do you feel about being commanded to be perfect?

Explain that many people feel overwhelmed and discouraged when they read this verse of scripture, because they feel it is impossible to become perfect.

Have class members find and read footnote *b* to Matthew 5:48. Explain that the Greek word which has been translated as "perfect" more accurately means "complete, finished, fully developed." Becoming perfect does not mean never making a mistake. It means repenting of our sins and learning from our mistakes and working to become complete, fully developed, righteous people, like our Father in Heaven and Jesus Christ. Becoming this kind of person is not an event that happens all at once; it is a process that we must work at all our lives.

Jesus Christ Is Our Model for Perfection

Scripture
discussion

Have class members read and mark 3 Nephi 12:48 and compare it to Matthew 5:48. Point out that both verses contain words spoken by Jesus Christ.

- How is 3 Nephi 12:48 different from Matthew 5:48? (3 Nephi 12:48 refers to the perfection of Jesus Christ as well as the perfection of our Father in Heaven.)

Explain that Matthew 5:48 was spoken while Jesus was alive on the earth, while 3 Nephi 12:48 was spoken during Jesus' visit to the Nephites after his Resurrection. Although Jesus was without sin, he did not become perfect—complete, finished, fully developed—until after he was resurrected (see Luke 13:32; see also the conference address by Elder Nelson listed in the "Preparation" section). Likewise, we will not be perfected until after we are resurrected. But our Father in Heaven and our Savior expect us to begin the process of perfection while we are on the earth and to make a sincere daily effort toward becoming perfect.

Explain that as the first person to be resurrected and become perfect, Jesus Christ set an example for us to follow. Have class members find and mark the last two sentences of 3 Nephi 27:27 (from *Therefore* to the end of the verse). Have a class member read these sentences aloud.

- What does this verse suggest about how we begin to work toward perfection? (We work toward perfection by becoming as much like Christ as possible.)

Have class members find and read Moroni 10:32.

- According to this verse, what must we do to "come unto Christ, and be perfected in him"? ("Deny [ourselves] of all ungodliness, and love God with all [our] might, mind and strength.")

Explain that "deny yourselves of all ungodliness" means "give up your sins." We must strive to give up our sins and demonstrate that we love God with all our might, mind, and strength. If we do this throughout our lives, then Jesus Christ, through his Atonement, will help us become perfect.

How Can I Direct My Life toward Perfection?

Chalkboard
discussion

On the chalkboard draw a pathway with many stepping-stones (see the illustration on the following page). Explain that this pathway represents the process of working toward perfection. Write *Perfection* at the top of the pathway.

Remind class members that while perfection cannot be entirely achieved in this life, we can make great progress toward it. The Lord expects us to do all we can toward giving up our sins and becoming perfect, and he has given us the gospel to help us do this.

- According to the fourth article of faith, what are the first principles and ordinances of the gospel?

Write *Have faith in Jesus Christ, Repent, Be baptized,* and *Receive the Holy Ghost* on four stepping-stones at the beginning of the path.

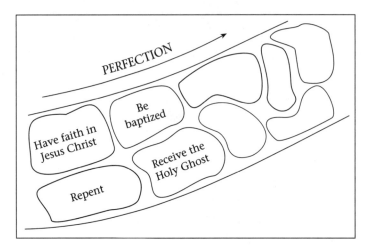

Discussion

- How does faith in Jesus Christ help us grow toward perfection? (We can follow his example as the one perfect person. He also makes repentance and baptism effective in our lives.)

- How can repentance help us progress? (When we repent, we abandon our sins, which keep us from improving and progressing.)

- How does baptism help make perfection possible? (We can be forgiven of our sins after we have been baptized. Also, through baptism we become members of The Church of Jesus Christ of Latter-day Saints, which has been organized to help us learn and do what Heavenly Father and Jesus Christ want us to do.)

- How can receiving the Holy Ghost help us grow and progress? (We can seek and follow his promptings. These promptings will always lead us to right actions.)

Chalkboard activity Have each class member, in turn, think of and write on a stepping-stone another gospel principle that helps us move toward perfection.

Examples:

Pray
Keep the Word of Wisdom
Honor the Sabbath
Be honest
Be dependable
Sustain leaders
Study the scriptures
Serve others

Teacher presentation

Point out that perfection is a very individual process. In one sense we are all on the same path, because we are all striving to become like Jesus Christ. At the same time, however, our paths are very different. We have all been given different strengths and weaknesses, so the order in which we learn these principles of perfection and the time it takes to grow and develop in each one will vary widely. One person may be very faithful in keeping the Word of Wisdom but find it difficult to pay tithing, while another may find it easy to pay tithing but struggle for years to overcome selfishness.

Remind class members that because perfection is such an individual process, we should not become discouraged by comparing ourselves to other people. Nor should we criticize those who may not be as strong as we are in a particular area. Heavenly Father and Jesus Christ will not compare us to each other but will evaluate our progress according to our own individual capabilities and efforts.

Situations and discussion

Remind class members that perfection is not attained suddenly. When we feel overwhelmed at how far we seem to be from perfection, we can focus on learning and growing in one or two areas at a time. Using the following situations (or others applicable to class members), discuss how improving in individual areas of the gospel can help us move toward our ultimate goal of perfection.

1. Tim works part-time at his uncle's store.

- How can Tim progress toward perfection in the payment of tithes? How will Tim's attitude about tithing affect his progress?

Write *Pay tithing* on a stepping-stone.

2. Peggy's parents are active members of the Church, and they encourage her to live Church standards. Peggy often hears her friends speak disrespectfully of their parents and ignore their counsel.

- How can Peggy grow toward perfection in honoring her parents? How can honoring her parents help her progress in other areas?

Write *Honor parents* on a stepping-stone.

3. Elizabeth has set a goal to be more faithful in attending her Church meetings.

- How can this goal help Elizabeth progress toward perfection? What does Elizabeth need to do besides simply show up in order to reach her goal?

Write *Attend Church meetings* on a stepping-stone.

We Must Endure to the End to Attain Perfection

Scripture discussion

Have class members read and mark Matthew 24:13.

- What does it mean to "endure to the end"? (To remain faithful throughout our lives.)

Point out that enduring to the end does not mean reaching a certain level of progress and then simply maintaining that level. It means working every day to become a more righteous person.

| Quotation | Read or have a class member read the following statement from Elder Russell M. Nelson of the Quorum of the Twelve Apostles: |

"Brothers and sisters, let us do the best we can and try to improve each day. When our imperfections appear, we can keep trying to correct them. We can be more forgiving of flaws in ourselves and among those we love. . . . We need not be dismayed if our earnest efforts toward perfection now seem so arduous and endless. Perfection . . . awaits all who love [the Lord] and keep his commandments" (in Conference Report, Oct. 1995, 118; or *Ensign,* Nov. 1995, 88).

| Testimony | Remind class members that while perfection cannot be completely achieved in this life, we are expected to begin the process and make a sincere effort to overcome our sins and become like Jesus Christ. Testify of the role of Christ and his Atonement in our eventual perfection. |

Remind class members not to become discouraged if perfection seems far away. Encourage each class member to choose one principle of the gospel and make a special effort this week to work toward perfection in that area.

**Enrichment
Activities**

You may want to use one or more of these activities during the lesson.

1. You may want to use this activity in place of the chalkboard activity at the beginning of the lesson:

   Write each of the letters *P E R F E C T I O N* on a small piece of paper. If you have more than ten class members, add blank pieces of paper until you have one piece of paper for each class member.

   Pin or tape at least one piece of paper to the back of each class member. (If there are more than ten class members, some will have blank papers; if there are fewer than ten class members, some will have two or three letters on their backs.)

   Allow class members to walk around the classroom and read each other's letters. Give them two or three minutes to figure out what word is spelled by the letters.

   When class members have guessed the word or time has run out, collect all the pieces of paper and pin or tape them to a piece of posterboard or stiff paper so they spell the word *Perfection.*

2. Bring to class an item carved out of wood and a piece of rough wood, or an item carved out of stone and a rough stone or rock. Allow class members to hold and examine the two items (if you do not want class members to handle the items, instead display them in front of the class). Point out that the carved item was once a piece of raw material similar to the rough item. Explain that the carved item did not become beautiful or useful all at once; it had to be carefully and gradually shaped and polished by the person who made it. Likewise, we do not become perfect all at once. We gradually and carefully "shape" and "polish" ourselves by following Christ's example and striving to live his teachings.

3. Draw the following illustration on the chalkboard:

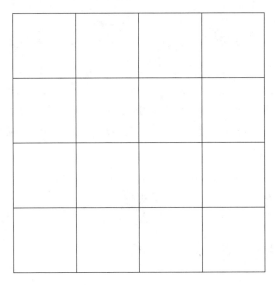

• How many squares are in this illustration?

Give class members an opportunity to count and give their answers, and then tell them that there are actually 30 squares in the illustration. Give class members a few more moments to find the 30 squares. If they cannot, point out the following squares:

1 square of the illustration as a whole

1 square containing four blocks, in the exact center of the illustration

4 squares containing four blocks each, one in each corner

4 squares containing four blocks each, one centered on each side

4 squares containing nine blocks each, one in each corner

16 squares containing one block each

• How many of you found all 30 squares the first time you looked at the illustration? How did you find all 30 squares?

Point out that just as finding all 30 squares may take a person several tries and help from others, attaining perfection in any area will take many attempts and help from family members, Church leaders, and Heavenly Father and Jesus Christ. We may not do an activity or live a principle perfectly the first time we try it, but our abilities will improve as we continue to do the activity or live the principle. (If any class members were able to find all 30 squares the first time, congratulate them, but assure them that there will be many other areas in which perfection does not come so easily.)

Lesson 23

Obedience:
The First Law of Heaven

Purpose	To help class members understand that God gives us commandments because of his love for us and that we should obey the commandments because of our love for him.

Preparation	1. Prayerfully study 1 Samuel 9:17; 10:24; 13:13–14; 15:28; Luke 22:41–44; John 6:38; 14:15, 21; Mosiah 2:41; 3 Nephi 11:11; Doctrine and Covenants 130:20–21; Moses 1:39.
	2. Materials needed:
	a. The picture Jesus Praying in Gethsemane (picture 4 in the picture section of the manual; 62175; Gospel Art Picture Kit 227).
	b. A set of scriptures and a scripture marking pencil for each class member. Continue to encourage class members to bring their own scriptures to class each week.
Note to the teacher	*We show our love for Heavenly Father by obeying his commandments. It is important to remember that Heavenly Father gives us commandments because he loves us. He wants us to be like him and return to his presence. Help class members understand that it is by keeping the commandments that we are able to receive all of the blessings of the plan of salvation.*

Suggested Lesson Development	**The First Law of Heaven**
Chalkboard discussion	Write on the chalkboard *The First Law of Heaven*. Then ask class members the following question:
	• What do you think the first law of heaven is?
	Write class members' responses on the chalkboard. Acknowledge their thoughts and ideas, even if no one mentions obedience.
	When all class members have had an opportunity to respond, write the word *obedience* on the chalkboard, or circle that word if it was mentioned.
	• Why do you think obedience is the first law of heaven?
Quotation	Read the following statement by Elder Joseph B. Wirthlin of the Quorum of the Twelve Apostles:
	"The windows of heaven are open wide to the faithful and righteous; nothing closes them faster than disobedience. . . .
	" . . . Diligent, enduring obedience to God's laws is the key that opens the windows of heaven. Obedience enables us to be receptive to the mind and will of the Lord. 'The Lord requireth the heart and a willing mind; and the willing

and obedient' are those who receive the blessings of revelation through the open windows of heaven" (in Conference Report, Oct. 1995, 101; or *Ensign*, Nov. 1995, 75–76; see also D&C 64:34).

Explain that every blessing we receive is based on our obedience (see D&C 130:20–21; note that *irrevocable* means unable to be taken back and *predicate* means establish).

Obeying God and His Chosen Servants

Scripture story and discussion

Tell class members that you are going to share two stories. One of the stories shows the consequences of disobedience, and the other shows the consequences of obedience.

Have class members read and mark the following scripture passages about Saul, the first king of Israel: 1 Samuel 9:17; 10:24; 15:28.

• In a short time, Saul went from being chosen by the Lord as king to being rejected by the Lord as king. What do you think could have happened to change Saul's standing with the Lord?

Allow class members to respond to this question. Then have them read and mark 1 Samuel 13:13–14.

• What was the main reason for Saul being rejected by the Lord? (He was disobedient to the Lord and His servants.)

• For Saul, disobedience made the difference between being king and not being king. What difference does our obedience or disobedience make in our lives?

Story and discussion

Explain that part of obeying God is following the counsel of those he has called to lead us. Share the following story told by President Gordon B. Hinckley, fifteenth President of the Church:

"Years ago I was on a mission in England. I had been called to labor in the European Mission office in London under President Joseph F. Merrill of the Council of the Twelve, then president of the European Mission. One day three or four of the London papers carried reviews of a reprint of an old book, snide and ugly in tone, indicating that the book was a history of the Mormons. President Merrill said to me, 'I want you to go down to the publisher and protest this.' I looked at him and was about to say, 'Surely not me.' But I meekly said, 'Yes, sir.'

"I do not hesitate to say that I was frightened. I went to my room and felt something as I think Moses must have felt when the Lord asked him to go and see Pharaoh. I offered a prayer. My stomach was churning as I walked over to the Goodge Street station to get the underground train to Fleet Street. I found the office of the president [of the publishing company] and presented my card to the receptionist. She took it and went into the inner office and soon returned to say that the president was too busy to see me. I replied that I had come five thousand miles and that I would wait. During the next hour she made two or three trips to his office; then finally he invited me in. I shall never forget the picture when I entered. He was smoking a long cigar with a look that seemed to say, 'Don't bother me.'

"I held in my hand the reviews. I do not recall what I said after that. Another power seemed to be speaking through me. At first he was defensive and even belligerent. Then he began to soften. He concluded by promising to do something. Within an hour word went out to every book dealer in England to return the books to the publisher. At great expense he printed and [placed] in the front of each volume a statement to the effect that the book was not to be considered as history, but only as fiction, and that no offense was intended against the respected Mormon people. Years later he granted another favor of substantial worth to the Church, and each year until the time of his death I received a Christmas card from him.

"I came to know that when we try in faith to walk in obedience to the requests of the priesthood, the Lord opens the way, even when there appears to be no way" ("If Ye Be Willing and Obedient," *Ensign*, July 1995, 4–5).

- Why was it difficult for young Elder Hinckley to obey the counsel of his mission president? Why is it sometimes difficult for us to be obedient?

- How was Elder Hinckley blessed for his obedience?

- What counsel has the Lord given recently through Church leaders? How are we blessed when we follow the counsel of our Church leaders?

God Gives Us Commandments Because He Wants Us to Live with Him Again

Scripture discussion

Have class members read and mark Moses 1:39.

- What is God's work and glory, or main purpose?

As class members answer this question, make sure they understand the terms *immortality* and *eternal life*. Immortality is a state of living forever, never to die again. Eternal life is living forever in the presence of God. It is the gift given to those who are exalted in the highest degree of the celestial kingdom (see lesson 8).

- How does our obedience play a part in Heavenly Father's work and glory?

Point out that we will all be resurrected and receive immortality. However, we must obey Heavenly Father's commandments to be able to receive eternal life. Heavenly Father gives us commandments because he loves us and wants us to become like him and dwell in his presence forever.

Point out that another reason Heavenly Father has given us commandments is to help us be happy. Have class members read and mark Mosiah 2:41.

- How have you seen that obedience to the commandments brings happiness?

If class members have difficulty answering this question, you may want to offer a few examples, such as when we obey the commandment to fast properly, we can enjoy spiritual growth; and when we obey the commandment to repent, we can be forgiven and freed from the burden of guilt. After you give examples, allow class members more time to think of examples of their own.

As you discuss this question, you may want to point out that obedience to the commandments does not guarantee that we will never experience difficulties or challenges. However, even when we are disappointed or sad about circumstances in our lives, we can be happy about our lives in general because of our faith in God and our assurance that he is pleased with our efforts to be obedient.

Jesus Christ Set a Perfect Example of Obedience

Scripture discussion

Tell class members that Heavenly Father showed his great love for us when he sent his Son to atone for our sins. By doing what Heavenly Father wanted him to do, Jesus Christ set a perfect example of complete obedience. Have class members read and mark John 6:38 (you may want to explain that Jesus is speaking in this verse).

• Why did Jesus come down from heaven?

Show class members the picture of Jesus praying in Gethsemane. Have them read and mark Luke 22:41–44.

• How did Jesus show complete obedience before he suffered for our sins and afflictions in the Garden of Gethsemane?

Explain that Jesus asked to be spared the pain that he knew would come in the Garden of Gethsemane. However, he put Heavenly Father's will before his own and willingly partook of the "bitter cup" the Father gave him (see 3 Nephi 11:11).

• What are some situations in which we might need to say, "Nevertheless not my will, but thine, be done"?

We Obey the Commandments Because We Love Heavenly Father and Jesus Christ

Discussion

• What are some reasons why people obey the commandments?

You may want to list class members' responses on the chalkboard. Answers may include the following:

People obey because:

1. They are afraid of being punished for disobedience.

2. They want the rewards that come from obedience.

3. They want other people to see them and think that they are righteous.

4. They feel peace and joy when they are obedient.

5. They love Heavenly Father and Jesus.

Have class members read and mark John 14:15.

• Why do you think love for Heavenly Father and Jesus is such an important reason for obeying the commandments?

Obedience Prepares Us to Serve God

Story and discussion

Explain that when we are obedient, we are better prepared to serve God and those around us. Then share the following story related by Elder Richard G. Scott of the Quorum of the Twelve Apostles:

"Two missionaries . . . had spent an active day establishing a branch of the Church in a remote village. At 5:30 that morning, they had taught a family before the husband left for the fields. Later they had struggled to plaster their adobe walls to keep out blood-sucking insects. During the week they had laid a small cement floor and had hung a five-gallon can with a shower head to keep clean. They had begun a sanitation facility and put new gravel and sand in their water filter. For part of the day they had worked beside men in the fields to later teach them. They were exhausted and ready for welcome rest.

"There came an anxious knock at the crude wooden door. A small girl was crying. She had been running and was gasping for air. They struggled to piece together her message, delivered amid sobs in a torrent of words. Her father had suffered a severe head injury while riding his donkey in the darkness. She knew he would die unless the elders saved his life. Men of the village were at that moment carrying him to the missionaries. She pled for her father's life, then ran to help him.

"The seriousness of their desperate situation began to engulf them. They were in a village with no doctors or medical facilities. There were no telephones. The only means of communication was a rough road up a riverbed, and they had no vehicle.

"The people of the valley trusted them. The missionaries were not trained in medicine. They did not know how to care for a serious head wound, but they knew someone who did. They knelt in prayer and explained their problem to an understanding Father in Heaven. They pled for guidance, realizing that they could not save a life without His help.

"They felt impressed that the wound should be cleansed, closed, and the man given a blessing. One companion asked, 'How will he stand the pain? How can we cleanse the wound and bless him while he is in such suffering?'

"They knelt again and explained to their Father, 'We have no medicine. We have no anesthetic. Please help us to know what to do. Please bless him, Father.'

"As they arose, friends arrived with the injured man. Even in the subdued candlelight, they could see he had been severely hurt. He was suffering greatly. As they began to cleanse the wound, a very unusual thing occurred. He fell asleep. Carefully, anxiously, they finished the cleansing, closed the wound, and provided a makeshift bandage. As they laid their hands on his head to bless him, he awoke peacefully. Their prayer had been answered, and his life saved. The trust of the people increased, and a branch of the Church flourished" (in Conference Report, Apr. 1989, 46; or *Ensign*, May 1989, 35).

- What commandments did these missionaries obey? (Answers may include that they served others, prayed for help, and followed the guidance of the Spirit.) How did the missionaries' obedience help them in their efforts to receive guidance from the Lord? How did their obedience affect their success in missionary service?

- How might this situation have been different if the missionaries had not been obedient?

After class members have discussed these questions, read Elder Scott's comments about the missionaries:

"The missionaries were able to save a life because they trusted the Lord. They knew how to pray with faith for help with a problem they could not resolve themselves. Because they were obedient to the Lord, the Lord trusted them and answered their prayer. They had learned how to recognize the answer when it came as a quiet prompting of the Spirit. You have that same help available to you if you live for it" (in Conference Report, Apr. 1989, 46; or *Ensign,* May 1989, 35–36).

Point out that although our Heavenly Father always hears our prayers, we are more prepared to receive his answers when we are obedient.

Testimony

Tell class members how you feel about the love Heavenly Father and Jesus Christ have for us. Express your gratitude for the commandments, and testify that Heavenly Father has given us commandments to help us receive eternal life and happiness.

Encourage class members to show their love for Heavenly Father and Jesus Christ by keeping the commandments.

Enrichment Activities

You may want to use one or more of these activities during the lesson.

1. If *Family Home Evening Video Supplement* (53276) is available, show "The Commandments Are for Our Protection," a six-minute segment.

2. Sing or read the words to the hymn "Love One Another" (*Hymns,* no. 308; or *Children's Songbook,* 136). Ask class members to think about how the words of this hymn apply to the Savior's counsel in John 14:15.

3. Read or tell in your own words the following story told by President Wilford Woodruff, fourth President of the Church:

"I will now give an example from my own experience of the result of not obeying the voice of the Spirit.

"Some years since I had part of my family living in Randolph, Rich County [Utah]. I was there on a visit, with my team [of horses], in the month of December.

"One Monday morning my monitor, the Spirit watching over me, said: 'Take your team and go home to Salt Lake City.'

"When I named it to my family who were at Randolph they urged me strongly to stop longer.

"Through their persuasion I stayed until Saturday morning, with the Spirit continually prompting me to go home. I then began to feel ashamed to think that I had not obeyed the whisperings of the Spirit to me before.

"I took my team and started early on Saturday morning. When I arrived at Woodruff, the Bishop urged me to stop until Monday and he would go with me.

"I told him, 'No, I [have] tarried too long already.'

"I drove on sprightly, and when within fifteen miles of Wasatch, a furious snow storm overtook me, the wind blowing heavily in my face.

"In fifteen minutes I could not see any road whatever, and knew not how or where to guide my horses.

"I left my lines loosely on my animals, went inside my wagon, tied down the cover, and committed my life and guidance into the hands of the Lord, trusting to my horses to find the way, as they had twice before passed over that road.

"I prayed to the Lord to forgive my sin in not obeying the voice of the Spirit to me, and implored Him to preserve my life.

"My horses brought me into the Wasatch [train] station at 9 o'clock in the evening, with the hubs of my wagon dragging in the snow.

"I got my horses under cover, and had to remain there until the next Monday night, with the snow six feet deep on the level, and still snowing.

"It was with great difficulty at last that I saved the lives of my horses by getting them into a [railroad] box car and taking them to Ogden; while if I had obeyed the revelation of the Spirit of God to me, I should have traveled to Salt Lake City over a good road without any storm.

"As I have received the good and the evil, the fruits of obedience and disobedience, I think I am justified in exhorting all my young friends to always obey the whisperings of the Spirit of God, and they will always be safe" (*Leaves from My Journal* [1881], 90–91).

4. Make copies of the "Obedience Puzzle" on the next page. Since there will not be time to do this activity in class, give each class member a copy of the puzzle to take home. Encourage class members to complete the puzzle by themselves or with their families in family home evening.

OBEDIENCE PUZZLE

Copy the letters from each circle to the corresponding numbered spaces in the box below it.

OPEN UP THIS OBEDIENCE OPTION:

Share

Obey the
Word of Wisdom

Work hard

Stay pure and clean

Control
your temper

Be honest

Respect others'
property

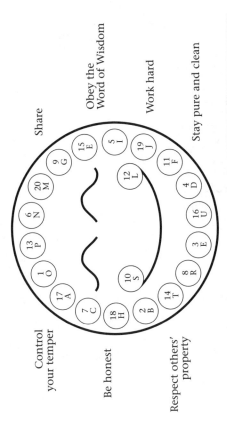

* ‾1‾ ‾2‾ ‾3‾ ‾4‾ ‾5‾ ‾6‾ ‾7‾ ‾15‾ ‾6‾ ‾7‾ ‾3‾ :
  ‾7‾ ‾17‾ ‾6‾ ‾2‾ ‾8‾ ‾5‾ ‾6‾ ‾9‾

* ‾7‾ ‾1‾ ‾6‾ ‾11‾ ‾5‾ ‾4‾ ‾3‾ ‾6‾ ‾7‾ ‾15‾

* ‾10‾ ‾3‾ ‾12‾ ‾11‾ ‾8‾ ‾3‾ ‾10‾ ‾13‾ ‾15‾ ‾7‾ ‾14‾

* ‾14‾ ‾8‾ ‾16‾ ‾10‾ ‾14‾ ‾11‾ ‾8‾ ‾1‾ ‾20‾ ‾1‾ ‾14‾ ‾18‾ ‾3‾ ‾8‾ ‾10‾

* ‾9‾ ‾1‾ ‾1‾ ‾4‾ ‾18‾ ‾3‾ ‾17‾ ‾12‾ ‾14‾ ‾18‾ ‾19‾ ‾1‾ ‾2‾ ‾10‾ '

* ‾17‾ ‾6‾ ‾4‾ ‾11‾ ‾8‾ ‾5‾ ‾6‾ ‾4‾ ‾10‾ ‾2‾ ‾12‾ ‾3‾ ‾10‾ ‾10‾ ‾5‾ ‾6‾ ‾9‾ ‾10‾

* ‾14‾ ‾3‾ ‾20‾ ‾13‾ ‾12‾ ‾15‾ ‾11‾ ‾15‾ ‾7‾ ‾14‾ ‾11‾ ‾8‾ ‾3‾ ‾15‾ ‾4‾ ‾1‾ ‾20‾

* ‾13‾ ‾3‾ ‾8‾
  ‾17‾ ‾6‾ ‾4‾ ‾9‾ ‾1‾ ‾4‾ ‾18‾ ‾1‾ ‾1‾ ‾4‾

DECIPHER THIS DISOBEDIENCE DILEMMA:

Be selfish

Be lazy

Steal

Smoke and drink

Be unkind

Lie

Be unclean

Cheat

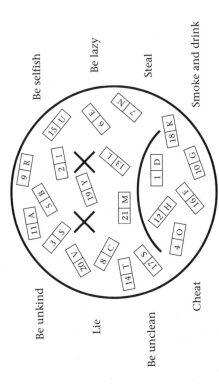

* ‾1‾ ‾2‾ ‾3‾ ‾4‾ ‾5‾ ‾6‾ ‾1‾ ‾2‾ ‾6‾ ‾7‾ ‾8‾ ‾6‾ :
  ‾8‾ ‾11‾ ‾7‾ ‾5‾ ‾9‾ ‾2‾ ‾7‾ ‾10‾

* ‾5‾ ‾11‾ ‾1‾ ‾12‾ ‾6‾ ‾11‾ ‾13‾ ‾14‾ ‾12‾

* ‾15‾ ‾7‾ ‾14‾ ‾9‾ ‾15‾ ‾6‾ ‾16‾ ‾9‾ ‾2‾ ‾6‾ ‾7‾ ‾1‾ ‾17‾

* ‾13‾ ‾11‾ ‾8‾ ‾18‾ ‾4‾ ‾16‾

* ‾8‾ ‾4‾ ‾7‾ ‾16‾ ‾2‾ ‾1‾ ‾6‾ ‾7‾ ‾8‾ ‾6‾

* ‾13‾ ‾11‾ ‾8‾ ‾18‾ ‾4‾ ‾16‾ ‾14‾ ‾9‾ ‾15‾ ‾17‾ ‾14‾

* ‾16‾ ‾9‾ ‾4‾ ‾21‾ ‾4‾ ‾14‾ ‾12‾ ‾6‾ ‾9‾ ‾17‾

* ‾17‾ ‾13‾ ‾11‾ ‾20‾ ‾6‾ ‾9‾ ‾19‾ ‾14‾ ‾4‾ ‾17‾ ‾11‾ ‾14‾ ‾11‾ ‾7‾

Lesson
24

Self-Mastery

Purpose	To help class members realize that lasting joy and happiness are achieved through self-mastery.

Preparation	1. Prayerfully study Matthew 16:24; Luke 22:39–46.
	
	2. If *Family Home Evening Video Supplement* (53276) is available, prepare to show "The Consequences of Our Choices (The Pump)," a nine-minute segment.
	
	3. Materials needed:
	  a. A picture of a beautiful new car from a magazine or newspaper (optional).
	  b. A pen or pencil and a piece of paper for each class member.
	  c. A set of scriptures and a scripture marking pencil for each class member. Continue to encourage class members to bring their own scriptures to class each week.

Note to the teacher	*Many youth are concerned most with what they want at the present moment. They may have difficulty thinking about the long-term consequences of their actions. Help class members see that most worthwhile things in life, both temporal and spiritual, can only be achieved by mastering ourselves.*

Suggested Lesson Development	**Living without Self-Mastery Is Dangerous**
Picture discussion	Display the picture of a car (if you do not have a picture, describe such a car). Ask class members:

- Would you like to ride in or drive this car? Why? What do you like about this car?

Allow class members a few moments to comment on the car.

- Would you want to ride in or drive this car if it had no brakes? Why not?

Point out that no matter how beautiful a car is or how good its engine or tires may be, if it does not have brakes it will soon be the cause of an accident. It would be very dangerous to ride in such a car.

Explain that today's lesson is about something that is as important to our lives as brakes are to a car: self-mastery (also called self-control or self-discipline).

Discussion and quotation	• What do you think self-mastery is?

Allow a few moments for comments, then have a class member read the following statement from Elder Russell M. Nelson of the Quorum of the Twelve Apostles:

"You consist of two parts—your physical body, and your spirit which lives within your body. You may have heard the expression 'mind over matter.' . . .

I would like to phrase it a little differently: 'spirit over body.' That is self-mastery" (in Conference Report, Oct. 1985, 38; or *Ensign,* Nov. 1985, 30).

Explain that self-mastery is the ability of your spirit to control your body, the ability to do what you know you should do even if a part of you does not want to do it. You exercise self-mastery when you do God's will instead of your own.

- How is a person without self-mastery like a car without brakes? Why is it important to exercise self-mastery?

Self-Mastery Brings Blessings

Scripture discussion

Explain that Jesus taught us that we must be able to master ourselves if we are to be his disciples.

Have class members read and mark Matthew 16:24.

- Why must a person "deny himself [or herself]" to be a follower of Jesus Christ?

Point out that the Joseph Smith Translation of Matthew 16:24 (see footnote *d* in the Latter-day Saint edition of the Bible) clarifies that we are to deny ourselves "all ungodliness." We are to give up unrighteous actions and replace them with righteous ones. Exercising self-mastery involves using our agency to choose to live righteously.

Help class members understand that exercising self-mastery does not mean denying oneself everything that is enjoyable or fun. When we practice self-mastery, we give up some things or experiences in order to receive things or experiences we want more. For example, when we fast, for a time we give up eating, which is enjoyable, in order to receive spiritual strength and growth. On a larger scale, we give up sin (which may sometimes *appear* enjoyable) in order to have peace of mind and the opportunity to live with Heavenly Father and Jesus Christ again.

Video presentation and discussion

Show the video segment "The Consequences of Our Choices (The Pump)." Then discuss the following questions:

- How does this man's experience show the need for self-mastery? (Because he lacked self-mastery, he satisfied his immediate desire instead of preparing for the future.)

- How would his experience have been different if he had exercised self-mastery? (If he had primed the pump before taking a drink, he would have had all the water he needed.)

- How is this man's decision (whether to drink the water in the bottle or prime the pump with it) comparable to spiritual decisions each of us must make?

We Can Exercise Self-Mastery

Chalkboard discussion

- What are some ways you demonstrate self-mastery? (If class members have difficulty coming up with answers, point out that they show self-mastery when they fast for spiritual strength despite being hungry or when they get up on time even though their bodies want to stay in bed.)

Explain that self-mastery, like other skills, is developed through practice. In some instances, we practice self-mastery simply by doing the desired action each day and thus forming a habit. Self-mastery in other areas, however, may require more effort.

Write the heading *Self-Mastery* on the chalkboard.

• What actions can help us exercise self-mastery?

List class members' answers on the chalkboard under *Self-Mastery,* and discuss each suggestion. You may want to include the following suggestions in the discussion:

1. Work to achieve appropriate goals.

When we recognize areas in our lives that require greater self-mastery, we can set goals with clear achievable steps to help us. For example, if we need greater self-mastery in getting ready for church on time, we can plan what things need to be done on Saturday in order to achieve this goal.

2. Replace bad habits with good ones.

It is easier to break a bad habit if we replace it with a better habit or activity. For example, a person trying to increase self-mastery over procrastination can replace a habit of leaving homework until the last minute with a better habit of doing it at a specific time every day.

3. Ask friends or family members to help.

Sometimes simply telling someone else about a goal we have set or a habit we are trying to develop can motivate us to work harder. Friends and family members can also give us encouragement and assistance as we work to exercise greater self-mastery.

4. Pray and read the scriptures.

When we pray, we can ask Heavenly Father to give us the strength we need to reach our goals or change our habits. As we study the scriptures, we can be guided by the Lord's counsel and the example of others who have exercised self-mastery, such as Daniel or Joseph of Egypt. If we are receptive to the influence of the Holy Ghost, he can also help us achieve self-mastery.

We Can Accomplish Great Things with Self-Mastery

Story and discussion

Tell in your own words the following story about a man who exercised self-mastery:

"Many years ago [Roger Bannister] participated in the Olympic Games as a champion in the one-mile race. He was supposed to win, but he wound up finishing in fourth place. He went home from the Olympics discouraged, disillusioned, and embarrassed.

"He had his mind set on giving up running. He was a medical student at the time, and his studies were so demanding. He decided that he'd better get on with life and devote all of his time in preparing for medicine and forget his hopes about running the world's record in the four-minute mile. He went to his coach and told him, 'Coach, I'm through. I'm going to devote all my time to studying.' His coach said, 'Roger, I think you are the man who can break the four-minute mile. I wish you'd give it one last try before you quit.'

138

"Roger . . . went home knowing not what to say or to do. But before the night was over, he had convinced himself that he would develop an iron will before he quit running. He was going to break the four-minute mile.

"He knew what this meant. He would have to set a pattern and live by it. He realized he would have to study seven, eight, or even nine hours a day to get through medical school. He would have to train for at least four hours a day. . . . He knew he would have to eat the best foods. He knew he would have to go to bed early every night and sleep nine or ten hours, to let his body recuperate and constantly build up for the great day. He determined within himself that he was going to follow the rigid pattern he and the coach knew was necessary for victory and achievement.

"On May 6, 1954, the four-minute-mile barrier was broken by Roger Bannister, . . . a man committed to a winning pattern which would bring him recognition worldwide. . . . Roger Bannister set the pattern many years ago and followed it with total commitment, self-discipline, and a will of iron" (Marvin J. Ashton, in Conference Report, Oct. 1990, 25–26; or *Ensign,* Nov. 1990, 22).

- What did Roger do to exercise self-mastery?

- How might Roger's life have been different had he not exercised self-mastery?

Personal experiences

Give class members a few minutes to think of examples of how they or someone they know accomplished something that required self-mastery, such as overcoming a handicap or personal problem, learning to play a musical instrument, developing a spiritual gift, developing a sports ability, or achieving a special honor at school. Invite several class members to share their examples, and ask each of these class members the following questions:

- How did you (or the person involved) realize this achievement?

- How much time did it take? How much work and effort were required?

- How do you feel about this achievement? Was it worth the time and effort required?

Remind class members that self-mastery can require hard work, but it also brings great blessings.

Scripture discussion

Read Luke 22:39–46 with class members.

- How did the Savior exercise self-mastery? (He did what Heavenly Father wanted, not what he wanted to do.)

- What were the results of his self-mastery? (He suffered for our sins and made salvation possible for us when we repent.)

Point out that as we develop self-mastery, we develop a greater ability to say, as Jesus did, "Father, . . . not my will, but thine, be done."

We Must Decide Now to Master Ourselves

Quotation

Read or have a class member read the following statement:

President David O. McKay urged us to remember that "the greatest battle of life is fought out within the silent chambers of your own soul" (in Conference Report, Apr. 1969, 95; or *Improvement Era,* June 1969, 30).

• What do you think this statement means?

Activity

Give class members pens or pencils and paper and ask them to write down their answers to the following question (assure them that no one else will see their answers):

• What is one thing you can do this week to increase your self-mastery?

Encourage class members to keep their papers in a place where the papers will remind them to work on the action they have written down.

Testimony

Bear your testimony about the rewards you have received as you have learned to master yourself.

Encourage class members to pray for help in exercising self-mastery. Remind them that all the blessings promised to the faithful in the plan of salvation come to those who learn to deny themselves of all ungodliness and follow the Lord.

Enrichment Activities

You may want to use one or more of these activities during the lesson.

1. Invite to class a ward or branch member who has recently achieved a notable goal, such as doing well in an athletic event; performing in a concert or play; or graduating from high school, seminary, or college. Give the guest a few minutes to tell class members how self-mastery enabled him or her to reach the goal.

2. Explain that many ancient cities had walls around them to protect the inhabitants. A city whose walls were missing or in poor condition was vulnerable to attack.

   Have class members read and mark Proverbs 25:28.

   • How is a person who "hath no rule over his own spirit," that is, a person without self-mastery, "like a city that is broken down, and without walls"? (Such a person has no defense against temptation and is vulnerable to Satan's attacks.)

   Divide the class into small groups and give each group a piece of paper and a pen or pencil. Have the members of each group create one or more proverbs, like Proverbs 25:28, that show the danger of living without self-mastery. (Another example is the comparison that begins this lesson: "A person without self-mastery is like a car without brakes.")

   When all groups are finished, have a member of each group read and explain the proverbs the group has written.

3. Make for each class member a card with the following statement on it:

   Never give up what you want most for what you want at the moment.

   Give each class member a card, and discuss what the statement means and how it relates to self-mastery. You may want to point out that the man in the video segment used in the lesson gave up what he wanted most (survival) for what he wanted at the moment (a drink of water).

Controlling Our Anger

Purpose	To teach class members how to recognize and overcome feelings of anger.

Preparation	1. Prayerfully study Proverbs 16:32; Matthew 5:43–44; Mark 11:15–17; Ephesians 4:31–32; Colossians 3:8; James 1:19–20; 2 Nephi 1:26; 3 Nephi 11:29–30; Doctrine and Covenants 60:2; 63:32; 84:24.
	2. Materials needed:
	a. A picture of an angry person (cut one from a magazine or newspaper or draw one yourself).
	b. A set of scriptures and a scripture marking pencil for each class member. Continue to encourage class members to bring their own scriptures to class each week.
Note to the teacher	*President Howard W. Hunter, fourteenth President of the Church, said: "We need to be slower to anger and more prompt to help. We need to extend the hand of friendship and resist the hand of retribution. In short, we need to love one another with the pure love of Christ . . . for that is the way God loves us" (in Conference Report, Apr. 1992, 84; or* Ensign, *May 1992, 61). In this lesson, class members can learn ways to recognize and overcome feelings of anger. All of us can and must control these powerful emotions if we wish to receive a place in God's kingdom.*

Suggested Lesson Development	**What Is Anger?**
Picture discussion	Show the picture of an angry person.
	• How do you think this person is feeling?
	• What kinds of things make you angry? (Allow only a minute or two for discussion of this question.)
	• What is the world's attitude toward anger?
	Using popular books, songs, movies, or television shows as examples, if possible, point out that many people in the world believe that anger is an acceptable reaction to situations we do not like and that violence and revenge are acceptable ways of dealing with anger.
Scripture discussion	• What is the Lord's attitude toward anger?
	To answer this question, have class members read and mark 3 Nephi 11:29–30 and Ephesians 4:31–32. Have one or two class members read these verses aloud.
	Point out that in 3 Nephi 11:29–30 Christ tells us that anger is not part of his gospel and "should be done away." In Ephesians 4:31–32 the Apostle Paul emphasizes that anger and similar feelings must be "put away."

Discussion	• How can anger be harmful to us? (Discuss with class members how anger affects us physically, emotionally, and spiritually.)
	• What would the world be like if people did not get angry?

Allow class members to discuss this question for a few minutes. Answers may include that disagreements would be solved more easily; people would have more peace and spiritual strength; and there would be happier families and neighborhoods, fewer violent crimes, less abuse, little or no divorce, and probably fewer problems between nations.

Explain that anger is a natural human response, but it is one we must overcome to become like Heavenly Father and Jesus Christ. Learning to recognize our anger and deal with it appropriately can help us overcome it.

Recognizing Reasons for Anger

Story and discussion

Write on the chalkboard (at least several inches from the top) *We get angry because:* and then relate the following incident:

Janice and Denise were in the same school club and had become friends. One day Janice told Denise that she thought the club president was cute. Denise, who also thought this boy was cute and wanted his attention, began saying unkind things about Janice to other club members, including the president, hoping to make Janice look bad.

• How do you think Janice feels? Do you think Janice has a right to be angry at Denise? Why or why not?

Under the first phrase on the chalkboard, write *We feel we have been treated unfairly.*

Quotation

Have a class member read the following statement:

"Anger is [used] to control others. Some people have learned this art very well. They get what they want by becoming loud and angry. . . . Anger thus has the unrighteous goal of attempting to diminish the freedom of others" (Burton C. Kelly, "The Case Against Anger," *Ensign,* Feb. 1980, 10).

Add to the list on the chalkboard *We want to get our own way.*

Story and discussion

Tell the following story:

When five-year-old Tommy went to the store with his mother, he spotted the rack of candy bars and headed straight for them. He asked his mother for a candy bar, but she told him he could not have one. Tommy immediately became angry and began screaming, crying, and stomping his feet. His mother was embarrassed and let him have a candy bar so he would be quiet. She vowed not to bring Tommy to the store again.

• Why did Tommy throw a tantrum? (To get his mother to buy him a candy bar.)

• Do youth and adults sometimes show anger for selfish reasons? Can you give an example?

| Story and discussion | Tell the following story to illustrate a third reason we sometimes become angry: |

Tell the following story to illustrate a third reason we sometimes become angry:

Terry loved his little brother but sometimes thought he was a nuisance. One day while Terry was away at school, his little brother got into his room and took everything out of the closet and piled it on the bed.

When Terry got home and found the mess, he flew into a rage. He stormed around the house. When he could not find his brother, he became even angrier. Finally he found his brother playing in the neighbor's yard. He yelled at him, "Did you come in and mess up my bedroom?"

His little brother, shaking with fear, said, "I didn't mess up your room. I was cleaning the closet for you."

Add to the list on the chalkboard *We misunderstand.*

- How do you think Terry felt after his little brother explained what he was doing?

- How might Terry have reacted to the mess in his bedroom if he had correctly understood the situation? (You may want to point out that correctly understanding a situation does not necessarily make the situation all right, but it can help us deal with the situation in a more constructive way.)

- Have you ever become angry because you misunderstood someone else's intentions?

We Can Control Our Anger

Scripture discussion

Explain that regardless of the reason we become angry, we can control how we deal with our anger. On the chalkboard, above the list of reasons we get angry, write in large letters *We choose how to respond.*

Have each class member find and read one of the scriptures below. Have a class member read each scripture aloud, and discuss with class members what each scripture teaches us about controlling our anger.

1. Proverbs 16:32
2. Colossians 3:8
3. James 1:19–20

Chalkboard discussion

Remind class members of the story about Janice and Denise.

- How might Janice respond to Denise's unkind actions? (Have class members give as many possibilities as they can think of.)

- What might be the results of each of these responses? Which response would be best for Janice? for Denise?

Point out that some possible responses, such as seeking revenge, could be spiritually or physically harmful to both Janice and Denise.

- What are some positive ways we can deal with anger?

Discuss the following positive ways to deal with anger and any other methods class members suggest. List each method on the chalkboard as you discuss it.

1. Talk it out.

When we are angry with another person, we should talk with that person, if possible. As we talk, we should be calm and direct. Discussing problems calmly and directly can help dispel tensions and help us better understand the other person's actions.

2. Wait.

We should delay any action until we find a constructive way of dealing with our anger. For example, talking with the person who made us angry may be a good idea, but we may need to wait until we have calmed down first. Sometimes it helps to count to ten (or even more) before speaking or doing anything.

3. Pray.

Through prayer, we can ask Heavenly Father to help us deal with a particular situation that makes us angry. We can also ask him to take away our anger and help us forgive.

4. Exercise.

Getting involved in physical activity away from the tense environment helps release the tension that anger produces.

Discussion

• How can controlling your feelings of anger bring you more satisfaction than seeking revenge or expressing anger in other ways?

Remind class members that our responsibility is to control our own behavior, including dealing appropriately with our anger. We should let the Lord take care of those who may have truly wronged us.

Overcoming Our Anger Helps Us Become More like Jesus Christ

Discussion

Explain that learning to control our actions when we get angry is an initial step in learning to overcome anger. Our ultimate goal is to learn not to become angry in the first place.

• Does the Lord become angry?

Ask class members to explain why they answered yes or no.

Class members may mention that the scriptures speak of the wrath (or anger) of God and that Christ was angry when he drove the money changers from the temple (see Mark 11:15–17). Point out that the Lord was not angry as we generally consider anger. He was not antagonistic; he showed no hostility or desire for revenge; he was not out of control. His anger is often called righteous anger. Its motivation is to bless God's children, manifest truth, and destroy wickedness (see 2 Nephi 1:26; D&C 60:2; 63:32; 84:24).

Quotation

Point out that Christ has given us guidelines on how to act when faced with a situation where anger is the usual response. Have a class member read the following statement by Elder ElRay L. Christiansen, who was an Assistant to the Twelve:

"Jesus set the example in personal conduct regarding anger when, although he had been falsely accused and made the subject of railings and mockery, he stood

144

majestically and completely composed before the perplexed Pontius Pilate. He did not retaliate in anger. Rather, he stood erect, poised, unmoved. His conduct was divine. What an example for all of us!

"Listen to these marvelous words of the Savior, the master teacher:

"'Ye have heard that it hath been said, Thou shalt love thy neighbour, and hate thine enemy.

"'But I say unto you, Love your enemies, bless them that curse you, do good to them that hate you, and pray for them which despitefully use you, and persecute you.' (Matt. 5:43–44.)" (in Conference Report, Apr. 1971, 28; or *Ensign,* June 1971, 38).

Discussion

• How can we show love for those who mistreat us?

• How can first controlling and then overcoming anger make us more like Christ?

Testimony

Testify that we must learn to overcome anger if we want to mature spiritually and become more like Heavenly Father and Jesus Christ. Remind class members that we can pray for Heavenly Father's help in overcoming anger. You may wish to share a personal experience in which Heavenly Father helped you deal with anger.

Referring to the list on the chalkboard, encourage class members to use one of these positive responses next time they become angry.

Enrichment Activities

You may want to use one or more of these activities during the lesson.

1. Bring enough hymnbooks for class members to read the words to "School Thy Feelings" (*Hymns,* no. 336). Have all class members read the words in unison, or have one class member read the words aloud while the others follow along silently.

After the words have been read, tell the following story about the origin of this hymn:

The words to this hymn were written in 1869 by Charles W. Penrose, who later became a member of the Quorum of the Twelve Apostles. Elder Penrose had been serving in the presidency of the Birmingham (England) Conference of the Church, and he had brought his own furniture to use in the office. When he was released from the calling and took his furniture home, he was accused by another Church member of stealing furniture belonging to the Church. This accusation hurt Elder Penrose's feelings and made him angry toward the other man. Elder Penrose initially wanted to get back at the man, but instead he wrote the words to this hymn to help himself calm down and control his anger. (See George D. Pyper, *Stories of Latter-day Saint Hymns* [1939], 158–60; see also Orson F. Whitney, "A Hymn with a History," *Improvement Era,* Oct. 1924, 1109–12.)

Read again the words to the chorus of the hymn, and remind class members that they will be able to act more wisely if they control their anger.

2. If *Family Home Evening Video Supplement* (53276) is available, show "Family Communication," a five-minute segment.

3. Explain that by controlling our own anger, we can help others control their anger as well. Have class members read and mark Proverbs 15:1.

   Put class members in pairs and give each pair one of the statements below to discuss (you may need to create more statements if you have a large class). Ask class members to think of two responses to their statements: one response containing "grievous words" that will create more anger and one "soft answer" that will defuse anger. When all pairs have thought of two answers, have each pair demonstrate their answers in a role play for the rest of the class.

   a. "Why don't you watch where you're going? You almost knocked me over."
   b. "Your brother's shirt is ugly."
   c. "I didn't vote for your sister for class president."
   d. "Can't we watch another television show? This one is dumb."
   e. "Why haven't you cleaned up that mess yet?"
   f. "You broke a family rule, so you can't go to the party."

The Wisdom of the Word of Wisdom

Lesson

26

Purpose	To help class members understand that obeying the Word of Wisdom provides spiritual blessings as well as good health.
Preparation	1. Prayerfully study Doctrine and Covenants 10:4; 88:124; 89.
	2. Make for each class member a copy of the handout "Blessings That Come from Obeying the Word of Wisdom," found at the end of the lesson (page 153).
	3. Make a copy of the story about Erroll Bennett in next week's lesson. At the end of class, give each numbered section to a different class member. Ask these class members to prepare to tell their sections of the story, in their own words, in class next week.
	4. Materials needed: a. A pen or pencil for each class member. b. An owner's manual for a vehicle or appliance (optional). c. A set of scriptures and a scripture marking pencil for each class member. Continue to encourage class members to bring their own scriptures to class each week.
Note to the teacher	*All people, even those with little or no knowledge of modern revelation, can become more healthy by observing the principles of the Word of Wisdom. Obedience to the Word of Wisdom develops and strengthens the body and the mind, and its principles apply to everyone. But the Word of Wisdom is much more than a health plan. Those who are obedient to it are promised "treasures of knowledge, even hidden treasures" (D&C 89:19). Help class members recognize the treasures, or blessings, that are ours when we obey the Word of Wisdom.*

Suggested Lesson Development	**A Plan for Protecting Our Bodies**
Object lesson	Explain that when a consumer purchases a new vehicle or appliance, the manufacturer provides instructions on the care and maintenance of the machine. (If you brought an owner's manual, show it to class members with a short explanation of what it contains.) By following the recommended instructions, a person can expect better performance and longer use from the vehicle or appliance.
	• What may happen if the owner ignores the manufacturer's instructions? (The machine may break down or even become dangerous.)
	Tell class members that each of them has a wonderful mechanism. This mechanism can repair itself when it has minor breakdowns, it has automatic "windshield wipers" and an automatic cooling system, and it usually works more efficiently the more it is used.

147

- What is this wonderful mechanism? (The human body.)

- What revelation could be considered an "owner's manual" for our bodies? (The Word of Wisdom.)

Explain that just as a manufacturer provides instructions on the care of a machine, the Creator of our bodies has provided instructions on how to take care of these bodies. If we follow these instructions, many of which are included in the Word of Wisdom, we can expect better performance from our bodies and minds. This does not mean that we will never get sick or that our bodies will never need repairs, but the Lord will bless us as we try to keep our bodies in good condition.

Scripture and chalkboard discussion

Ask a class member to read aloud the heading and summary of Doctrine and Covenants 89 while the other class members follow along in their own scriptures.

- When was this revelation received? How was it received? (The Prophet Joseph Smith inquired of the Lord regarding the use of tobacco, and the Lord gave this revelation in answer.)

Write on the chalkboard *The Word of Wisdom,* and write the headings *Do Use:* and *Do Not Use:* under this title.

- What does the Word of Wisdom teach us about how to take care of our bodies? (If class members are already familiar with the principles contained in the Word of Wisdom, only a brief review is necessary here. If class members are not familiar with the principles, read and discuss Doctrine and Covenants 89:5–17.)

Write or have class members write their answers under the appropriate headings on the chalkboard.

THE WORD OF WISDOM

Do Use:	Do Not Use:
Grains	Wine or strong drinks
Fruits	(alcohol)
Herbs (plants, especially	Tobacco
vegetables)	Hot drinks (tea and
Meat (sparingly)	coffee)

Point out that not everything harmful is mentioned by name in Doctrine and Covenants 89. For example, these verses do not specifically mention drugs, but prophets and medical experts have taught us that drugs are harmful when used outside of specific medicinal purposes. Explain that the message of the Word of Wisdom is to avoid all substances that are harmful to our bodies. Add to the "Do Not Use" column on the chalkboard "drugs" and any other harmful substances mentioned by class members.

Explain that the Lord has given other revelations in modern times concerning health care. Have class members read and mark Doctrine and Covenants 88:124 and 10:4.

- What additional rules of good health are given in these verses?

Add these points to the appropriate column on the chalkboard.

We Will Follow the Lord, Not Conspiring Men

Scripture discussion

Have class members read and mark Doctrine and Covenants 89:4.

- What is meant by "conspiring men"? (Dishonest people who lure others into harmful or evil practices.)

- According to the scripture, when would these people try to lure others into evil? (In the last days, which are now.)

Teacher presentation

Tell class members that although the revelation in section 89 was given over 150 years ago, it applies directly to our time. In 1833, the advertising methods we see today were unknown. There were no radios or televisions, and printed material was limited. Since that time, advertising has become commonplace. People who are concerned only with making money often use sophisticated advertising to sell bad products as well as good ones. Much advertising is aimed directly at young people, trying to convince them that harmful substances and products are commonplace and acceptable.

Discussion

Mention a harmful product that is commonly advertised in your area, and ask class members to think about the advertisements they have seen for that product.

- What methods do advertisers use to try to convince you that this product is desirable? (Answers may include showing glamorous people and places or promising acceptance and popularity to those who use the product. For example, many beer advertisements show good-looking people having lots of fun, suggesting that the people have fun because they drink beer.)

Point out that advertisements often ignore the harmful effects of the products they sell. For example, beer advertisements never show people getting drunk and hurting themselves or others.

- How can we resist the efforts of people who want us to use things that are harmful to our bodies and spirits?

Help class members realize that when the Lord revealed the Word of Wisdom in 1833, he knew what practices would develop in our time. He gave us this revelation to help us know the truth about what things are and are not good for our bodies and spirits.

Treasures Are Promised to the Obedient

Discussion

Explain that occasionally a news item reports the discovery of a "hidden treasure," such as a valuable book or work of art that had been stored in an attic, a sunken ship carrying gold, or an ancient tomb filled with rare artifacts and precious gems.

- Would you like to find a plan directing you to a hidden treasure? What would you do if you had such a plan?

Point out that we have been given such a plan, but it leads to hidden treasures of spiritual wealth, not material wealth.

Scripture discussion

Have class members read and mark Doctrine and Covenants 89:18–19.

- What blessings are promised to those who obey the Word of Wisdom?

- What "treasures of knowledge" and "hidden treasures" might be included in this promise?

Activity

Give each class member a pen or pencil and a copy of the handout "Blessings That Come from Obeying the Word of Wisdom." Discuss each "treasure," or blessing, listed and how it comes as a result of obeying the Word of Wisdom.

Point out that at the time the Word of Wisdom was revealed, most people did not know about the unhealthful effects of products such as tobacco and alcohol. Today, scientists have confirmed what the Lord told Joseph Smith over 150 years ago, and many people avoid such products in order to live more healthfully. Explain that the physical advantages of obeying the Word of Wisdom are the same for those who believe in the revelation and those who do not. However, those who obey the Word of Wisdom because it is a commandment of God receive additional spiritual blessings.

Have class members look at their handout and identify which treasures come from simply following wise health practices and which come from obeying the commandments of God.

After the discussion, have each class member choose the four treasures that are most desirable to him or her right now and mark them on the handout. Have class members take the handout home, and encourage them to discuss it with their families, perhaps in family home evening or at dinnertime.

Testimony

Bear testimony of the importance of the Word of Wisdom in keeping us physically and spiritually healthy. You may want to tell class members about the effect of the Word of Wisdom in your life or the life of someone you know.

Encourage class members to obey the Word of Wisdom so they can receive the physical and spiritual blessings promised.

Enrichment Activities

You may want to use one or more of these activities during the lesson.

1. Play the game "Don't Get Poisoned." Set a folding chair in the middle of the classroom. On one piece of paper, write *alcoholic drinks,* and on another piece of paper, write *tobacco.* Tape the label "alcoholic drinks" to the top of the chair and the label "tobacco" to the seat of the chair. Pass a six-foot-long string through the space between the backrest and the seat (see the illustration on the next page), and place a ring on the string. Tell class members that the object of this game is to pass the ring from one end of the string to the other without touching the poisons "alcoholic drinks" and "tobacco."

Invite a class member to try to do this alone. If other class members want to try, allow them to do so. Then have the first class member choose a partner, and have the two work together to pass the ring. (They will probably find it easier than the person working alone did.) Ask the first class member:

• Was it easier to accomplish this task by yourself or with another person?

Point out that keeping the Word of Wisdom is easier when you have the help and support of other people. Encourage class members to support each other in their commitment to keeping the Word of Wisdom. Briefly discuss ways they might do this.

Note to the teacher: For information on other games that teach, see Teaching— No Greater Call, *143–44.*

2. If the following video segments are available, show one of them (do not show a segment you have already shown during another lesson):

a. "Addiction versus Freedom," a three-minute segment of *Family Home Evening Video Supplement 2* (53277).
b. "True to the Faith," a nine-minute segment of *Family Home Evening Video Supplement* (53276).

After showing the video segment, discuss how choosing to obey or disobey the Word of Wisdom affects one's freedom to make future choices (see lesson 2).

3. Before class, glue a piece of candy, money, or some other desirable object to the tongue of a mousetrap. In class, set the mousetrap and display it on a table or box.

• How many of you would be willing to try to take the object? (Do not allow anyone to actually try this.)

Point out that the object is glued to the mousetrap.

• How many of you would still be willing to try to take the object from the trap? Why not?

Explain that Satan sets spiritual traps for us. To entice us into these traps, he will promise us anything we want, but he has no intention of keeping his promises. Many of Satan's traps involve the Word of Wisdom. To get us to disobey the Word of Wisdom, Satan promises us that doing so will bring us desirable things. For example, he tells us that drinking or using drugs will make us beautiful or popular or make us feel good. But disobeying the Word of Wisdom will never bring lasting beauty, popularity, or happiness. It is a trap that will ultimately cause pain and unhappiness.

Blessings That Come from Obeying the Word of Wisdom

Physical health:	Your body will be more resistant to disease and weakness.
Emotional health:	You will have less stress and guilt and more peace of mind.
Health for your descendants:	Your children will be free from inherited deformities and weaknesses caused by drug abuse, smoking, and drinking.
Faith:	Your faith will be strengthened as you see that the Lord blesses those who obey.
Spiritual sensitivity:	You will be better able to receive and follow inspiration from the Holy Ghost.
Freedom:	You will not be a slave to drug abuse or other addictive habits.
Wisdom and knowledge:	You will have a clear mind, the desire to learn, and the ability to distinguish truth from falsehood; you will perform better in school and employment.
Self-discipline:	You will be in control of yourself and will strengthen your ability to say no to people or things that would harm you.
Financial advantage:	You will not spend money on cigarettes, liquor, or other harmful substances; you will not need to pay medical expenses caused by use of these substances.
Ability to serve:	You will not cause harm to others (by driving drunk, smoking around them, and so on); you will have the health and strength necessary to serve others.

Lesson 27

Not of the World

Purpose	To encourage class members to live righteously despite worldly pressures.

Preparation	1. Prayerfully study 1 Samuel 8; 1 Timothy 4:12; Alma 5:57; Doctrine and Covenants 3:5–8.
	2. The week before the lesson is to be given, make a copy of the story about Erroll Bennett and give each numbered section to a different class member. Ask these class members to prepare to tell their sections of the story in their own words.
	3. Materials needed: a. A pen or pencil and a piece of paper for each group in the group activity (see page 156). b. A set of scriptures and a scripture marking pencil for each class member. Continue to encourage class members to bring their own scriptures to class each week.
Note to the teacher	*We left our heavenly home to live on this earth and to progress according to the plan of salvation. While providing us with this opportunity, the world also presents us with many challenges, temptations, and pressures. Teenagers, particularly, are faced with great pressures from a worldly society. As they learn to deal with challenges according to gospel principles, they are strengthened and continue their eternal progression. Help class members understand that it is of eternal importance that we learn to be in the world but not of the world.*

Suggested Lesson Development	**Recognizing Worldly Influences**
Chalkboard discussion	Remind class members of the previous lesson on the Word of Wisdom.
	• Has anyone you know ever tried to convince you to disobey the Word of Wisdom? Have you ever felt pressure from friends or acquaintances to do other things that you knew were wrong?
	• What arguments do people often use when they are trying to persuade others to do something wrong?
	List class members' answers on the chalkboard (leave this list on the chalkboard for the group activity in the third section of the lesson). You may want to use the following examples to stimulate class members' thinking:
	1. "No one will know."
	2. "Everyone does it."
	3. "Just once won't matter."

• Why are these arguments so often effective?

Point out that we all want to be liked and accepted. This is not wrong, but the desire to be liked and accepted can lead us into trouble if we want to be accepted by other people more than we want to be accepted by the Lord.

Explain that part of living on this earth is learning to deal successfully with unrighteous influences. It is easier to deal with these influences when we recognize them and understand the results that yielding to them can bring.

Peer Pressure and the Desire to Be like Others

Teacher presentation

Explain that influence to do certain things often comes from our peers—people around our own age and in circumstances similar to ours. This kind of influence is often called "peer pressure." Peer pressure can be positive or negative, depending on whether your peers are influencing you to do righteous or unrighteous things.

Point out that sometimes our peers make a deliberate effort to influence our behavior, and sometimes we are influenced by our peers simply because we want to be like those we admire. Either way, we need to consciously consider what we are being influenced to do and whether or not these are right things to do.

Scripture story and discussion

Explain that Satan has used negative peer pressure and the desire to be accepted as his tools throughout the ages. In Old Testament times the children of Israel experienced a desire to be like other people around them. Discuss with class members the situation found in 1 Samuel 8.

To answer the following questions, have class members find and read the indicated scriptures. You may want to have class members take turns reading the verses aloud while the rest of the class follows along.

• The children of Israel asked the prophet Samuel to appoint a king to rule over them. Why did the children of Israel want a king? (1 Samuel 8:4–5; they wanted to be "like all the nations.")

• What did Samuel do when the people asked for a king? (1 Samuel 8:6.) What did the Lord tell Samuel to do? (1 Samuel 8:7, 9; he told Samuel to explain to the people what life would be like if they had a king.)

• What did the Lord, through Samuel, tell the Israelites about the results of having a king? (1 Samuel 8:10–11, 13–18.)

• Would you want a king if you knew he would enslave your children and take your property? Do you think the Israelites changed their minds about wanting one? (1 Samuel 8:19–22.)

• Why do you think the Israelites still wanted a king, even after they were told how bad life would be under a king?

Explain that the results Samuel prophesied did come to the children of Israel. The first few kings that ruled over them helped them to become a strong nation, but later kings enslaved them, took their possessions, and eventually contributed to the downfall of the entire nation.

- Are we ever like the Israelites, rejecting the counsel of the Lord's servants so we can be more like everyone else?

- What can we learn from the Israelites' experience?

Emphasize that unrighteous influences can be powerful and can have devastating consequences. In order to progress in life, we must learn to know when we are being pressured in the wrong direction and how to resist that pressure.

Resisting the Pressures of the World

Discussion

Point out that while our peers often have great influence on how we think and act, pressure to do wrong things can come from other areas as well.

- What other people or things may influence us to do things we know are wrong? (Answers may include famous movie, music, or sports personalities; songs or literature that are against Church standards; or advertising that entices us to sin.)

Scripture discussion

Have class members read and mark Alma 5:57. Explain that this verse is part of Alma's teachings to the people in Zarahemla who wanted to be followers of Christ ("the good shepherd").

- What do you think Alma meant when he told the people to "come ye out from the wicked, and be ye separate, and touch not their unclean things"?

- How can we live in today's world and still follow Alma's counsel?

After class members have had time to discuss this question, explain that today it is not possible or desirable to isolate ourselves completely from all people who do not believe as we do. But by maintaining our standards and striving to live righteously, we can withstand worldly pressures and exert a positive influence on those around us. A phrase often used to describe this situation is being "in the world but not of the world." This means that we live in the world, but we do not live according to worldly standards and beliefs.

Group activity

Explain that one way to increase our ability to resist worldly pressures is to prepare our resistance ahead of time. Divide class members into small groups and give each group a pen or pencil and a piece of paper for making notes. Assign each group one or more items from the list of arguments you put on the chalkboard at the beginning of the lesson. Have group members work together to develop ways they could respond if someone used these arguments to try to persuade them to do something wrong. When all groups are finished, have each group share its responses with the other class members. (See the third enrichment activity for a variation on this activity.)

Discussion

- What has helped you do the right thing when you have felt pressure to do otherwise?

Story

Explain that as we strive to resist worldly influences, we should remember that God desires our success and stands ready to help us. Have the class member who was given the first part of the Erroll Bennett story tell it now:

1. Erroll Bennett's father was upset when he heard that Erroll planned to be baptized into The Church of Jesus Christ of Latter-day Saints. He demanded:

   "'Have you gone mad? You'll have to give up everything—*everything* you've worked for. . . . If you do this, I don't want to know you. Take everything in this house that belongs to you and don't ever set foot across this door again.'

   "It was not the first time . . . that deep parental misgivings have been a barrier to embracing the gospel. But there was more to this opposition than objections to new religious doctrines. For Erroll Bennett, joining the Church could well mean the end of his spectacularly successful career as the top soccer star in Tahiti."

   Erroll Bennett and his wife had been introduced to the Church by a friend. They recognized the truth of the gospel and decided to be baptized. Erroll knew that as a member of the Church he would need to keep the Sabbath day holy, but all of his soccer league's games were played on Sundays. Erroll was a very valuable player, and when the league president heard that Erroll was going to join the Church, he called the stake president to ask if Erroll could get some kind of special permission to play on Sundays. The stake president told the league president that the decision about whether or not to play on Sundays was up to Erroll.

Discussion
Ask all class members:

• How do you think Erroll felt about the pressure he was receiving from his family, teammates, and league officials? If you were Erroll, what would you do?

Story continued
Have the assigned class members tell the second and third parts of the story:

2. Erroll again spoke to his father regarding his decision to join the Church and again was rejected, but Erroll's commitment to the Church was strong. He decided to seek counsel from the friend who had introduced him to the Church. This friend told him about priesthood blessings, and another friend gave Erroll a blessing that promised that his problems would be resolved and his father would accept his baptism.

   "The next day, Erroll again drove out to his father's home. As he approached the house, he could see his father standing by the gate to the front garden. There were tears in his eyes. 'I want you to forgive me, Erroll,' he said. 'I couldn't sleep last night for thinking about it. . . .' Then he continued: 'You know that thousands of people will be disappointed in you. It will mean the end of your career if you won't play on Sundays. You know that [the league president] isn't going to change the entire [soccer] league schedule just to accommodate you. Still, this is your decision. . . .'"

3. Erroll received pressure from family and friends until the day he was to be baptized. "'I remember my feelings on that day,' Brother Bennett now says. . . . 'We had gone through a lot of pressure, and we knew what we had to do. Yet somehow I felt I needed a final confirmation, a last indication from the Lord that all was well and that we should proceed.

   "'I remember going up the side of the mountain near my home where I like to jog, and privately pouring out my feelings to my Heavenly Father. I asked for confirmation, perhaps some message that I was about to take the right step. Halfway down the mountain on the way home, I offered the same prayer again.

"'As I drew near my home, there was a car parked outside. It belonged to Gabriel Vaianui, a member who had been [less active] for about ten years, attending church only intermittently. Gabriel had been at the market and had overheard someone say that Erroll Bennett had decided not to join the Mormon Church after all. He had then driven over to my home immediately to find out for himself.'

"Erroll recognised Brother Vaianui as the messenger he had sought and promptly asked him, 'Gabriel, should I be baptised today?' Without hesitation, the answer came: 'Erroll, whatever you do, you must be baptised. Do not turn your back on the Church.'"

Erroll was very grateful for this counsel. He said, "'It was just what I needed— that little extra to give me the courage I lacked.'"

Chalkboard discussion

- How did Erroll find the courage to resist outside pressure and do what was right?

List class members' responses on the chalkboard. The list may include:

1. He sought help from priesthood leaders and followed their counsel.

2. He asked for and was given a priesthood blessing.

3. He prayed earnestly.

4. He stayed in tune with the Holy Ghost so he could recognize the answer to his prayer.

Point out that each of us can follow Erroll's example when we feel pressure to do something wrong. God will help us resist the pressures of the world.

Story concluded

End the discussion by noting that sometimes standing up to the pressures of the world can have surprising results. Have the assigned class member tell the conclusion of Erroll Bennett's story:

4. "The baptisms went ahead as scheduled, and afterwards Erroll Bennett had time to think. . . . It was no good agonizing over an elusive compromise. . . . He wasn't going to play on Sundays. The following day he would talk to [his team president] and withdraw from active soccer, leaving his position open to some other hopeful.

"[The president's] reaction was a surprising one. 'Hold off for a few days,' he said. 'Wait until after the meeting of the league later this week.'

"When Erroll heard the news a few days later, he could hardly believe it. [The team president] had advised league officials that the Central club had decided not to play on Sundays. . . . A vote was then called for, and the decision was unanimous. From now on, all Honours Division games would be played on weekday evenings" (Michael Otterson, "Erroll Bennett, Tahitian Soccer Star: His Courage Changed the Rules," *Ensign*, Oct. 1982, 15–17).

Point out that things turned out well for Erroll Bennett, but Erroll made his decision to be baptized without knowing how things would turn out. He decided to do the right thing no matter what the personal consequences might be. Remind class members that choosing the right will lead to eternal blessings, even if the immediate situation does not turn out the way we want.

Setting a Good Example

Scripture discussion and story

Explain to class members that as they face worldly influences, they may have to deal with feelings of loneliness and rejection. But they can ease these feelings by seeking ways to exert "positive peer pressure," influencing their friends to do what is right.

Have class members read and mark 1 Timothy 4:12.

• How can you be "examples of the believers"?

Discuss with class members ways they can set good examples, helping each other and their other friends to live according to the Lord's standards. You may want to have a class member read the following description of how some Latter-day Saint students dealt with unrighteous pressures:

"I was one of four LDS students among 1,055 in our high school and we found the only way to avoid Friday night loneliness was to provide a fun alternative to the drinking and carrying on of many of our fellow students.

"We invited friends to come to our house to make root beer and doughnuts from scratch, as well as pizza, sweet rolls and candy. We'd play games, both indoors and out, dance, sing and even had pie-eating and pyramid-building contests.

"We found lots of our friends and their friends enjoyed this alternative 'fun' and we appreciated the opportunity to set a good example and be subtle missionaries" (Leslie E. Hartsock, in "How to Keep Standards Despite Temptations," *Church News,* 30 Jan. 1982, 15).

Resisting Worldly Influences Brings Eternal Rewards

Scripture discussion

Explain that early in his service to the Lord, the Prophet Joseph Smith gave in to Martin Harris's repeated requests to borrow 116 pages of the translation of the Book of Mormon. The Lord had instructed Joseph not to give these pages to Martin Harris, but Joseph continued to ask the Lord until He finally consented. The pages were subsequently lost. Have class members read and mark Doctrine and Covenants 3:5–8, the Lord's counsel to Joseph Smith about being influenced by other people.

• What did the Lord tell Joseph Smith about "fear[ing] man more than God"? What did the Lord promise Joseph if he would be faithful?

• Why is it worth the effort to resist the negative influences of the world and stand up for what we believe in?

Testimony	Testify that pleasing God is more important than pleasing other people. Pleasing God will bring eternal rewards, even if it brings a loss of popularity. You may want to share an experience in which you resisted worldly influences and kept the commandments of God.

Encourage class members to be in, but not of, the world and to set good examples for their peers.

Enrichment Activities

You may want to use one or more of these activities during the lesson.

1. Remind class members that peer pressure can be very subtle. Sometimes we are not specifically asked to do wrong things but are made to feel inferior or unpopular because we do right things. Read the following situations and have class members discuss how they would react if they were in these situations:

   a. Joe and a friend are walking toward a group of boys who are looking at a magazine. When the boys see Joe coming, they hide the magazine and say, "This stuff is too rough for Joey! If he saw it he'd have to go confess to his bishop!" They all laugh.

      • How do you think Joe feels? What could he do? What should he do?

      • If you were Joe's friend, what would you say to Joe?

   b. Michelle enters a classroom where some other girls are noisily laughing. She hears someone say, "She's so self-righteous. She dresses like her mother picks out her clothes." When the girls see Michelle, they suddenly become silent and look away.

      • How do you think Michelle feels? What should she do?

2. Tell the following story to remind class members that they can set good examples for others:

   "It had been a great year for me, and now my high school years were coming to an end. I was standing in a large group of noisy, excited [students] signing yearbooks when a girl I didn't know asked me if she could sign my book. I thought it was a little unusual, but I . . . handed [the book] over. She gave me a big smile and hurried off to a desk in one of the classrooms.

   "That night as I was looking through my yearbook and smiling at all the things my friends had written, I came to a small paragraph that began, 'You don't know me, but I have been watching you all year.'

   "I was shocked. I read that sentence over and over. I hadn't been living my life as if someone might be watching me. I had only been thinking of what a good time I was having. I read on. This girl . . . also wrote that she had noticed how active I was in seminary and that she was determined to be just like me.

   "While I was proud she had chosen me to admire, what I mostly felt at that moment was a profound sense of relief that I had not unknowingly led her down the wrong path by my actions. . . .

"I never saw that girl again. But I have always remembered the moment she changed my life by asking to sign my yearbook. I have tried since that day to live each minute as though someone is watching—because someone usually is" (Kaye Garner, "Just Like Me?" *New Era,* Oct. 1995, 9).

Have class members silently consider the following question:

- If you found out that someone had been watching you and following your example, would you be pleased or embarrassed by the example you had set?

3. You may want to use the following group activity instead of the one on page 156:

Divide class members into small groups and give each group a pen or pencil and a piece of paper. Have each group write down one or two things their peers might do to pressure them to do something wrong (for example, a group of friends might try to convince them to see an inappropriate movie).

When each group has written down one or two examples, have the groups trade papers. Have each group look at the examples on their new paper and come up with ways a person in those situations could resist peer pressure. When the groups are finished discussing, have them share their suggestions with the rest of the class.

Remind class members that one way to increase our ability to resist worldly influences is to decide before we experience them how we will react to these influences.

Lesson 28

Remember the Sabbath Day, to Keep It Holy

Purpose	To encourage class members to keep the Sabbath day holy.

Preparation	1. Prayerfully study Exodus 20:8–11; Isaiah 58:13–14; Luke 24:1–3; Doctrine and Covenants 59:9–12.
	2. Make a copy of the "Personal Sabbath Survey," found at the end of the lesson (page 168), for each class member.
	3. Materials needed: a. A pen or pencil for each class member. b. The pictures Passing the Sacrament (62021; Gospel Art Picture Kit 604) and Family Prayer (62275; Gospel Art Picture Kit 606). c. A set of scriptures and a scripture marking pencil for each class member. Continue to encourage class members to bring their own scriptures to class each week.
Note to the teacher	*It is sometimes difficult for young people to feel gratitude for the Sabbath. Too often they associate it only with rules and restrictions and forget that it is a blessing from a loving Father in Heaven. Understanding why Heavenly Father has commanded us to keep the Sabbath day holy can help us enjoy the Sabbath and be grateful for it. Help class members see that honoring the Lord on the Sabbath day brings us great blessings.*

Suggested Lesson Development	**The Sabbath Is a Day of Rest and Worship**
Story	Read or tell the following story:

Eli Herring was a football player on the Springville (Utah) High School team. The team had just won the state championship, and Eli appeared to be headed for a college and even professional football career. As Eli talked with his parents about the possibilities, they cautioned him to remember the values he had been taught.

Several universities invited Eli to play for them after high school, but he chose to attend Brigham Young University, in part because the coaches there would allow him to leave on a mission after his freshman year. After Eli returned from his mission, he rejoined the team and became one of the best college football players in the United States.

As Eli realized that he had a good chance at a career playing professional football, he thought about how much he would enjoy it and how much money he could make. But he also realized that as a professional football player, he would have to play football on the Sabbath.

Eli knew he could do good things with the money he could earn as a professional football player. He could pay his children's college and mission expenses; he could

162

go on missions with his wife; he could do whatever he wanted after his football career was over without worrying about money.

As Eli struggled to make his decision, he remembered reading about Erroll Bennett (see lesson 27). When Erroll joined the Church, he decided to stop playing soccer on Sunday, even though he was a top soccer star in Tahiti and not playing on Sunday would mean he would have to quit his team. Eli Herring was very impressed by Erroll Bennett. Eli said, "I knew I wanted to be a man like that, with that kind of commitment and dedication to what I knew was right."

Eli's parents and wife let him know they would support him in whatever he decided. Eli talked to many people and then fasted and prayed about his decision. He also read the scriptures intensively. It took him six months to come to a final decision.

Ultimately Eli decided that for him, keeping the Sabbath day holy was more important than playing professional football and making lots of money. "I read my scriptures, and time after time I would see more and more and more reasons that I felt in my heart that I needed to observe the Sabbath more than I needed to play football," Eli said. He turned down the offers from the professional teams and now teaches and coaches at a high school. He does not make a lot of money, but he is happy. He said: "The paychecks now, in spite of being low, are more than we were making when we were students. We're happy to have more than we had before. Occasionally I think we could have a brand-new car or a nice house, but I have never had any serious doubts about the decision." (See Joseph Richardson, "To Keep It Holy," *New Era,* Oct. 1997, 34–37.)

Explain that this lesson is about the blessings we receive when we obey the Lord's commandment to keep the Sabbath day holy.

Honoring the Sabbath Day

Scripture discussion

Have class members read and mark Exodus 20:9–11.

- When was the Sabbath day first made holy?

Explain that after the Lord made "heaven and earth, the sea, and all that in them is" in six days, he rested on the seventh day. He hallowed the seventh day. In other words, he made it holy. Explain that until the Resurrection of Jesus Christ, the Sabbath was observed on the seventh day (Saturday). Today the Sabbath is observed on Sunday in remembrance of the Savior's Resurrection on that day (see Luke 24:1–3).

- What does it mean to keep something holy? (To honor it, to dedicate it to righteous use, to keep it sacred and deserving of reverence.)

- Why should we keep the Sabbath day holy?

Quotation and chalkboard discussion

Have a class member read the following statement by Elder James E. Faust, who was at the time a member of the Quorum of the Twelve Apostles:

"Why has God asked us to honor the Sabbath day? The reasons I think are at least threefold. The first has to do with the physical need for rest and renewing. Obviously God, who created us, would know more than we do of the limits of our physical and nervous energy and strength."

Write *Physical renewal* in the top left corner of the chalkboard. Then have a second class member continue with Elder Faust's statement:

"The second reason is, in my opinion, of far greater significance. It has to do with the need for regeneration and the strengthening of our spiritual being. God knows that left completely to our own devices without regular reminders of our spiritual needs, many would degenerate into the preoccupation of satisfying earthly desires and appetites. This need for physical, mental, and spiritual regeneration is met in large measure by faithful observance of the Sabbath day."

To the right of *Physical renewal,* write *Spiritual strength.*

• Why is the blessing of spiritual strength more important than the blessing of physical rest and renewal?

Have a third class member read the rest of Elder Faust's statement:

"The third reason [for honoring the Sabbath day] may be the most important of the three. It has to do with obedience to commandments as an expression of our love for God. Blessed are those who need no reasons other than their love for the Savior to keep his commandments" (in Conference Report, Oct. 1991, 46–47; or *Ensign,* Nov. 1991, 35).

To the right of *Spiritual strength,* write *Love for God.*

• How is reverent observance of the Sabbath day "an expression of our love for God"? Why might this be the most important reason for honoring the Sabbath?

Scripture and chalkboard discussion

Have class members read and mark Doctrine and Covenants 59:9–12 (explain that the word *oblations* in verse 12 refers to things we do to serve God and other people). As they read these verses, have them look for phrases that fall under each of the three categories you have written on the chalkboard. Write their answers on the chalkboard under the appropriate categories, as shown below:

PHYSICAL RENEWAL	SPIRITUAL STRENGTH	LOVE FOR GOD
"Rest from your labors" (verse 10).	"Keep thyself unspotted from the world" (verse 9).	"Pay thy devotions unto the Most High" (verse 10).
	"Confessing thy sins" (verse 12).	"Offer thine oblations and thy sacraments unto the Most High" (verse 12).

Making the Sabbath a Delight

<table>
<tr><td>Scripture
discussion</td><td>Have class members read and mark Isaiah 58:13–14. Help them discuss the following phrases and questions:</td></tr>
</table>

1. "Turn away . . . from doing thy pleasure."

- What do you think Isaiah meant when he said this?

Explain that Isaiah was not saying that we should not enjoy the Sabbath; he was saying that the Sabbath is a day to forget our own desires and follow God's will.

2. "Call the sabbath a delight."

- How is the Sabbath a delight?

3. "Honour him."

- How might this phrase serve as the standard for all our activities during the Sabbath?

4. "Not doing thine own ways."

- How can this phrase be a caution to us when we wonder what we should and should not do on the Sabbath?

5. "Delight thyself in the Lord."

- How does worshiping God make us happy?

<table>
<tr><td>Quotation
and discussion</td><td>Have someone read the following words from President Thomas S. Monson of the First Presidency:</td></tr>
</table>

"The Lord has given the Sabbath day for your benefit and has commanded you to keep it holy. Many activities are appropriate for the Sabbath. Bear in mind, however, that Sunday is not a holiday. Sunday is a holy day" (in Conference Report, Oct. 1990, 61; or *Ensign*, Nov. 1990, 47).

- What is the difference between a holiday and a holy day? What can we do to make the Sabbath a holy day and a delight for us?

<table>
<tr><td>Chalkboard activity</td><td>Show the pictures Passing the Sacrament and Family Prayer. Ask class members to take turns coming to the chalkboard and listing things they can do at church and at home to keep the Sabbath day holy. If class members have questions about appropriate Sabbath-day activities, refer to the fourth enrichment activity.</td></tr>
<tr><td>Activity</td><td>Give each class member a pen or pencil and a copy of the "Personal Sabbath Survey." Have each class member write his or her answers to the questions on the survey. Allow five to seven minutes, and then discuss class members' answers to questions 1 through 4 (allow them to keep private their answers to question 5).</td></tr>
<tr><td>Testimony</td><td>Bear your testimony of the blessings and joy that have come to you through proper observance of the Sabbath day.</td></tr>
</table>

Encourage class members to make each Sunday delightful by putting into practice the commitment or commitments they wrote on their "Personal Sabbath Survey" (question 5).

**Enrichment
Activities**

You may want to use one or more of these activities during the lesson.

1. Read the following comments:

"An almost totally deaf sister was once asked how she managed to come to sacrament meeting each week [and remain] genuinely interested in what was being said. . . . [She said]: 'I look forward to being in the physical presence of those whom I love and who love the gospel. I can share in their spirit without hearing a word, and if I am really in tune, the Lord whispers to me'" (Robert K. Thomas, "Listening with the Spirit," *Ensign,* Jan. 1978, 40).

   • What can we do in sacrament meeting to be "in tune" like this sister was?

2. Read the words to the hymn "Sabbath Day" (*Hymns,* no. 148). Discuss what the hymn says about Sabbath-day observance at church and at home. Since this hymn might be unfamiliar to class members, you may want to play a recording of it.

3. Tell the following story related by Elder James E. Faust:

"A . . . miracle occurred at the Wells Stake Welfare Tannery some years ago where hides of animals were tanned into leather. On regular work days, the hides were removed from the vats and fresh lime placed in the vats, after which the hides were returned to the lime solution. If the hides were not turned on holidays, they would spoil. But the change was never made on Sunday, and there were no spoiled hides on Monday. Explained J. Lowell Fox, the supervisor of the tannery at the time:

"'This brought a strange fact to our minds: holidays are determined by man, and on these days just as on every week day, the hides need to have special care every twelve hours. Sunday is the day set aside by the Lord as a day of rest, and He makes it possible for us to rest from our labors as He has commanded. The hides at the tannery never spoil on Sundays. This is a modern-day miracle, a miracle that happens every weekend!'" (in Conference Report, Oct. 1991, 46; or *Ensign,* Nov. 1991, 35).

4. Refer to the following statements if class members have questions about appropriate Sabbath-day activities:

Things We Can Do on the Sabbath

President Spencer W. Kimball said: "The Sabbath is a day on which to take inventory—to analyze our weaknesses, to confess our sins to our associates and our Lord. It is a day on which to fast. . . . It is a day on which to read good books, a day to contemplate and ponder, a day to study lessons for priesthood and auxiliary organizations, a day to study the scriptures and to prepare sermons, a day to nap and rest and relax, a day to visit the sick, a day to preach the gospel, a day to proselyte, a day to visit quietly with the family . . . , a day for proper courting, a day to do good, a day to drink at the fountain of knowledge and of instruction, a day to seek forgiveness of our sins, a day for the enrichment of our spirit and our soul, a day to restore us to our spiritual stature, a day to partake of the emblems of [Jesus'] sacrifice and atonement, a day to contemplate the glories of the gospel and of the eternal realms, a day to climb high on the upward path toward our Heavenly Father" (*The Teachings of Spencer W. Kimball*, ed. Edward L. Kimball [1982], 216).

Things We Should Avoid on the Sabbath

Elder Ezra Taft Benson, then a member of the Quorum of the Twelve Apostles, said:

"It seems to me that the following should be avoided on the Sabbath:

"Overworking and staying up late Saturday so that you are exhausted the next day.

"Filling the Sabbath so full of extra meetings that there is no time for prayer, meditation, family fellowship, and counseling.

"Doing gardening and odd jobs around the house.

"Taking trips to canyons or resorts, visiting friends socially, joy riding, wasting time, and engaging in other amusements. . . .

"Playing vigorously and going to movies.

"Engaging in sports and hunting 'wild animals' which God made for the use of man only 'in times of famine and excess of hunger.' (See D&C 89:15.) . . .

"Reading material that does not contribute to your spiritual uplift.

"Shopping or supporting with your patronage businesses that operate on Sunday, such as grocery stores, supermarkets, restaurants, and service stations" ("Keeping the Sabbath Day Holy," *Ensign*, May 1971, 6–7).

Working on the Sabbath

Elder Earl C. Tingey of the Seventy said: "We know that there are essential businesses that must be open on Sunday. These are emergency, medical, transportation, and some forms of protective services, such as police and fire" (in Conference Report, Apr. 1996, 12; or *Ensign*, May 1996, 10–11).

Employees of such "essential businesses" can keep the Sabbath day holy even when their services are required on Sunday. For example, they can read the scriptures during breaks at work and attend Church meetings before or after work.

Personal Sabbath Survey

1. Which purposes and blessings of the Sabbath are important to you?

2. What activities seem to take away from the purpose of the Sabbath for you?

3. What activities help you feel the Spirit on the Sabbath?

4. What could you do before Sunday to make the Sabbath a more delightful day?

5. What will you do to keep the Sabbath day holy and enjoy it more?

Paying Tithing with the Right Attitude

Purpose	To encourage class members to pay tithing cheerfully and with faith.

Preparation	1. Prayerfully study Malachi 3:8–12; 2 Corinthians 9:6–7; Moroni 7:6–8; Doctrine and Covenants 104:14–15; 119:4.
	2. Materials needed: A set of scriptures and a scripture marking pencil for each class member. Continue to encourage class members to bring their own scriptures to class each week.
Note to the teacher	*Paying tithing is a privilege. It allows us to show our gratitude to and love for the Lord. We need to pay tithing much more than God needs us to do so, yet it greatly pleases him when we pay with faith and with a willing and happy heart. The spirit with which we give is, in fact, as important as the act of giving. Help class members understand that paying tithing is more than giving money; it is a demonstration of faith, gratitude, and humble obedience.*

Suggested Lesson Development	**Paying Tithing Demonstrates Faith and Obedience**
Story	Tell the following story shared by Elder Joe J. Christensen of the Seventy:
	"I remember vividly an experience I had near the end of my mission. . . .
	"At that time I was working in the mission home with the president of the Mexico and Central America Mission. He called my companion and me into his office one day and told us that he was sending us to Oaxaca. He handed us a list of the names of all the people who had joined the Church during the brief time missionaries had served there; they had been withdrawn some months previously. Our assignment was to look up everyone on the list, see how they were getting along, and, if possible, arrange for a sacrament meeting so that the members could meet together and partake of the sacrament. Then we were to bring back a report.
	"We made the overnight trip on the little narrow railway, arriving very early the next morning. As soon as we got off the train, we began tracking down addresses.
	"The first place we went to was a street lined with long adobe walls with doorways in them. When we found the address we were looking for and walked through the doorway, we found a whole group of homes inside. Tucked back in one corner was the home of the woman we were seeking. She lived there with her eight-year-old son and infant daughter.
	"As she came out of her small house, she recognized us by the way we were dressed, and rushed to give us a warm Mexican greeting. Then, without saying another word, she turned around and went back into her home.

"Moments later she returned, carrying a small clay jar. She reached into the jar and pulled out some pesos and centavos (Mexican money). She told us that her family had saved ten percent of what they had earned. Most of that tithing had come from her son, who worked at the plaza in the center of the city, shining shoes. When he returned each day, he immediately put his tithing into the little jar so that the money could be turned in to the missionaries whenever they returned.

"I can remember my feelings as that woman handed me the money. She was standing there in threadbare clothes and no shoes, and her children were in the same circumstances. I knew that there were things she would have loved to buy her children. I knew that there were many things that they desperately needed money for.

"At first I wanted to give the money back to her and to encourage her to spend it where it was most needed. But then I realized that that was not my right. She and her son had saved that money carefully, knowing that it belonged to the Lord and wanting Him to have it. I realized, too, that they would be blessed for it.

"I learned a great lesson that day about the importance of paying tithing and the blessings it can bring. I also learned a lesson about faith. That little boy and his mother had not known if missionaries would ever return to their home, but they were committed to the gospel principles, and they had faith that, if they were obedient, the Lord would bless them" (quoted by Kellene Ricks, in "Friend to Friend," *Friend,* Jan. 1991, 6).

Tell class members that this lesson is about tithing. Explain that the lesson answers three questions about tithing:

What is tithing?
What blessings will we receive when we pay tithing?
What should be our attitude about paying tithing?

What Is Tithing?

Discussion and quotation

• What does it mean to pay a full tithe?

Share the following statement by President Spencer W. Kimball:

"Inquiries are received at the office of the First Presidency from time to time from officers and members of the Church asking for information as to what is considered a proper tithe.

"We have uniformly replied that the simplest statement we know of is the statement of the Lord himself, namely, that the members of the Church should pay 'one-tenth of all their interest annually' which is understood to mean income (see D&C 119:4)" (in Conference Report, Oct. 1980, 113; or *Ensign,* Nov. 1980, 77).

Explain that whenever we receive money, we are asked to pay tithing by giving ten percent of that money to the Lord.

Scripture discussion

Have class members read and mark Malachi 3:8–9.

• How do people "rob God" by not paying tithing?

Discussion
and quotation

• What are tithing funds used for?

Give class members a chance to respond. Then read the following statement by Elder Dallin H. Oaks of the Quorum of the Twelve Apostles:

"The Lord has directed by revelation that the expenditure of his tithes will be directed by his servants, the First Presidency, the Quorum of the Twelve, and the Presiding Bishopric (see D&C 120). Those funds are spent to build and maintain temples and houses of worship, to conduct our worldwide missionary work, to translate and publish scriptures, to provide resources to redeem the dead, to fund religious education, and to support other Church purposes selected by the designated servants of the Lord" (in Conference Report, Apr. 1994, 46; or *Ensign,* May 1994, 35).

What Blessings Will We Receive When We Pay Tithing?

Scripture
discussion

Point out that we receive blessings when we pay tithing. Have class members read and mark Malachi 3:10.

• What do you think the Lord meant when he said "Prove me now herewith"? (To pay tithing and see that he really does keep his promises. Note that in this verse, the word *prove* means test.)

• How might the Lord "open . . . the windows of heaven" to bless us when we pay tithing?

Explain that the blessings the Lord may provide to people who pay tithing include the ability to earn enough money to provide for their needs, the ability to use money wisely, protection from costly catastrophes, and the joy of sharing and giving. Obedience to the law of tithing, like obedience to other commandments, also helps us feel the influence of the Holy Ghost in our lives.

Quotation and
discussion

Have a class member read the following statement by President David O. McKay, ninth President of the Church:

"Tithing makes its greatest appeal to the sincere mind because of its spiritual significance. It is an unfailing source of spiritual power. True and constant obedience to this law will give as much spiritual development as will obedience to any other principle of the gospel" (*Gospel Ideals* [1953], 199).

• The Lord has promised to give us spiritual and material blessings when we pay a full tithe. How has the Lord blessed you or someone you know for paying tithing faithfully? (You may want to share an experience from your own life.)

What Should Be Our Attitude about Paying Tithing?

Story and
discussion

Point out that we should not pay tithing just so we can receive blessings. We should pay tithing with the right attitude—willingly, cheerfully, and with faith.

Explain that in the past, tithing was often paid "in kind." In other words, Church members gave one-tenth of their increase in things such as crops and livestock. Tell the following story told by a man who as a child learned to pay tithing in kind:

171

"Grandpa Vanisi's spirituality inspired an awe in me as a child. I remember following him daily to his plantation. He would always point out to me the very best of his taro, bananas, or yams and say: 'These will be for our tithing.' His greatest care was given to these 'chosen' ones. During the harvest, I was often the one assigned to take our load of tithing to the branch president. I remember sitting on the family horse. Grandfather would lift onto its back a sack of fine taro which I balanced in front of me. Then with a very serious look in his eyes, he said to me, 'Simi, be very careful because this is our tithing.' From my grandfather I learned early in life that you give only your best to the Lord" (quoted by Dallin H. Oaks, in Conference Report, Apr. 1994, 46; or *Ensign,* May 1994, 35).

- What was Grandpa Vanisi's attitude about paying tithing?

- Now that we usually pay tithing with money, how can we give our very best to the Lord? (Answers may include that we can pay with the proper attitude and pay tithing first, before we use our money to buy things we need or want.)

Scripture discussion

Have class members read and mark 2 Corinthians 9:6–7.

- How can paying tithing relate to being "a cheerful giver"?

Have class members read and mark Moroni 7:6–8.

- What does it mean to offer a gift "with real intent"? (To offer it with sincerity, really wanting to give it.)

- What does it mean to offer a gift grudgingly? (Giving a gift but not really wanting to do so.)

- When we pay tithing, are we giving a gift to God? Why or why not?

Point out that everything we have belongs to God (see D&C 104:14–15). Although the words in 1 Corinthians 9:6–7 and Moroni 7:6–8 can be applied to the way we pay tithing, it is important to remember that when we pay tithing, we are merely giving back one-tenth of what God has already given us.

- Why do you think our attitude and motivation are important when we pay tithing to the Lord?

Story and discussion

Explain that having faith is another part of paying tithing with the right attitude. Then share the following story told by Elder Dallin H. Oaks:

"My attitude toward the law of tithing was set in place by the example and words of my mother, illustrated in a conversation I remember from my youth.

"During World War II, my widowed mother supported her three young children on a schoolteacher's salary that was meager. When I became conscious that we went without some desirable things because we didn't have enough money, I asked my mother why she paid so much of her salary as tithing. I have never forgotten her explanation: 'Dallin, there might be some people who can get along without paying tithing, but we can't. The Lord has chosen to take your father and leave me to raise you children. I cannot do that without the blessings of the Lord, and I obtain those blessings by paying an honest tithing. When I pay my tithing, I have the Lord's promise that he will bless us, and we must have those blessings if we are to get along'" (in Conference Report, Apr. 1994, 43–44; or *Ensign,* May 1994, 33).

- How was paying tithing a demonstration of Sister Oaks's faith in the Lord?

- What can we do to pay our tithing with the right attitude—willingly, cheerfully, and with faith?

Testimony

Bear your testimony of tithing. Encourage class members to pay tithing willingly, cheerfully, and with faith in the Lord.

Enrichment Activities

You may want to use one or more of these activities during the lesson.

1. If *Doctrine and Covenants and Church History Video Presentations* (53912) is available, show "Windows of Heaven," an eleven-minute segment. This segment dramatizes a time when President Lorenzo Snow, fifth President of the Church, taught the blessings of tithing to Church members experiencing a severe drought.

2. Bring to class a Tithing and Other Offerings form. Show class members where to list the amount of tithing they pay. You may also want to point out the spaces for fast offerings and other donations and explain why these donations are made. Explain that we give this form and our tithing and offerings to the bishop (or branch president) because he is the Lord's representative in our ward (or branch).

3. Read the following story:

President George Albert Smith, eighth President of the Church, was talking to a longtime friend after they had both attended a Church conference. The friend explained to President Smith how he paid tithing.

"'Well,' he said, 'if I make ten thousand dollars in a year, I put a thousand dollars in the bank for tithing. I know why it's there. Then when the bishop comes and wants me to make a contribution for the chapel or give him a check for a missionary . . . , if I think he needs the money, I give him a check. . . . Little by little I exhaust the thousand dollars, and every dollar of it has gone where I know it has done good. Now, what do you think of that?'"

- Had this man paid tithing? Why or why not?

President Smith answered him: "I think you are a very generous man with someone else's property. . . . You have not paid any tithing. You have told me what you have done with the Lord's money. . . . You have taken your best partner's money, and have given it away" ("The Story of a Generous Man," *Improvement Era*, June 1947, 357; see also *Sharing the Gospel with Others,* comp. Preston Nibley [1948], 44–47).

- Who was the man's "best partner"? (The Lord.)

Emphasize that paying tithing faithfully includes doing it in the way the Lord has established. It is not our responsibility to determine how tithing should be used.

Lesson
30

The Blessings of Work

Purpose	To help class members understand that work builds character, enriches our lives, and helps us become self-reliant.

Preparation	1. Prayerfully study Proverbs 14:23; Words of Mormon 1:18; Mosiah 2:14; 27:5–7; Moses 4:25.
	2. Make a copy of the quotations numbered 1 through 4 on page 176. Then cut the copy in four pieces so each quotation is on a separate piece of paper. (If you do not have access to a copy machine, write the quotations on four separate pieces of paper.)
	3. Ask a few class members to bring to class an object that represents work they have done. For example, a class member who has worked with her family to paint their house could bring a paint brush. A class member who has worked to develop artistic talent could bring a picture he has drawn or a poem he has written. Have these class members prepare to answer the questions on page 177 of this lesson under the subheading "Presentations by class members."
	4. Materials needed: a. The picture A Family Working Together (62313). b. A set of scriptures and a scripture marking pencil for each class member. Continue to encourage class members to bring their own scriptures to class each week.
Note to the teacher	*Many people do not understand that work is a blessing. More and more, the modern world emphasizes ease and play. Help class members see the value of work in building character and improving our lives. Few things compare to the sense of accomplishment and well-being that comes to a person who has worked hard and done a job well.*

Suggested Lesson Development	**Work Is Essential**
Discussion	Ask class members the following questions:

• Do you like to work? Why or why not?

Class members' responses may be negative or even humorous. Accept whatever they say, using the discussion to get their attention and promote participation.

• What would the world be like if everyone stopped working?

Let class members have fun with this discussion. Answers might include the following: Garbage and dirty dishes would pile up; there would be no teachers;

we would have to wear dirty clothes; we would have little or no food. Help class members see that although a world without work might seem attractive at first, without work the world would not be a very pleasant place.

God Expects Us to Work

Scripture discussion

Have class members read and mark Proverbs 14:23 through the word *profit.*

- What do you think the statement "In all labour there is profit" means? (We benefit from our work.)

Have class members read and mark Moses 4:25 through the word *bread.* Explain that this verse contains some of the Lord's words to Adam just before Adam and Eve were cast out of the Garden of Eden.

- What did the Lord mean when he said this to Adam? (He meant that Adam would have to work to obtain food.) How would this help Adam and Eve? How does work help us?

Quotation

Read the following statement by President Marion G. Romney, who was a First Counselor in the First Presidency:

"In Eden the Lord said to Adam:

"' . . . Because thou hast . . . eaten of the fruit of the tree of which I commanded thee, saying—Thou shalt not eat of it, cursed shall be the ground for thy sake; in sorrow shalt thou eat of it all the days of thy life.

"'By the sweat of thy face shalt thou eat bread, until thou shalt return unto the ground. . . . ' (Moses 4:23, 25.)

"Now this was not a vindictive decree. The Lord was not retaliating against Adam. He was simply placing Adam in a situation where he would have to work to live.

"The ground was cursed in the manner prescribed for Adam's sake, not to his disadvantage. Had Adam and his posterity been able to live without working, the human race would never have survived" (in Conference Report, Oct. 1973, 105; or *Ensign,* Jan. 1974, 89).

Scripture discussion

Point out that God expects all his children to work. Righteous political and religious leaders in the Book of Mormon worked to support themselves even though kings and other leaders traditionally lived off taxes paid by their people. Have class members read and mark Mosiah 2:14, which contains words of King Benjamin, and Mosiah 27:5, which is about Nephite priests and teachers.

- How do you think the people responded when they saw their leaders working with them?

- What do you think were the results of these leaders' efforts? (See Words of Mormon 1:18; Mosiah 27:6–7. Note that although there were many reasons for the peace and prosperity of the people, the leaders' willingness to work with the people contributed greatly to the Nephites' success at the time.)

Work Builds Character

Quotation and
discussion

Read the following statement by President Spencer W. Kimball, twelfth President of the Church:

"Few miracles in our [Church] history exceed that of establishing our settlements in a desolate land no one else wanted and then making the desert blossom as a rose. Our people not only survived but flourished because of their faith and their family solidarity. Our pioneer character was molded [by] hard work, sacrifice, pulling together, and depending upon the Lord.

"How well I remember my boyhood years in Arizona. Our living came from the soil. There was little money and seldom enough to go around. Going without and making do was our way of life. We learned to share: we shared the work" (in Conference Report, Apr. 1981, 107; or *Ensign*, May 1981, 79).

- What positive effects did hard work have on the pioneers and on young Spencer Kimball?

- How is our character "molded [by] hard work"? (Answers may include that hard work helps us learn to discipline ourselves, finish tasks we have begun, and make wise decisions.)

Quotations and
chalkboard
discussion

Display the picture of the family working together. Then hand out the papers containing the quotations below. Explain that they are statements made by four brothers who often worked together with their family (quoted by Dean Jarman, in Conference Report, Oct. 1982, 126; or *Ensign*, Nov. 1982, 87). As a class member reads each quotation, have another class member list on the chalkboard the benefits of work that are mentioned.

1. "An eighteen-year-old boy writes, 'Since I can remember, I have been taught the value of hard work and honoring all of your responsibilities and your family name. As I look back to my experience in family projects, I can see how they have shaped my character and personality by letting me make many important decisions. I have gained confidence by meeting new people and am better able to express myself. But the most important thing about family work projects is that your family comes closer together in love and respect.'"

2. "A thirteen-year-old who has been mowing lawns for four years writes, 'Family projects have really helped me to understand how to work. The harder you work, the better you feel. I am grateful for a closer relationship with my brothers and parents.'"

3. "A sixteen-year-old said, 'Working on family projects has taught us the importance of being honest and dependable. It has taught us to make a lot of sacrifices in order to keep our name in good standing.'"

4. "A fifteen-year-old said, 'The family work projects have helped me manage my money. When I buy my clothes and other things, I take care of them because I know how much they cost and how much work it takes to buy them. When my parents bought my things, I honestly thought there was an endless supply of money, so I wouldn't take care of them. Also, work gives me a feeling of satisfaction.'"

Have class members look at the list on the chalkboard and talk about work experiences that have helped them reap the same benefits. To begin this discussion, you may want to ask the following questions:

• How has work helped you be a better person? How have your relationships with friends and family members been affected by working with them to accomplish a common goal?

Work Gives a Sense of Accomplishment

Presentations by class members

Invite the assigned class members to show and briefly discuss the objects they have brought to class. Then ask them the following questions:

• What was the hardest thing to do as you worked on this project?

• What was the most rewarding part of working on this project? (Note that the answer to this question may be the same as the answer to the previous question.)

• As you worked on this, did you ever get frustrated or tired of working? How did you overcome those feelings?

• How would your feelings about this project be different if someone had done it all for you?

Quotation and discussion

Read the following statement by Brigham Young:

"I have believed all my life that, that which was worth doing was worth doing well, and have considered it as much a part of my religion to do honest, reliable work, such as would endure, for those who employed me, as to attend to the services of God's worship on the Sabbath" (quoted by Dean C. Jessee, in "The Prophet's Letters to His Sons," *Ensign,* Mar. 1974, 68).

• What did President Young say about the importance of the quality of our work? How would work done with this attitude bring us a sense of accomplishment?

Testimony

Tell the class about work you have done that has brought joy and a sense of accomplishment to your life.

Encourage class members to each pick a job that they have been doing only out of duty and do their best to have a good attitude about doing that job in the coming week. Encourage them to remember the value of work, always making an effort to do their best.

Enrichment Activities

You may want to use one or more of these activities during the lesson.

1. Several hymns, such as "Put Your Shoulder to the Wheel" (*Hymns,* no. 252), teach the necessity and joy of work. Sing or read the words to one or more of these hymns with class members.

2. Tell the following story related by Elder Loren C. Dunn of the Seventy:

"While we were growing up in a small community, my father saw the need for my brother and me to learn the principle of work. As a result, he put us to work on a small farm on the edge of town where he had been raised. He ran the local newspaper, so he could not spend much time with us. . . . And sometimes we made mistakes.

"Our small farm was surrounded by other farms, and one of the farmers went in to see my father one day to tell him the things he thought we were doing wrong. My father listened to him carefully and then said, 'Jim, you don't understand. You see, I'm raising boys and not cows'" (in Conference Report, Oct. 1974, 12; or *Ensign,* Nov. 1974, 11).

- What did Elder Dunn's father mean when he said, "I'm raising boys and not cows"? (His primary purpose for having a farm was to give his sons the opportunity to work.) What do you think his sons might have gained from this experience?

Your Attitude Makes a Difference

Purpose	To help class members understand that much of their happiness depends on their attitude.

Preparation	1. Prayerfully study 1 Nephi 2:16; 3:4–7; Helaman 15:7.
	2. Make a copy of the "Attitude Indicator," found at the end of the lesson (page 184), for each class member.
	3. Materials needed: a. A pen or pencil for each class member. b. A set of scriptures and a scripture marking pencil for each class member. Continue to encourage class members to bring their own scriptures to class each week.
Note to the teacher	*Because we have a knowledge of the gospel of Jesus Christ and know that we are spirit children of God, we should be the most positive-thinking people in the world. We know that our loving Father in Heaven has put us on earth to succeed, not to fail. Help class members understand that living the gospel of Jesus Christ can help us develop a positive attitude and create happiness, peace, and contentment in our own and others' lives.*

Suggested Lesson Development	**Attitude Is a Powerful Influence**
Chalkboard discussion	Ask class members to think of two or three things they know they should do but do not always feel like doing. Ask one class member to list these items on the chalkboard as class members share their ideas. After class members have a chance to respond, ask the following questions:

- Why is it sometimes difficult to do these things? What blessings do you receive when you do these things?

- What would help you do the things you know you should do?

- How does your attitude about a task affect how well or how fast you do it?

Explain that when we choose to have a positive attitude, we usually perform our work better and faster, and we usually enjoy it more. A positive attitude can also help us as we strive to live the gospel of Jesus Christ.

Quotation	Have a class member read the following statement from President Spencer W. Kimball:

"I remind you . . . that regardless of your present age, you are building your life; . . . it can be full of joy and happiness, or it can be full of misery. It all depends upon you and your attitudes, for your altitude, or the height you climb, is dependent upon your attitude or your response to situations" (in Conference Report, Oct. 1974, 112–13; or *Ensign,* Nov. 1974, 80).

Explain that today's lesson discusses the importance of attitude and how to develop a more positive attitude.

Story and discussion

Relate in your own words the following story told by Elder Thomas S. Monson when he was a member of the Quorum of the Twelve Apostles:

"In the mission over which I presided, there was a small branch; it consisted of two families. I had been invited to be the speaker at one of the meetings. I was not accustomed to such small branches; the ward over which I presided had 1,050 people. That Sunday we went into the place where the Saints met. It was a rented hall. We didn't meet on the main floor; we met in a room [in] the basement, about nine people in all.

"After the meeting, the branch president asked if he could visit with me. He said, 'We would like to have a chapel in our branch.' I said, 'Someday.' Then he opened a copy of one of the Church magazines and showed me pictures of chapels of Australia and New Zealand. He said, 'This is the one we would like to build,' and he pointed to a building that would house maybe four hundred people, that would cost far more money than they had.

"I said, 'Oh, you will not be able to afford that until you have several hundred members.' He said, 'We intend to have many hundreds of members.' And then he asked me if I would send six missionaries into his branch. He indicated that his family would personally share the gospel with the city, and this he did.

"One day, with the missionaries in his little store, he said, 'Elders, let's pray.' And they got down upon their knees and prayed. This branch president then said, 'This is the greatest day in the city of St. Thomas. This is the day when the gospel shall really begin to be preached with effectiveness in this city. This is the day when we begin to build our new chapel.'

"The missionaries asked, 'Whom are we going to teach? We have no investigators.' The branch president said, 'Hand me the telephone directory.' And he turned to the back of the directory where men of all professions were listed. He said, 'If we are going to build a new chapel, we need an architect who is a Mormon. And since we don't have an architect who is a member of this branch, we must convert one.' Then he went down the list and said, 'Who shall be the first Mormon architect in St. Thomas?' And he identified a name. Then he continued with a contractor or builder, and a plumber, and an electrician, and a doctor, and a lawyer. Then he personally went to each and invited him into his home so that the missionaries might present the message and he and his family could bear testimony after the missionaries had given their message.

"What was the result of that sharing? I am God's witness that in the three years that I served in eastern Canada, I saw that branch grow from two families to a branch of almost three hundred members. They constructed their beautiful chapel. I attended the meeting where that building held perhaps four hundred persons. What was the secret? It was the attitude 'we can achieve our goal'" (in Conference Report, Amsterdam Area Conference, Aug. 1976, 8–9).

- How did this branch achieve such amazing growth?

- What would have happened if the branch president and his family had just chosen to think about how hard the job would be? How did their attitudes affect what they were able to accomplish?

Our Attitude Affects Our Happiness

Story and
discussion

Tell the following story:

Two friends were preparing to go to the same summer camp for a month. Steven thought that summer camp was a waste of time and that all the popular kids were staying home, sleeping in and playing video games. He did not see any point in going to the classes or participating in any of the activities, but his parents had paid for the camp and insisted that he go. Richard, on the other hand, had been saving up for camp, doing yard work and other jobs to earn money. He loved learning new things and making friends. He packed his entire suitcase three days before he left, and as he walked out the door he promised to send postcards to each member of his family.

- If you asked Steven and Richard about their camp experiences when they got home, what do you think they would say? How might their responses be different? Why?

- How can our attitude towards life affect how happy we are?

Activity

Distribute a pen or pencil and a copy of the "Attitude Indicator" to each class member. Explain that each section of the "Attitude Indicator" contains two opposite attitudes with three empty boxes between them. Ask class members to read the handout and decide which attitude of each pair best describes them.

For example, in the first section, if they frequently count their blessings, they should mark the box next to that side of the section. If the other side describes them more accurately (if they often think about things that they do not have), then they should mark that side instead. If they sometimes feel either way, they should put a mark in the middle box. (You may want to remind class members that we all have different attitudes from time to time. Emphasize that the boxes they mark do not make them a good or bad person.)

After class members have had time to complete the "Attitude Indicator," discuss a few sections with them. Have class members explain why they can be happier if they have or develop the attitudes listed on the left side of the handout.

We Can Choose to Have a Positive Attitude

Discussion

- What challenges do you have right now that might be easier if you developed a positive attitude about them? (Answers might include doing homework, getting along with brothers and sisters, obeying parents, doing jobs around the house, attending Church meetings, and choosing good friends.)

Explain to class members that they can choose what their attitude will be. Each of us can develop a positive attitude that will bring us happiness and success.

Scripture and
chalkboard
discussion

Write *Ways to Change Your Attitude:* on the chalkboard.

Have class members read and mark 1 Nephi 3:4–7.

- What attitude did Laman and Lemuel have toward the instructions Lehi had received from the Lord? What was Nephi's attitude?

- On what did Nephi base his positive attitude about obtaining the plates? (His faith that he would be successful because the Lord would not ask him to do an impossible thing; see 1 Nephi 3:7.)

- How did Nephi's attitude help him? (He trusted the Lord and was able to obtain the brass plates.)

Write *Trust in the Lord* on the chalkboard under *Ways to Change Your Attitude.* Explain that having faith that the Lord will not ask us to do something impossible can help us maintain a good attitude while we seek a way to do what he has asked us to do.

- What are some other things you can do to develop a more positive attitude?

Discuss each answer briefly and add it to the list on the chalkboard. You may want to use the following answers to help class members get started:

1. Pray (see 1 Nephi 2:16).

- How does prayer help us keep a positive attitude?

2. Read the scriptures (see Helaman 15:7).

- If negative attitudes are influencing us, how can reading the scriptures bring a change in our lives?

As you finish this discussion, emphasize that a positive attitude does not always come to us naturally. We can use these suggestions as we work to improve our attitude.

Testimony

Testify to class members that they will be happier when they maintain a positive attitude. You may want to share a personal experience in which you were blessed for having or developing a positive attitude. Encourage class members to use the suggestions that have been discussed as they work for greater happiness.

Enrichment Activities

You may want to use one or more of these activities during the lesson.

1. Show the class several different kinds of seeds (from flowers, vegetables, weeds, and so on). Point out that the seeds are small but will grow into something much larger if they are planted and allowed to take root.

   Explain that our attitudes are seeds from which our actions grow, and as with seeds, we harvest more than we plant. A positive attitude grows and produces more positive attitudes, for ourselves and those around us. A negative attitude produces more negative attitudes.

   Set a blooming flower or another beautiful plant on the classroom table and place beside it an ugly weed (or show pictures of these plants).

   - If your "attitude seeds" keep growing, what will they become—beautiful flowers or ugly weeds? How can we plant good seeds?

2. Sing with class members or read the words to "Scatter Sunshine" (*Hymns*, no. 230). Discuss the hymn's message about how our attitudes can affect others.

3. Tell the following story:

Suzanne did not like gym class. She was tall and uncoordinated, and she felt like a failure in gym. One day the teacher asked for a volunteer to teach a younger boy to swim during gym class time. Suzanne thought nothing could be worse than playing basketball, so she volunteered.

Teaching Henry, a young mentally handicapped boy, turned out to be a real challenge. As the lessons progressed, Suzanne became very frustrated because Henry would not listen to her. She began to be rude and unkind to him. One night Suzanne prayed and asked Heavenly Father to soften Henry's heart so he would obey her. The next few days Henry acted just the same. However, Suzanne noticed that he had a nice smile. Then she laughed at something he did. Then she started talking with him instead of yelling at him. As Suzanne started being positive and kind to Henry, he became more willing to listen and follow her directions. By the end of the semester he had learned to swim the width of the pool. Suzanne realized that it wasn't Henry's heart that needed softening; it was her own. (See Suzanne C. Stewart, "Sink or Swim," *New Era,* Jan. 1994, 44–45.)

- How was Henry's behavior affected by Suzanne's attitude toward him?

- How can our attitude affect those around us?

- When has your attitude changed a negative situation in your life into a positive situation?

Attitude Indicator

I often count my blessings.				I often think about things that I do not have.
I am comfortable when I have enough money and possessions for necessities.				I often wish for great wealth and many possessions.
I am happy when I am busy.				I often complain that I have too much to do.
I treat everyone with respect.				I feel I am better than others.
I am willing to accept and follow through with responsibilities.				I would rather have others take responsibility.
I enjoy serving others.				I am too busy to help others.
I try to find good in others.				I often criticize others and find fault.
I try to develop my gifts and talents.				I often feel sorry for myself.
I have faith in the Lord Jesus Christ.				I am not sure Jesus Christ is important to me personally.
The gospel of Jesus Christ guides my life.				I don't think the gospel of Jesus Christ has any effect on my life.

The Worth of a Soul

Purpose	To give class members a sense of their infinite worth.

Preparation	1. Prayerfully study Ether 12:27; Doctrine and Covenants 18:10; 46:11–26; Moses 1:39.

2. For each class member, make a copy of the handout containing Doctrine and Covenants 18:10, found at the end of the lesson (if it is not feasible to make copies, write the scripture on a piece of paper for each class member). Cut each copy into six pieces to create a puzzle. Cut the puzzles so that no two puzzles are the same and no piece from one puzzle will fit another puzzle.

Following are some possible ways to cut the puzzles:

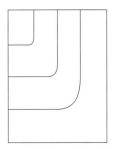 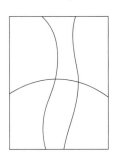 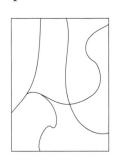

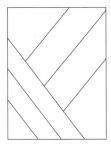 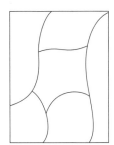 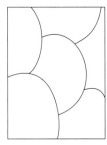

Put each puzzle into a separate envelope.

3. Materials needed:
   a. Several different colors of chalk, if possible, for the chalkboard activity (see page 186).
   b. A set of scriptures and a scripture marking pencil for each class member. Continue to encourage class members to bring their own scriptures to class each week.

Note to the teacher — *Some young people do not feel that they are valuable or important. In an attempt to feel important, some of them pursue the fads and lifestyles of the world. Help class members recognize and appreciate their worth as children of our Father in Heaven. Help them also recognize that each of them has talents and abilities that can bless their lives and the lives of others.*

Each Child of Heavenly Father Is of Great Worth

Activity

Give each class member an envelope with six puzzle pieces inside, and explain that each envelope contains a special message from the Lord. Divide the class into groups of three or four people. Have each member of a group put all but two of his or her pieces in a group pile (a separate pile for each group). Have the group members shuffle the pieces in their pile. Then ask them to find their own puzzle pieces and put their puzzles together, starting with the two pieces they kept.

When class members have finished, ask:

- What do you see when you compare your puzzle with the others? (They all have the same message: "Remember the worth of souls is great in the sight of God.")

- What does it mean to be of worth? (To be important or valuable.)

- If the message is the same on each puzzle, how did you know which pieces belonged to your puzzle?

Explain that each puzzle had the same message because each of us is of the same infinite worth to our Father in Heaven and our Savior, Jesus Christ. Each puzzle was made of differently-shaped pieces because each of us is a unique individual with different strengths and weaknesses.

Collect the puzzles or have class members put them away if they want to keep them.

Each of Us Has Strengths and Weaknesses

Note to the teacher

"A word of kindness creates warm, positive feelings. Enthusiasm is contagious. Class members know when you care for them and will respond in a warm, friendly manner" (Teaching—No Greater Call, *171*).

Discussion

- What is one thing that makes you unique among the members of the class? (Give each class member a chance to respond.)

Emphasize that though we all look, sound, and act different, we are all important in the sight of God. He has given each of us a unique combination of strengths and weaknesses.

Scripture
discussion

Have class members read and mark Doctrine and Covenants 46:11–12.

- Why are we each given different gifts? (So that we can share them and bless each other's lives.)

Have class members read to themselves Doctrine and Covenants 46:13–26, marking verses that are meaningful to them.

- What are the gifts of the Spirit mentioned in these verses?

As the gifts are mentioned, list them on the chalkboard.

Activity

Explain that in addition to the gifts of the Spirit mentioned in this scripture, we may have other strengths. Have class members think of other talents and abilities to add to the list of gifts already on the chalkboard. When the board is full or all suggestions have been given, invite a class member to draw a line that encloses some of the gifts and strengths he or she has. (If class members are reluctant to talk about their own strengths, let them draw for another member of the class.)

For example:

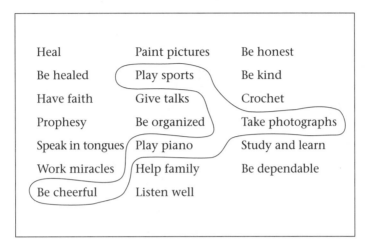

Have another class member enclose his or her gifts and strengths (using a different color of chalk, if possible). Repeat until at least three or four class members have done this. Point out that although two sets may contain some of the same gifts, no two sets are identical.

Scripture discussion

Point out that in addition to talents and gifts, we each have weaknesses. Have class members read and mark Ether 12:27.

- Why does the Lord give us weaknesses?

- What can we do to receive the Lord's help in overcoming our weaknesses?

Story and discussion

To illustrate the importance of working hard to overcome our weaknesses and develop our talents, tell class members about Demosthenes [*dih MAHS thuh neez*], who was a great orator in ancient Greece. Although Demosthenes was born with a serious speech impediment, he wanted to be a great speaker. To overcome his weakness in speaking, he would go to the beach and fill his mouth with pebbles. Then he would shout above the noise of the waves. Through constant practice he learned to speak so well that people came from long distances to hear the great speeches he gave. (See *Encyclopaedia Britannica,* 15th ed., s.v. "Demosthenes.")

Invite class members to tell of anyone they know who has overcome a weakness to develop a strength. Ask class members to identify from the list on the chalkboard those gifts or talents that were weaknesses for them before they developed them into strengths.

Develop and Share Your Gifts

Quotation

Have a class member read the following statement made by Elder Gordon B. Hinckley when he was a member of the Quorum of the Twelve Apostles:

"The work of the world is not done by intellectual geniuses. It is done by men [and women] of ordinary capacity who use their abilities in an extraordinary manner" (in Conference Report, Oct. 1972, 107; or *Ensign,* Jan. 1973, 92).

Chalkboard discussion	• What can we do to discover our gifts and talents and use them to the fullest?
	Erase the chalkboard, and list the answers that are given. Discuss how each item on the list can help us discover and use our gifts and talents.
	The list could include the following:
	Prepare for and receive a patriarchal blessing. Live worthy of the companionship of the Holy Ghost. Fulfill Church callings and responsibilities. Study the scriptures. Listen to the prophet and other Church leaders. Listen to parents. Try new skills.
Scripture discussion	Have class members read and mark Moses 1:39.
	• According to this scripture, what is Heavenly Father's primary concern?
	• How can we use our gifts and talents to aid in this work?
	• How can using our gifts and talents to the fullest increase our sense of worth? (If we use these abilities righteously, we can be an instrument in the Lord's hands to help others return to him. Knowing that we are helping in the Lord's work can increase our sense of worth.)
	• How can we help others understand who they are and what they can contribute to their family, the Church, and the community? (Answers may include share our gifts with them; recognize or compliment them for their gifts and talents; provide opportunities for them to share their gifts and talents with others.)
Quotation	Have a class member read the following statement from Elder Marvin J. Ashton, who was a member of the Quorum of the Twelve Apostles:
	"As children of God we are somebody. He will build us, mold us, and magnify us if we will but hold our heads up, our arms out, and walk with him. What a great blessing to be created in his image and know of our true potential in and through him!" (in Conference Report, Apr. 1973, 21; or *Ensign*, July 1973, 24).
Testimony	As the Spirit directs, bear your testimony of each person's worth and of God's plan for each one of us. Encourage class members to strive to see their own worth and the worth of others in the sight of God.

Enrichment Activities

You may want to use one or more of these activities during the lesson.

1. Before class, make individual lists of the gifts and talents that you see in each class member. If possible, contact each class member's parents during the week to find out more. Give each class member his or her list during class.

   • What do you think of your list? Does it contain more talents than you thought you had? What else could you add to the list?

   Ask each class member to pick one of the talents on the list and describe how he or she could use it to serve others.

2. Relate the following story:

"I remember the first time Jenni walked into my seminary class and said hi to me. She had a very difficult time speaking, her words were slurred and hard to understand, and she limped and hobbled as she tried to make her legs carry her frail body toward her desk. During Jenni's first week . . . in my class, she seemed content to be mostly ignored by her classmates, who appeared to be struggling to figure out how to interact with her.

"Jenni would try to speak, and very few students could understand her. . . . Most of them distanced themselves from her both physically and socially and, as a result, proceeded to politely ignore her.

"However, they weren't aware that inside Jenni's deformed body was a keen mind, a heart of gold, and an indomitable spirit crying out to be heard, to be understood, to be accepted, and to be loved. She wouldn't be ignored, politely or otherwise."

One day Jenni asked her teacher if she could say something in class. She asked for a friend to sit by her at lunch. The class was silent for a long moment, and then a girl named Treasure volunteered.

"'I'll be your friend, Jenni.' . . . This . . . gave Treasure's friend Wendy the confidence to raise her hand and tell Jenni that she would also be her friend and sit by her at lunch every day. . . .

"I noticed as the days turned into weeks that Treasure and Wendy began to translate Jenni's words when we couldn't understand her.

"As the students began to see what a beautiful, intelligent person Jenni was, they began to invite her to activities [and] help her with her difficulties. . . . Jenni's classmates helped her realize what a wonderful person she is. [They] included her in their circle of friends and helped her feel like she belonged; [they] saw through her handicap to the special needs of her heart—a young woman wanting to be accepted and understood" (Victor W. Harris, "The Miracle of Jenni," *New Era,* Mar. 1996, 12–14).

- Why did the class ignore Jenni at first?

- What did the class discover when they got to know Jenni?

- How can we learn to look beyond physical differences to understand each person's worth in the sight of God? (See 1 Samuel 16:7.)

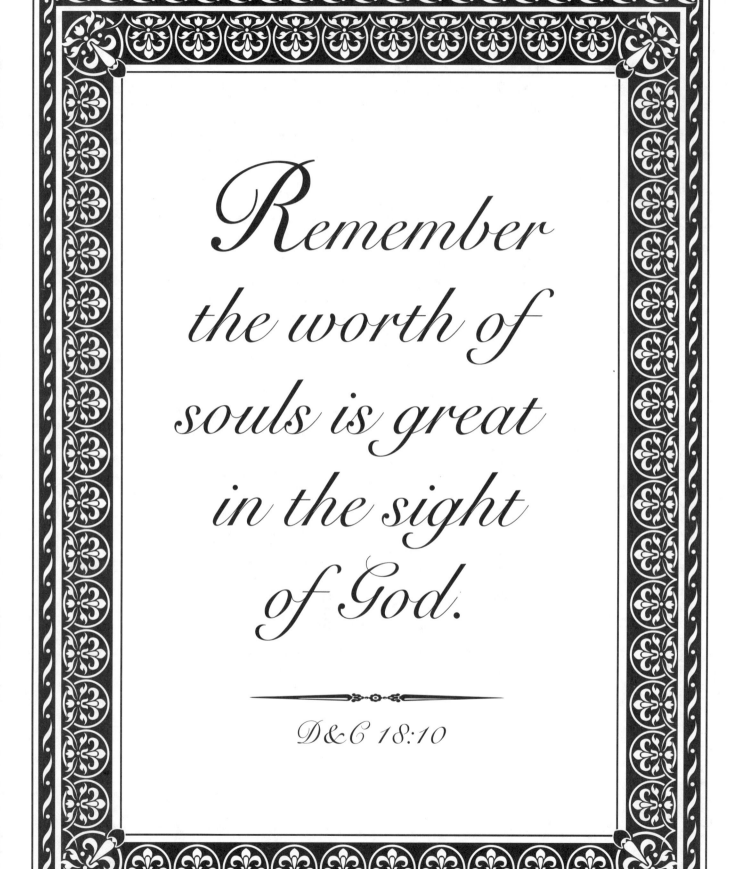

Remember
the worth of
souls is great
in the sight
of God.

D&C 18:10

Love Thy Neighbor

Purpose	To inspire class members to obey the Lord's commandment to "love thy neighbour" (Matthew 22:39).

Preparation	1. Prayerfully study Matthew 22:35–39; Mark 6:30–44; Luke 10:25–37; John 19:25–27; 1 John 4:20–21; 3 Nephi 17:7–13, 17–23; Moroni 7:46–48.
	2. Materials needed:
	a. The pictures Jesus Healing the Nephites (62541; Gospel Art Picture Kit 317); Jesus Praying with the Nephites (62542); The Good Samaritan (62156; Gospel Art Picture Kit 218); and Bedside Prayer (62217).
	b. A set of scriptures and a scripture marking pencil for each class member. Continue to encourage class members to bring their own scriptures to class each week.
Note to the teacher	*The Lord has commanded us to love our neighbor (see Matthew 22:39). Encourage class members to develop love for all people by following Jesus' example and by praying to be filled with charity, the pure love of Christ.*

Suggested Lesson Development	**Love: The Greatest Commandment**
Scripture discussion	Before disclosing the topic of the lesson, ask the following question:

- Of all God's commandments, which do you think is the greatest?

Allow class members to offer answers to this question. Then explain that a man once tried to trick Jesus by asking this same question (see Matthew 22:35–36). Have class members read and mark Jesus' response in Matthew 22:37–38.

Write *Love the Lord* on the chalkboard. Then have class members read and mark Matthew 22:39.

Write *Love thy neighbor* on the chalkboard.

- Why do you think these are the two greatest commandments?

- How would obeying these commandments make it easier to obey other commandments?

- How is the commandment to love our neighbor "like unto" the commandment to love the Lord?

Have class members read and mark 1 John 4:20–21.

- Why is it impossible to love God and hate other people?

Explain that the prophet Mormon also taught that we should love one another. Have class members read and mark Moroni 7:46–47.

- What is charity? (The pure love of Christ.)

- Why do you think Mormon said that "if [we] have not charity, [we] are nothing"?

- Why is it sometimes hard to have charity for all people?

Explain that this lesson discusses three things we can do that will help us have charity.

The Savior Set a Perfect Example of Love

Chalkboard and scripture discussion

Write the following on the chalkboard:

We can develop charity by:

1. Following the Savior's example

Read with class members the scripture passages listed below. Have class members mark phrases in the passages that show the Savior's perfect love for all people. After you read each passage, ask class members to share the phrases they marked and talk about why they chose those phrases.

1. 3 Nephi 17:7–13, 17–23. Jesus blesses the Nephites. (Display the pictures of Jesus healing the Nephites and Jesus praying with the Nephites as you discuss this passage. You may also want to use the video segment listed in the second enrichment activity.)

2. Mark 6:30–44. When people follow Jesus and his Apostles, Jesus teaches them rather than sending them away, as his Apostles request. When the people become hungry, he miraculously feeds them.

3. John 19:25–27. Jesus, while on the cross, asks that his mother be cared for.

- How did Jesus Christ treat others? What are some things we can do to follow his example?

Serving Others Helps Us Develop Charity

Chalkboard and scripture discussion

Add *2. Giving service* to the chalkboard.

Explain that once after Jesus explained the commandment to love our neighbor, a man asked him, "Who is my neighbour?" (see Luke 10:25–29). Jesus answered by telling a parable, or a story intended to teach a lesson.

Show the picture of the good Samaritan, and have class members read the parable of the good Samaritan in Luke 10:30–35. Then have them answer the question asked by the Savior:

- "Which now of these three . . . was neighbour unto him that fell among the thieves?" (Luke 10:36).

After class members have responded to the question, have them read the answer in Luke 10:37. Emphasize that all people are our neighbors. Invite class members to "go . . . and do thou likewise," as the Savior said.

• What are some things we can do to be good neighbors to all people? How will being a good neighbor help us develop charity?

Story and
discussion

Tell in your own words the following story:

"Snow fell lightly on the cold, bitter Canadian landscape. Overhead a dome of gray, lifeless clouds blended with the bare aspens on the ground, painting a gloomy picture. I gazed listlessly out the window of our [pickup truck]. The scene outside matched my own downcast spirits. My companion, Elder Hancock, was humming 'Joy to the World' to himself, half smiling and lightly tapping his fingers on the rim of the steering wheel. Christmas, my first one away from home, was in three days. I'd always enjoyed the same sort of traditional Christmas each year at home. But that was behind me now and far away like my family. I wanted this Christmas to be the same but knew inside that it wouldn't be. . . .

" . . . Our apartment was bare of any sign of Christmas. We didn't even have time to put up a tree. At first we had agreed to spend the entire Christmas day in active missionary work, but Elder Hancock soon sensed my lack of enthusiasm and arranged for us to have dinner with some members that night.

"'Elder,' he said as we drove into town, 'what you need more than a turkey dinner is a little TPLOC in your life.' He grinned to himself as if he'd just made a very witty remark. I stared out the window, pretending to ignore him. I always wondered how he stayed so cheerful. Trying to teach me the discussions, along with keeping track of the area we'd opened up, must have been hard for him; yet I never heard him complain or get despondent. Oh well, I did enough of that for both of us. I wondered what he meant by TPLOC. Probably some new missionary term no one had bothered to tell me about."

Write *TPLOC* on the chalkboard. Then continue with the story:

"We pulled off onto a wide street in the older part of town, parked our truck, and began tracting. The boardwalks raised above the frozen earth snapped in protest as we stepped on them. Houses on this street were rundown, unpainted, and inanimate. . . . Several houses were empty. At the first corner we encountered a small shack that, in comparison, made the other houses on the street look good.

"The house hid all signs of ever having been painted. There were no power outlets attached; here we would find no electricity. My companion knocked on the door. . . . Small timid footsteps started at the back of the house and worked forward toward the door. It creaked open, and I beheld a living museum piece.

"The woman stood four-and-a-half feet tall. Her face was full of wrinkles, so much so that it was only with effort I could make out two piercing, coal-black eyes peeking out of the crevasses. She invited us in. As I suspected, her home was also threadbare on the inside, yet it was spotless.

"Her name was Mrs. Ivar, and she was a 98-year-old immigrant from Poland. We tried to teach a discussion, but it was hard—she was so lonely. She had just learned that none of her children would be home for Christmas, and so she would be alone. I felt sorry for the lady, but we had work to do. We talked a little longer and then left.

"The next day we finished our preparations for Christmas. We had asked the Relief Society to bake us some cakes to take out to investigators. They responded in numbers, and soon our small apartment was lined with assorted cakes. One sister brought us three. She said she wanted to bake one for us, but reasoned that if she baked two we'd give them both away, so she had baked three. I smiled at that but couldn't help thinking how bare our place looked without a tree.

"Christmas came swiftly, on a bright clear day. My stomach tied itself in knots at the thought of barging into investigators' homes on Christmas day. If Elder Hancock was nervous, he hid it well. It took us most of the day to deliver our cakes. People were glad to see us, all of them, even one man who had thrown us out earlier. By dusk we had only one cake left, the cake that was ours, and our dinner was in half an hour. As we climbed in the truck I had visions of hot turkey and stuffing drenched in cranberries. Elder Hancock paused to look at something as he slid in. I looked and saw nothing—except that old row of houses we had tracted out earlier. They were leaning at crazy angles, Mrs. Ivar's being the worst.

"'That's whose house he's looking at,' I thought to myself. I knew my companion too well. 'He wants us to miss our dinner appointment and give our last cake to that old lady.' He turned and saw me eyeing the house, too. His eyes met mine, and he waited; he knew me pretty well also. This would be my decision.

"I thought of the member's home where we were expected—warm, inviting, full of life. It wasn't our fault that none of the old woman's kids could make it back home. She wasn't even good for a discussion, so why bother?

"I shifted my weight and thought of home. My sister would be back from school, and my brother would be there with his family. But what if, for some reason, none of us could make it? What if that were my mother all alone on Christmas? A lump as large as a grapefruit grew in my throat.

"I glanced at Elder Hancock and said, 'I never did go for cake much.'

"He grinned. We stopped to phone our excuses to the member family and then sped over to spend the rest of the day in the company of a great lady. She told us stories of her homeland and her Christmases as a girl. . . . Before we left, Mrs. Ivar had a new pile of wood for her stove and a half-eaten cake for her pantry.

"On the way back to our apartment I tried to tell Elder Hancock how I felt, but the words just wouldn't come. The phone was ringing as we stepped in. Elder Hancock answered it while I put on some hot chocolate.

"'Guess what?' he announced, after a brief discussion. 'I've been transferred.'

"I didn't know what to say, there was so much. Finally I blurted, 'Well, before you go there's one thing I want to know. What does TPLOC stand for?'

"'It stands for what you caught a feeling of today, Elder Johnson. TPLOC stands for "The Pure Love of Christ." And it tastes much better than a turkey dinner.' With that he began to pack" (Kelly Johnson, "The Secret of TPLOC," *New Era*, Aug. 1979, 40–42).

• What important lesson did Elder Johnson learn? How does this apply to us?

Point out that as we help other people, our love for them grows.

Heavenly Father Will Help Us Develop Charity

Chalkboard
and scripture
discussion

Explain that Mormon talked about another thing we can do to develop charity. Have class members read and mark Moroni 7:48.

Show the picture Bedside Prayer. Add 3. *Praying for help* to the list on the chalkboard.

- Why do you think prayer is important in our efforts to develop charity?

Explain that we need Heavenly Father's help to be filled with this kind of love. He will fill us with charity if we sincerely ask for that blessing and make an effort to follow the Savior's example in our relationships with others.

Testimony

Share your gratitude for the love Heavenly Father and Jesus Christ have for us, and testify of the joy that comes to us when we have charity for others.

Encourage class members to develop love for their neighbors by following Jesus Christ's example, giving service, and praying to be filled with "the pure love of Christ" (Moroni 7:47).

**Enrichment
Activities**

You may want to use one or more of these activities during the lesson.

1. Sing with class members "Love One Another" (*Children's Songbook,* 136). You may also want to teach class members the song in sign language, as shown on page 137 of the *Children's Songbook.*

2. If *Book of Mormon Video Presentations* (53911) is available, show "My Joy Is Full," a four-minute segment, in connection with your reading of 3 Nephi 17:7–13, 17–23.

3. Make a copy of the puzzle on the next page for each class member. Give each class member a copy of the puzzle and a pen or pencil. (If it is not feasible to make copies, prepare the puzzle on a poster and have class members work together.) Explain that one of the scriptural messages discussed in this lesson is hidden in the puzzle. Tell class members to start with the second letter in the puzzle, *C*, and write down every second letter in the blanks to find the message ("Charity is the pure love of Christ, and it endureth forever").

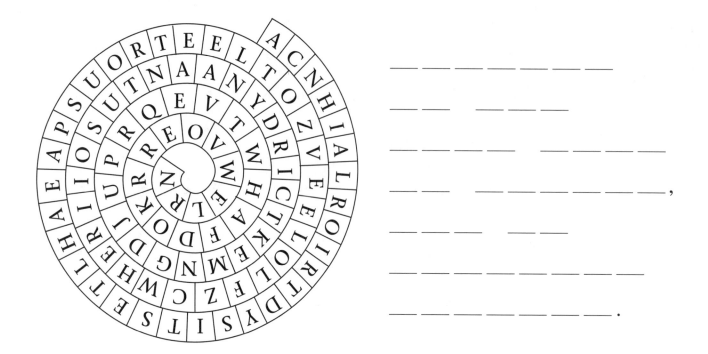

_____ _____ _____ _____

_____ _____ _____ _____

_____ _____ _____ _____

_____ _____ _____ _____ ,

_____ _____ _____ _____

_____ _____ _____

_____ _____ _____ .

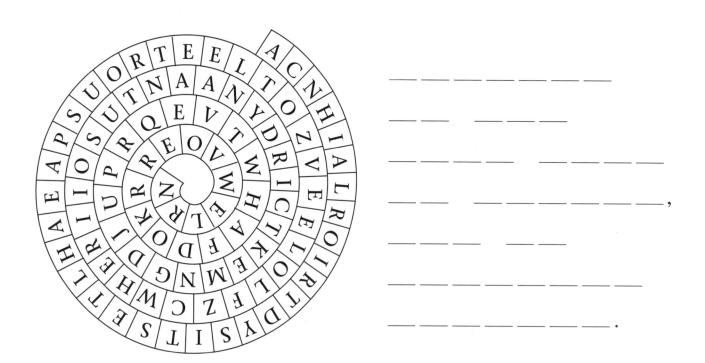

_____ _____ _____ _____

_____ _____ _____ _____

_____ _____ _____ _____

_____ _____ _____ _____ ,

_____ _____ _____ _____

_____ _____ _____ _____

_____ _____ _____ .

Forgiving Others

Purpose	To encourage class members to seek the peace that comes from forgiving others.

Preparation	1. Prayerfully study Genesis 45:1–15; Matthew 5:43–45; 18:21–22; Luke 15:11–32; 1 Nephi 7:8–21; Moroni 6:8; Doctrine and Covenants 64:9–10.
	2. Write each of the following scripture references on a separate piece of paper: Moroni 6:8; Matthew 18:21–22; Doctrine and Covenants 64:9–10; Matthew 5:43–45.
	3. Materials needed: a. A piece of paper from which to make a paper airplane (see page 198). b. Adhesive tape. c. A coin, small rock, or other small weight. d. A set of scriptures and a scripture marking pencil for each class member. Continue to encourage class members to bring their own scriptures to class each week.
Note to the teacher	*When we burden ourselves with anger, hate, and vengeance, we forfeit the blessings of having the guidance of the Holy Spirit. We invite the spirit of the adversary into our lives and thus limit our own progress toward exaltation when we are unforgiving. We invite the Holy Spirit into our lives when we follow the example of Jesus Christ and truly forgive.*

Suggested Lesson Development	**We Have Been Commanded to Forgive All People**
Discussion and quotation	• What does it mean to forgive someone?
	After class members have a chance to respond, ask a class member to read the following statement by Elder Richard G. Scott of the Quorum of the Twelve Apostles:
	"Forgiveness . . . allows the love of God to purge your heart and mind of the poison of hate. It cleanses your consciousness of the desire for revenge. It makes place for the purifying, healing, restoring love of the Lord" (in Conference Report, Apr. 1992, 45; or *Ensign*, May 1992, 33).
	Explain to class members that forgiving others does not mean approving of their wrongdoing or offense. Forgiving someone means that with the help of our Father in Heaven, we can cleanse our hearts of anger or hatred toward the offender, cease to dwell on the offense, and feel peace. This process is not always easy or quick, but Heavenly Father will help us as we try to forgive.
Scripture activity and discussion	Give each class member (or small group of class members) one of the pieces of paper you have prepared with a scripture reference on it.

Have class members locate and read their references. Allow enough time for each class member to understand the scripture's message. Then ask the following questions, and have class members answer by reading aloud the scripture that answers the question.

1. How often is the Lord willing to forgive? (Moroni 6:8.)

   • Why is it important for us to have this same willingness to forgive? (Emphasize that to become more like the Lord, we must strive to follow his example, even though it may be difficult sometimes.)

2. How often should we forgive others? (Matthew 18:21–22. You may want to point out that Jesus was not stating a precise number of times we must forgive; he was using the large number to show that we should forgive as often as necessary.)

   • How often do we ask the Lord to forgive us? (Remind class members that we all have a need to ask for the Lord's forgiveness. We should strive to show others the same kindness and mercy the Lord shows us.)

3. Why should we forgive others? (D&C 64:9–10.)

   • How can it be a greater sin to refuse to forgive someone? (When we refuse to forgive others, we can become filled with anger, hate, and a desire for revenge. These feelings can cause us to lose the companionship of the Holy Ghost and make it more difficult for us to live other gospel principles. Also, when we do not forgive someone, it can make it more difficult for that person to complete his or her own repentance process.)

4. What blessings does the Lord promise us if we are forgiving toward others? (Matthew 5:43–45.)

   • How can forgiving others make us "children of our Father in Heaven"?

Forgiving Others Brings Us Peace

Object lesson

Ask a class member to make a paper airplane, or make one yourself. Tape a coin, rock, or weight to one side of the airplane. Stand on the same side of the room as the class members, and ask a class member to throw the airplane gently toward the other side of the room. Next, pick up the airplane and remove the taped object. Have the class member throw the airplane again. After the class member has done so a few times, put the airplane away, and ask the following questions:

• How can just one small weight keep the plane from flying correctly?

Explain that taping a weight to the wing of a paper airplane is like holding a grudge. When we refuse to forgive others, we carry around a weight that keeps us from traveling the straight and narrow path our Father in Heaven wants for us. It is important to forgive others so that we can enjoy the companionship of the Holy Spirit and grow spiritually.

Quotation and discussion

Ask a class member to read the following statement made by Elder Gordon B. Hinckley when he was a member of the Quorum of the Twelve Apostles:

"There is no peace in harboring old grudges. There is no peace in reflecting on the pain of old wounds. There is peace only in repentance and forgiveness. This is the sweet peace of the Christ, who said, 'Blessed are the peacemakers; for they shall be called the children of God' (Matthew 5:9)" (in Conference Report, Oct. 1980, 88; or *Ensign*, Nov. 1980, 63).

- Why is it difficult to feel peace when we do not forgive others?

- How can forgiving others help us be peacemakers?

Note to the teacher

For stories to be effective, you must rehearse them so you can read them well or tell them in your own words. Teaching—No Greater Call, *pages 98–100, contains some suggestions for telling a story.*

Story and discussion

Read the following story, which was related in general conference by Bishop H. Burke Peterson when he was First Counselor in the Presiding Bishopric:

"During World War II there were terrible examples of man's inhumanity to man. After the war was over and the concentration camps were opened, there was much hatred among the weak and emaciated survivors. In one camp, observers noticed a native of Poland who seemed so robust and peaceful they thought he must have only recently been imprisoned. They were surprised to learn that he had been there over six years! Then, they reasoned, he must not have suffered the terrible atrocities to his family members that most of the prisoners had. But in questioning him, they learned how soldiers had come to his city, lined up against a wall his wife, two daughters, and three small sons, then opened fire with a machine gun. Though he begged to die with them, he had been kept alive because of his knowledge and ability in language translation.

"This Polish father said: 'I had to decide right then . . . whether to let myself hate the soldiers who had done this. It was an easy decision, really. I was a lawyer. In my practice I had seen . . . what hate could do to people's minds and bodies. Hate had just killed the six people who mattered most to me in the world. I decided then that I would spend the rest of my life—whether it was a few days or many years—loving every person I came in contact with' (George G. Ritchie with Elizabeth Sherrill, *Return from Tomorrow* [Waco, Texas: Chosen Books, 1978], p. 116)" (in Conference Report, Oct. 1983, 84–85; or *Ensign*, Nov. 1983, 60).

- What reasons might this man have given if he had chosen to be unforgiving?

- What might have happened to this man if he had spent all his time being angry and planning his revenge?

- How did his decision to forgive make a difference in his life?

The Scriptures Contain Many Examples of Forgiveness

Scripture discussion

Read and discuss with class members the following scriptural events that illustrate the concept of forgiveness:

1. Nephi exhorting his brothers to have faith in the Lord (1 Nephi 7:8–21).

- What had Laman and Lemuel done that Nephi needed to forgive?

- How long did it take Nephi to decide to forgive his brothers?

2. Joseph making himself known to his brothers, who had sold him into Egypt (Genesis 45:1–15).

- When Joseph revealed himself to his brothers, whom was he concerned with first? (His father and his brothers.)

- How did Joseph show his brothers that he had forgiven them? (He took care of them and their families during the famine.)

3. The prodigal son returning home (Luke 15:11–32).

- How did the prodigal son's father react when his son returned?

- How did the older brother react when the prodigal son returned? What can we learn from the father's response to his elder son?

Quotation and discussion

- Who gave us the best example of forgiveness to follow? (The Savior.)

Read the following statement about Christ's forgiving love:

"All his life he had been the victim of ugliness. As a newborn infant he had been spirited away to save his life at the instruction of an angel in a dream. . . . At the end of a hectic life he had stood in quiet, restrained, divine dignity. . . .

"He was beaten, officially scourged. He wore a crown of thorns. . . . He was mocked and jeered. He suffered every indignity at the hands of his own people. . . . He was required to carry his own cross. . . . Finally, with the soldiers and his accusers down below him, he looked upon the Roman soldiers and said these immortal words: *'Father, forgive them; for they know not what they do.'* (Luke 23:34)" (Spencer W. Kimball, *The Miracle of Forgiveness* [1969], 279–80).

- Think of some things others have done that have hurt or offended you. How can the Savior's example help you forgive others?

Emphasize that even though we will not experience anything as severe as the things the Savior experienced, we all have opportunities to forgive others. The Lord's commandment to forgive others applies to everyone.

Testimony

Testify of the importance of forgiving others in bringing us peace and helping us enjoy the companionship of the Spirit. As appropriate, you may want to share with your class members an experience that you have had with forgiveness.

Encourage class members to follow the Lord's example of forgiving others. Invite them to seek his help in forgiving so that they too can feel the peace that comes through forgiving others.

Enrichment Activities

You may want to use one or more of these activities during the lesson.

1. Sing or read with class members the second verse of "Did You Think to Pray?" (*Hymns*, no. 140).

- Why is it important that we pray when we are trying to forgive someone?

- How can praying for the Lord's help in forgiving someone help bring us rest?

2. Read the following statements to the class. After each statement, ask class members to decide whether the statement shows a forgiving or unforgiving attitude. Ask them to explain their choices.

   a. She didn't invite me to her party, so I'm not going to invite her.

   b. He ignored me when I asked for his help. Maybe he was worried about something else.

   c. He made fun of my hair, so I made fun of the way he dresses.

   d. I guess I'll forgive her, but I'm not going to talk to her.

   e. She never sits by me or talks to me during class. I wonder if she's shy.

3. Read or tell the following story:

   "It seemed like a silly thing to fight over, and 12-year-old Ava Rosenberg didn't want to fight. But another 12-year-old at school kept insisting that Ava had stolen her pen."

   The girl and her sister made frightening threats against Ava. One day, as Ava went to the drinking fountain at school, a group of people approached her, and one girl attacked her. She kicked and punched Ava and beat her head on the ground.

   "Ava's mother had come to the school to discuss the threats against her daughter. When she arrived, she found Ava in the office in a terrible state of shock—her face discolored, swollen and bleeding, her jaw severely dislocated.

   "'We spent many hours at the hospital,' Sister Rosenberg says. What followed was a nightmare of unsuccessful operations, culminating eventually in Ava receiving a bone graft from her lower jaw to her upper jaw, secured by a titanium plate and screws. As a result, her face was severely traumatized and she was in great pain."

   • How do you feel about the girl who assaulted Ava? How do you think Ava felt about her?

   Continue the story:

   "Ava finally came out of the hospital on a Saturday. The next day was fast Sunday, and during the testimony meeting Ava stood to speak. It was physically difficult to form the words, and tears filled her eyes. But Ava had something important to say. She asked the congregation to fast and pray— that the Lord would bless the girl that had done this to her.

   "'The scars from my injuries will heal,' Ava said. 'But the girl who attacked me has deep scars inside. I have a loving family and the gospel to get me through. She has neither. Pray for her. Pray that the missionaries can find her and teach her, so that she can turn from hate to love.'

   "Many in the congregation were moved by Ava's example of forgiveness. To her, however, it was simply a matter of doing what the Savior taught. 'We're supposed to love our enemies,' she says matter-of-factly. 'When I was in the hospital, I couldn't speak because I was in so much pain. But I could think, and I remember thinking to myself, What would the Savior do?'

Despite continued threats against her, repeated surgeries far from home, lingering pain, and a sometimes discouraging recovery, Ava's friends and family attest they have never heard her say a single word against the girl who beat her.

"'I will probably have a plate in my jaw all my life,' she says. 'But it doesn't matter because I know I will be healed in the celestial kingdom. I just hope and pray that [the girl who attacked me] will be healed too'" (Richard M. Romney, "Pray for Her," *New Era,* Oct. 1994, 44–45).

- When Ava stood up in testimony meeting, she asked the congregation to pray for the girl who attacked her. If Ava had done what people naturally do in her situation and had given way to anger, hatred, and a desire for revenge, what effect might that have had on her?

- What do you think about Ava's reaction to the events?

Give Yourself Away

Purpose	To encourage class members to give of themselves through service.

Preparation	1. Prayerfully study Matthew 25:34–40; Mosiah 2:17.
	2. Materials needed:
	a. A piece of paper and a pen or pencil for each class member.
	b. A set of scriptures and a scripture marking pencil for each class member. Continue to encourage class members to bring their own scriptures to class each week.
Note to the teacher	*Charity, the pure love of Christ, involves a desire to serve. For us to become more Christlike, each of us must be willing to serve others. Jesus taught, "Whosoever will be chief among you, let him be your servant" (Matthew 20:27). Help class members understand that they have the ability to serve, and encourage them to look for opportunities to help others.*

Suggested Lesson Development	**The Results of Service Can Be Far-Reaching**
Story and discussion	Read or tell the following story:
	"A young mother on an overnight flight with a two-year-old daughter was stranded by bad weather in [the] Chicago airport without food or clean clothing for the child and without money. She was two months pregnant and threatened with miscarriage, so she was under doctor's instructions not to carry the child unless it was essential. Hour after hour she stood in one line after another, trying to get a flight to Michigan. The terminal was noisy, full of tired, frustrated, grumpy passengers, and she heard critical references to her crying child and to her sliding her child along the floor with her foot as the line moved forward. No one offered to help with the soaked, hungry, exhausted child. Then, the woman later reported, 'Someone came towards us and with a kindly smile said, "Is there something I could do to help you?" With a grateful sigh I accepted his offer. He lifted my sobbing little daughter from the cold floor and lovingly held her to him while he patted her gently on the back. He asked if she could chew a piece of gum. When she was settled down, he carried her with him and said something kindly to the others in the line ahead of me, about how I needed their help. They seemed to agree and then he went up to the ticket counter [at the front of the line] and made arrangements with the clerk for me to be put on a flight leaving shortly. He walked with us to a bench, where we chatted a moment, until he was assured that I would be fine. He went on his way. About a week later I saw a picture of Apostle Spencer W. Kimball and recognized him as the stranger in the airport'" (Edward L. Kimball and Andrew E. Kimball, Jr., *Spencer W. Kimball* [1977], 334).

- What were the immediate effects of President Kimball's service? (The mother and her daughter were comforted and able to board the plane more quickly.)

Draw a simple stick figure on the left-hand side of the chalkboard. Label the figure *President Kimball.* Draw two more stick figures immediately to the right of that figure. Explain that they represent the mother and her daughter.

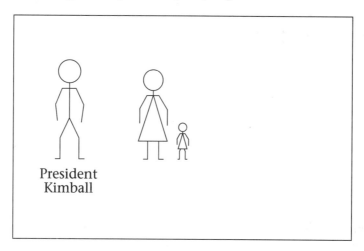

Explain that acts of service can also have far-reaching effects. Then ask a class member to read the following letter, which was sent to President Kimball many years after he helped the woman at the airport:

"Dear President Kimball:

"I am a student at Brigham Young University. I have just returned from my mission in Munich West Germany. I had a lovely mission and learned much. . . .

"I was sitting in priesthood meeting last week, when a story was told of a loving service which you performed some 21 years ago in the Chicago airport. The story told of how you met a young pregnant mother with a young screaming child in . . . a [condition of] distress waiting in a long line for her tickets. She was threatening miscarriage and therefore couldn't lift her child to comfort her. She had experienced four previous miscarriages which gave added reason for the doctor's orders not to bend or lift.

" . . . You comforted the crying child, and explained the dilemma to the other passengers in line. This act of love took the strain and tension off of my mother. I was born a few months later in Flint, Michigan.

"I just want to *thank you* for your love. *Thank you* for your example!" (quoted by Gordon B. Hinckley, in Christmas Devotional address, 18 Dec. 1983).

Chalkboard discussion

- When Elder Kimball helped the woman in the airport, the person who wrote this letter had not yet been born. How did Elder Kimball's act of service influence this person's life?

Ask a class member to draw on the chalkboard a simple figure representing the young man who wrote the letter. Then ask:

- Who else might have been influenced by this act of kindness?

For each person or group of people mentioned, have the class member at the chalkboard add another figure to the diagram. Discuss how the people mentioned might have been influenced by President Kimball's service. Answers may include the following:

The other people who were standing in line at the airport

The employees at the ticket counter

Family members and friends of the mother and her daughter

People in Germany who were taught the gospel by the young man who wrote the letter

President Kimball and his family (note that the first story was recorded by a son and a grandson of President Kimball)

Members of this class and others who have heard this story

Point out that one act of service has the potential to influence the lives of many people.

Service to Others Is Service to the Lord

Story

Have someone read the following story told about Emma Somerville McConkie, a widow who, despite her own illness, found time and energy to serve others who were suffering (the experience was related by Oscar McConkie, Sister McConkie's son):

"Mother was president of the [ward] Relief Society. . . . [A nonmember who opposed the Church] had married a Mormon girl. They had several children; now they had a new baby. They were very poor and Mother was going day by day to care for the child and to take them baskets of food. . . . Mother herself was ill, and more than once was hardly able to get home after doing the work at [this family's] home.

"One day she returned home especially tired and weary. She slept in her chair. She dreamed she was bathing a baby which she discovered was the Christ Child. She thought, Oh, what a great honor to thus serve the very Christ! As she held the baby in her lap, she was all but overcome. . . . Unspeakable joy filled her whole being. She was aflame with the glory of the Lord. It seemed that the very marrow in her bones would melt. Her joy was so great it awakened her. As she awoke, these words were spoken to her, 'Inasmuch as ye have done it unto one of the least of these my brethren, ye have done it unto me'" (quoted by Bruce R. McConkie, in "Charity Which Never Faileth," *Relief Society Magazine,* Mar. 1970, 169).

Scripture discussion

Have class members read and mark Matthew 25:34–40. Make sure they understand that "the King" in these verses is Jesus Christ.

- What did Jesus mean when he said, "Inasmuch as ye have done it unto one of the least of these my brethren, ye have done it unto me"?

If class members need help answering this question, have them read and mark Mosiah 2:17.

- How is service to others also service to God?

Refer back to the story about Sister McConkie, and ask the following questions:

- Why do you think Sister McConkie served this young family so diligently? In what ways do her actions show that she was serving out of more than just duty as a Relief Society president? How did this service show her love for the Lord?

- How do you think her actions influenced her feelings toward the family she served? How might they have affected her love for the Lord?

- By helping the husband in the family, she showed that she was willing to serve someone who was antagonistic toward the Church. Why should our service and love not be limited to Church members, family, and friends?

Help class members understand that some people serve only those they enjoy being around and avoid all others, showing that their love for others is limited. Jesus commanded us to love and serve everyone. We show our willingness to give of ourselves when we love and care about all people.

Read the following statement by Elder Hans B. Ringger of the Seventy:

"We need to look around us, and if we cannot see poverty, illness, and despair in our own neighborhood or ward, then we have to look harder. And remember, we cannot be afraid to go beyond our own social and cultural circles. We have to rid ourselves of religious, racial, or social prejudices and expand the boundaries of our service. Service should never discriminate and is hardly ever easy. Did not Jesus Himself mingle with those who were branded unfit by the self-righteous Pharisees? And were not those people the ones who needed Him the most?" (in Conference Report, Apr. 1990, 33; or *Ensign*, May 1990, 26).

We Should Look for Opportunities to Serve

Have someone read this statement by President Spencer W. Kimball:

"God does notice us, and he watches over us. But it is usually through another person that he meets our needs. Therefore, it is vital that we serve each other in the kingdom. The people of the Church need each other's strength, support, and leadership. . . . So often, our acts of service consist of simple encouragement or of giving mundane [ordinary] help with mundane tasks, but what glorious consequences can flow from mundane acts and from small but deliberate deeds!" ("Small Acts of Service," *Ensign*, Dec. 1974, 5).

- How do simple acts of service demonstrate love? What are some simple things we can do to show our love for others?

Read the following statement made by Elder M. Russell Ballard in an address at general conference:

"We observe vast, sweeping world events; however, we must remember that the purposes of the Lord in our personal lives generally are fulfilled through the small and simple things and not the momentous and spectacular."

Later in the same talk, Elder Ballard spoke about small and simple things we can do to help others, concluding:

"We must never ignore or pass by the prompting of the Spirit to render service to one another" (in Conference Report, Apr. 1990, 4, 7; or *Ensign,* May 1990, 6, 8).

Activity

Give each class member a piece of paper and a pen or pencil. Have each person privately list acts of service that he or she could perform at home, at school, in the neighborhood, at church, or in the community.

Testimony

Bear your testimony of the joy of service and the blessings of love and growth that come from serving others.

Ask class members to choose one item on their lists and perform the service they have identified. Encourage them to look for other opportunities to serve others.

Enrichment Activities

You may want to use one or more of these activities during the lesson.

1. Remind class members of lesson 33, which was about charity, the pure love of Christ. As was discussed in that lesson, one way to develop charity is to serve others. When we serve others we show our love for them and for Heavenly Father and Jesus Christ. This increases our love for Heavenly Father and Jesus, and our desire to serve them increases. This desire manifests itself in greater desire to serve others. As we serve others, our love continues to grow.

On separate pieces of paper, write the names of each member of your class, including the names of those who do not usually attend class. Put the pieces of paper in a bowl, and have each class member choose one and silently read the name written on it. (Instruct class members to select another name if they have chosen their own. If there are more pieces of paper than there are class members, some class members will need to choose more than one piece of paper.)

Invite class members to do something kind in the coming week for the people whose names they have chosen. Testify that as they do so, their love for the people they serve and for Heavenly Father and Jesus will increase.

2. If *Family Home Evening Video Supplement* (53276) is available, show "Serving Others with Love," a seven-minute segment.

3. Give each class member several paper hands, like those shown on page 208, to take home. Invite class members to look for opportunities to help their family members anonymously, leaving behind a helping hand when they have performed an act of service. They may be surprised at how quickly this activity catches on among family members.

You have been served by a helping hand. Now it's your turn. Leave this helping hand behind after you do something nice for a member of our family.

You have been served by a helping hand. Now it's your turn. Leave this helping hand behind after you do something nice for a member of our family.

You have been served by a helping hand. Now it's your turn. Leave this helping hand behind after you do something nice for a member of our family.

You have been served by a helping hand. Now it's your turn. Leave this helping hand behind after you do something nice for a member of our family.

You have been served by a helping hand. Now it's your turn. Leave this helping hand behind after you do something nice for a member of our family.

You have been served by a helping hand. Now it's your turn. Leave this helping hand behind after you do something nice for a member of our family.

Look beyond Yourself

Purpose	To help class members understand that they can grow closer to the Savior by thinking of others' needs before their own.

Preparation	1. Prayerfully study Ruth 1–2; 1 Samuel 19–20; Matthew 7:12; Luke 23:34.
	2. Materials needed: A set of scriptures and a scripture marking pencil for each class member. Continue to encourage class members to bring their own scriptures to class each week.
Note to the teacher	*According to an old saying, "The smallest of packages is a person wrapped up in himself." Many people in the world give little thought to what others think and feel. Selfishness seems to come easily and naturally, and it is the cause of many problems in the world. Remind class members that thinking of others is the Savior's way.*

Suggested Lesson Development	**Thinking of Others First**
Story and discussion	Write on the chalkboard *1+1=0* and *1–1=2*. Ask class members to try to figure out how these mathematical formulas can be true.

After class members have had a chance to respond, tell them the following parable:

One Monday morning when Rob and Janet arrived at school, they noticed that their teacher, Mr. May, had an interesting smile on his face. "I wonder what Mr. May is going to do today," Janet whispered to Rob. The other students in the class also seemed curious about what was behind Mr. May's intriguing smile.

It seemed to take forever for class to begin. When the bell signaled the start of class, Mr. May said, "Today I am going to give each of you three gifts. You may do whatever you wish with the gifts. But the object of receiving these gifts is to get more of them by the end of the week."

With that short explanation, Mr. May gave each student three small pieces of paper. Rob quickly looked at each one. On one piece of paper was the word "Smile." A second piece of paper read "Sincere compliment." The third simply read "Help."

A student raised her hand and asked, "What are we supposed to do with these?"

Mr. May smiled again. "You can figure it out," he said.

Determined to get more gifts, Rob stuffed the pieces of paper into his pocket so no one would be able to take them from him. Then he spent the rest of the week trying to get gifts from other people. He poked fun at one of the students in the class and then looked around to see how many people had smiled at him.

209

When he got a good grade on a spelling test, he showed his grade to several people, hoping that someone would give him a sincere compliment. And he reminded Tom of a favor he had done for him once, saying, "We'll be even if you will help me with my book report." By the end of the week, all Rob had was three crumpled pieces of paper in his pocket and a sick feeling in his stomach.

Janet didn't really think about Mr. May's assignment. She just went about her week as she always did. She greeted everyone with a smile. When she noticed that Emily had done especially well on a math quiz, she congratulated her. Later that week she noticed that Loren was having a hard time with his science project. She helped him with the problem that was frustrating him. By the end of the week, Janet was happier than she had been before, even though she had forgotten about Mr. May's challenge to get more gifts.

Rob was confused. He had tried hard to get more gifts, but he had failed. Meanwhile, he noticed that even though Janet had not done anything different, everyone smiled at her. People were always giving her sincere compliments. And when she needed help with something, someone always seemed to notice and offer assistance.

- For Rob, how did one plus one equal zero? (After trying all week to add to his own store of "gifts," he seemed to have less than he had when the week began.) How did one minus one equal two for Janet? (Rather than trying to get smiles, compliments, and help from others, she gave those gifts away. However, in the process, she received those gifts from others and felt even happier than she had felt when the week began.)

Explain that Rob approached Mr. May's assignment selfishly but Janet was selfless, spending the week thinking of others. Although she gave her gifts away, she never lost anything (for example, she didn't lose her smile when she smiled at others). Likewise, when we give of ourselves, we often find that we don't lose anything at all. Instead, we receive gifts of love, friendship, and greater happiness.

Selfishness versus Selflessness

Chalkboard discussion

- What does the word *selfish* mean to you?

Following the discussion, read the dictionary definition of *selfish:* "Seeking or concentrating on one's own advantage, pleasure, or well-being without regard for others" (*Merriam-Webster's Collegiate Dictionary,* 10th ed., s.v. "selfish").

- What are some characteristics of a selfish person?

List class members' responses on the chalkboard, including some of the following characteristics:

SELFISH

　　Self-centered
　　Greedy
　　Unkind
　　Insensitive
　　Lustful
　　Unpleasant

- What are some results of selfishness?

Write class members' responses on the chalkboard. Answers may include the following:

RESULTS OF SELFISHNESS

Dishonesty (lying, cheating, stealing)
Jealousy
Poor family relationships
Unwillingness to serve in the Church
Immorality
War and crime

- How does selfishness bring these results?

Point out that the opposite of selfishness is selflessness. Selfless people think of others before they think of themselves.

- What are some characteristics of a selfless person?

You may want to list class members' responses on the chalkboard, or you may simply help them see that a selfless person will have characteristics opposite to those of a selfish person. For example, a selfless person is generous and kind rather than greedy and unkind.

- What are some results of selflessness?

Help class members see that just as the characteristics of selflessness are opposite to those of selfishness, so are the results of selflessness opposite to the results of selfishness. Selflessness leads to love, service, and peace.

Situations and discussion

Discuss with class members the following situations:

1. Max knew that his mother had made a pie for dessert. Because he was hungry on his arrival home from school, he cut the pie and ate nearly half of it. When his mother confronted him, he said that he had wanted his pie early and that since he was the biggest in the family he deserved the biggest share.

   - Who was Max thinking of?
   - What could he have done differently?

2. One Saturday afternoon six girls decided to go to lunch and see a movie together. Five of the girls chose to see a certain movie, but Joan insisted they attend the one her favorite actor was playing in at a theater across town. When the other girls outvoted Joan, she said that if they wouldn't go to her movie she would not go at all. Angrily she stomped out of the room.

   - What do you think of Joan's behavior?
   - How might Joan have been more considerate of her friends' feelings?

Ask class members to think silently about the following questions:

- What would you do in the same situation as Max or Joan? In what ways are you a selfish or selfless person?

Developing a Selfless Attitude

Quotation
and discussion

President Spencer W. Kimball spent his life thinking of others and the Lord instead of himself. Have a class member read the following advice from President Kimball to young people:

"To do the special things given to this generation, you will need to guard against selfishness. One of the tendencies most individuals have which simply must be overcome is the tendency to be selfish. All that you can do now while you are young and are more pliant to become less selfish and more selfless will be an important and lasting contribution to the quality of your life in the years, indeed in the eternity, to come. You will be a much better wife or a much better husband, a better mother or a better father, if you can curb the tendency to be selfish" ("President Kimball Speaks Out on Planning Your Life," *New Era,* Sept. 1981, 51).

- Why did President Kimball emphasize the importance of learning to be selfless "while you are young and pliant"? (*Pliant* means "easily influenced." President Kimball was saying that it is easier to change when we are young than when we are old and may have established bad habits.)

- How can being selfless improve our lives now and in eternity?

Scripture
discussion

Have class members read and mark Matthew 7:12. Explain that many people refer to this teaching as the Golden Rule.

- How can this teaching help us be more selfless?

- What are some specific things we can do to overcome selfishness?

Help class members see that we can do such things as:

Show courtesy and kindness.
Compliment others sincerely.
Avoid sarcasm.
Put ourselves in the other person's position.
Avoid thoughts of resentment, envy, or jealousy.
Be genuinely interested in other people.
Show love for others.

Following the Examples of Selfless People

Scripture stories
and discussion

Tell the class that there are many great examples in the scriptures of men and women who were unselfish. Instead of thinking of themselves, they thought of others. Many of these people suffered danger, trouble, pain, and disappointment to be able to help others.

Relate the following scripture stories. After each story, have class members discuss the person's example of unselfishness.

Jonathan

Jonathan was the son of King Saul. Normally he would have been next in line to be king. However, the prophet Samuel anointed David to succeed Saul as king.

In 1 Samuel, chapters 19 and 20, we read that Jonathan protected his friend David when Saul tried to kill David.

- How might Jonathan have acted if he had been selfish? How did Jonathan show that he was unselfish?

Ruth

When Ruth's husband died, she decided to leave her homeland and go to Bethlehem with her mother-in-law, Naomi, who was also a widow. When they arrived in Bethlehem, Ruth provided food for Naomi by picking up, or gleaning, corn or grain that was left in the fields after the harvest. (See Ruth 1–2.)

- What reasons could Ruth have had to stay in her homeland rather than go with Naomi?
- How did Ruth show that she was unselfish?

Joseph Smith

The Prophet Joseph Smith suffered humiliation and abuse from enemies of the Church while he translated the Book of Mormon and established the restored Church of Jesus Christ. He later gave his life for his testimony.

- What blessings have we received because of Joseph Smith's selflessness?
- How can we, like Joseph Smith, give more of ourselves in the Lord's service?

Jesus Christ

Jesus Christ taught us to be unselfish, and he always practiced what he taught, giving us an example to follow. One great example of his selflessness was shown on the cross. Referring to the Roman soldiers who had nailed him to the cross, he said, "Father, forgive them; for they know not what they do" (Luke 23:34).

- Who was Jesus thinking of at that moment of personal agony?
- What are some other examples of unselfishness from Jesus' life and teachings? How was the Atonement of Jesus Christ a selfless act?

Testimony

Testify that Jesus Christ gave us the perfect example of selflessness. Encourage class members to follow that example, working to become less selfish during the coming week.

Enrichment Activities

You may want to use one or more of these activities during the lesson.

1. Have class members sit in a circle. Explain that seeing good in other people is part of being selfless. Then have class members take turns sharing one thing they admire about the person to their left.

2. Invite class members to talk about how they felt when they performed an act of service as they were asked in lesson 35. Be sure they talk about things they *felt* rather than specific things they did.

3. With class members, sing or read the words to "Have I Done Any Good?" (*Hymns,* no. 223). Focus on the words in the chorus: "Then wake up and do something more / Than dream of your mansions above." Ask class members the following questions:

- Why is it selfish to focus only on our own salvation in "mansions above"? How could this attitude prevent us from reaching those mansions?

Honest in All Things

Purpose	To help class members commit to make a constant, conscious effort to be honest in all things.

Preparation	1. Prayerfully study Exodus 20:16; Ecclesiastes 5:4–5; 1 Nephi 4:31–33, 35–37; Alma 27:26–27; Doctrine and Covenants 3:5; 14:7; 20:77; 82:10; 89:19; 124:15; Moses 4:4; Articles of Faith 1:13.
	2. Materials needed: A set of scriptures and a scripture marking pencil for each class member. Continue to encourage class members to bring their own scriptures to class each week.
Note to the teacher	*Honesty includes being true to oneself as well as being honest with others and with the Lord. It is a gospel principle that affects many other eternal principles. Help class members see that the blessings of honesty are many: self-respect, love of others, and eventually all the blessings that the Lord can offer.*

Suggested Lesson Development	**Honesty in Word and Deed**
Story and discussion	Relate the following story to the class:
	Even though Tony had poor study habits, he got passing grades. Everyone thought he was good at taking tests. But in reality, he had simply learned how to cheat.
	Tony's parents wanted him to go to college, but they were worried because he never seemed to study or do homework. They frequently asked how he felt about school. He always told them that he was doing fine.
	One day Tony's father asked him some questions that required an understanding of simple algebra. Tony was unable to answer them, but he said that he had received passing grades in his algebra class, so the questions must have been too difficult for a high school student.
	When Tony's grandmother asked him about the books he had been reading in his literature class, she found that he had little or no understanding of them. She questioned Tony about this, but he responded that he had passed his literature class, so he knew all he needed to know.
	One day Tony's parents asked him if he felt prepared to go on to college. He replied that he thought he would be fine. He insisted that his passing grades proved that he was ready. He challenged his parents to wait and see how well he would do at college.
	After the discussion, Tony had an empty feeling. He had mastered skills for cheating that never failed to get him through his classes, but he knew he really

hadn't applied himself and hadn't learned much of anything in school. He wondered if he would find a college where he would be able to cheat and bluff his way through the classes the way he had so far.

- With whom had Tony been dishonest? (With his teachers, his classmates, his parents, his grandmother, and himself.)

- What other kinds of dishonesty are there besides cheating? (Answers may include stealing, lying, telling only part of the truth, remaining silent when someone says something that isn't true, and so on.)

Quotation

Explain that although Tony's dishonesty was obvious, some forms of dishonesty are more subtle. Ask a class member to read the following statement by Elder Marvin J. Ashton, who was a member of the Quorum of the Twelve Apostles:

"[After] 50 years . . . some former students recall with lasting appreciation the words one teacher had her class repeat at the beginning of each day. Every school morning this [teacher] implanted the meaning of honesty into our minds by having us recite 'A lie is *any* communication given to another with the intent to deceive.' A lie can be effectively communicated without words ever being spoken. Sometimes a nod of the head or silence can deceive" (in Conference Report, Apr. 1982, 10; or *Ensign*, May 1982, 9).

Emphasize that anytime we cause or allow someone to believe something that is not true, we are being dishonest. To be exalted in the celestial kingdom, we must learn to be honest with ourselves, with others, and with the Lord.

Being Honest with Ourselves

Discussion

Refer back to the story about Tony, and ask the following questions:

- Who was hurt most by Tony's dishonesty? (Tony himself.) How was he hurt?

- How was Tony dishonest with himself? (He tried to make himself believe that cheating was not serious because the things he did not know were not important anyway.)

- If Tony's lack of honesty continues, how do you think it will affect his life?

Scripture discussion

Have class members read Moses 4:4. Explain that in this verse the Lord is speaking.

- In what ways did Satan's influence affect Tony? (Tony was deceived or "blinded" into thinking that his dishonesty was not a serious problem. His dishonesty with himself caused him to deceive others also.)

Chalkboard discussion

Write *Honesty with oneself* on the left side of the chalkboard.

- What does it mean to be honest with ourselves? (Answers may include accepting responsibility for our decisions instead of blaming other people or circumstances; recognizing that our decisions have consequences; and being willing to recognize our strengths and our weaknesses.)

- Why is it important to be honest with ourselves? (If we are honest with ourselves about our own thoughts and actions, we will know what we must do to become more like the Lord. We can ask for his help in overcoming our weaknesses, and we can thank him for our blessings.)

- How can we develop this kind of honesty?

Being Honest with Others

Chalkboard discussion

- How does being true to ourselves help us to be honest with others? (When we are honest with ourselves, we develop a sense of honor and self-respect. We can apply this same respect in our relationships with others.)

Write *Honesty with others* under *Honesty with oneself* on the chalkboard.

- What things keep us from being honest with others?

List class members' answers on the right-hand side of the chalkboard. Answers may include:

Pride
Greed
Manipulation
Hate
Rationalization
Fear of being found out

- How do these things keep us from being honest with others? (If we are filled with pride, for example, we may be so concerned about our reputation that we are willing to lie to make others think highly of us.)

Scripture discussion

Ask class members to turn back to Moses 4:4 and reread this verse.

- How can lies cause us to be led captive?

Emphasize that if we are dishonest and do not repent, we may continue in more dishonest behavior. For example, imagine that someone steals a neighbor's bike. When the neighbor asks if anyone has seen it, the person who stole the bike can either admit it or say no (another dishonest act). To keep the bike, the person who stole it will have to hide it from the owner or sell it to someone else (other dishonest acts). Thus, if we commit one dishonest act and do not repent, we often have to continue being dishonest to avoid being caught. This pattern of dishonesty can greatly harm our relationships with others and with the Lord.

Have someone recite or read the thirteenth article of faith.

- How can being honest help us in "doing good to all men"?

Have class members read and mark 1 Nephi 4:31–33.

- Why do you think Nephi spoke to Zoram, the servant of Laban, with an oath or promise? Do you think he intended to keep his promise?

Have class members read and mark 1 Nephi 4:35–37.

- What happened when Zoram responded to Nephi's promise with a promise of his own?

Explain that in the time of Nephi and Zoram, an oath was sacred and would not be broken. Therefore when Zoram promised to leave Jerusalem and follow Nephi and his family into the wilderness, Nephi had no fear that Zoram would try to escape and return to his home. Likewise, Nephi's oath assured Zoram that he would be treated kindly and fairly by Nephi and his family.

- What are some promises we make to others? (To fulfill Church assignments, to do jobs around the house, to be home at a certain time, or to do our own schoolwork.)

- If our promises to others were as solemnly observed as Nephi's and Zoram's, how would our relationships with others be improved? How would our communities, and even the world, be improved? (Have class members read and mark Alma 27:26–27.)

- What experiences have you had in which you were blessed for being honest with other people?

Being Honest with God

Scripture and chalkboard discussion

Have class members read and mark Ecclesiastes 5:4–5. Explain that a vow is an earnest promise.

Write *Honesty with God* under *Honesty with others* on the chalkboard.

- What are some of the vows we have made with God?

Erase the right side of the chalkboard, and list the responses toward the top of the right side. The list should include:

1. Take upon us the name of Christ.

2. Remember him always.

3. Keep his commandments.

Read Doctrine and Covenants 3:5, and have class members note the phrase "the promises." Explain that God has made marvelous promises to us.

- What are some of the promises God has made to us if we live the gospel?

List class members' answers near the bottom of the right-hand side of the chalkboard. If they have difficulty answering, have them read the scripture references below. The list on the chalkboard should include:

1. The Lord's Spirit to be with us always (see D&C 20:77).

2. Great treasures of knowledge (see D&C 89:19).

3. Eternal life (see D&C 14:7).

Have class members read and mark Doctrine and Covenants 82:10.

- Why is it important to be honest in keeping our covenants with God?

Testimony

Bear your testimony about the blessings and importance of honesty in all things.

Urge class members to always be honest with themselves, with others, and with the Lord. Encourage them to remember the promises the Lord has made to those who are honest and faithful. Conclude by reading Doctrine and Covenants 124:15 to class members and challenging them to develop the kind of integrity (honesty) that Hyrum Smith had.

Enrichment Activities

You may want to use one or more of these activities during the lesson.

1. Relate the following story:

   A seminary teacher had been teaching his class the importance of honesty and had stressed that often we do not know when our honesty is being tested. One day he gave a quiz in class and collected the papers. He graded them at home that night and recorded the scores, but did not mark any of the papers. The next day, he returned the papers and asked the students to grade their own tests and report their scores. Most students reported high scores. "John?" "85." "Susan?" "95." "Harold?" "80." "Arnold?" "90." "Mary? . . . Mary?" The response was very quiet: "45." Once all the scores were recorded the difference between the two scores was revealing. Many students had reported higher scores than the teacher had recorded when he graded the tests himself.

   An unusual silence settled over the class when the teacher explained what he had done: "This was a different kind of test. This was a test for honesty. I noticed that many of you looked at Mary when she announced her score of 45. I want each of you to know that in my book Mary just achieved the highest score in class" (*Family Home Evening Resource Book* [1983], 195).

2. Sing with class members or read the words to "True to the Faith" (*Hymns,* no. 254). Ask class members to think about how honesty helps us defend "truth and right" (verse 1).

3. Before class, arrange the following role play with one of the class members:

   Explain that you will be asking her (or him) why she was late coming home from school. Tell her to make up whatever reasons she can think of to keep you from finding out that she went to her friend's house instead of coming straight home as she was told. You will need a long piece of string or yarn for this activity.

   Begin the role play by asking a simple question such as "Why were you late getting home from school today?" As the class member answers falsely, wrap a long string or yarn around her once. Then ask a follow-up question (for example, "Why did you have to stay after school?"). As she answers falsely again, wrap another length of string or yarn around her. Continue to ask questions, wrapping the string around her each time she answers falsely.

   Explain to the class that you asked the person to give wrong answers to help show how one lie leads to another and how quickly we can become trapped by our lies. (For suggestions on effective role plays and dramatizations, see *Teaching—No Greater Call,* 141–42.)

4. If *Family Home Evening Video Supplement* (53276) is available, show "Honesty Leads to Integrity," a six-minute segment.

5. Have class members describe several situations in which it is easy to be dishonest and list reasons why it might be tempting to be dishonest in each of these situations. (Reasons may include to avoid embarrassment, to gain some advantage, to hurt others, and to excuse poor performance.) Then discuss the damage that could be caused by dishonesty in each situation and the blessings that could come from being honest. Emphasize to class members that even when honesty seems to cause immediate difficulties (for example, you do poorly on a test for which you did not study), it provides eternal rewards.

6. Read or tell the following story told by Elder Jeffrey R. Holland when he was president of Brigham Young University:

"One night I came home quite late from work. My nine-year-old daughter . . . seemed visibly distressed. . . . She walked softly into the living room and said, 'Daddy, I have to talk to you.' I held her hand and . . . she started to cry.

" 'I was at [the store] this morning and saw a ladies' compact I knew Mother would love. I was sure it was quite expensive, but I picked it up just to admire it. . . . It fell out of my hands onto the floor. I quickly picked it up, but Daddy, the mirror was cracked. I didn't know what to do! I didn't have enough money to pay for it, and I was all alone. . . . I put the compact back on the shelf and left the store. Oh, Daddy, I think I've been dishonest.' And then she wept and wept.

"I held her in my arms as that little nine-year-old body shook with the pain of sin being expelled. She said, 'I can't sleep and I can't eat and I can't say my prayers. What will I do? I won't ever get it out of my mind.'

"Well, Mother joined us, and we talked quite a while that night. We told her that we were very, very proud of her honesty . . . and we would have been disappointed if she had been able to eat or sleep very well. I told her . . . the compact probably wouldn't cost *too* much, and that we would go back to the store manager, tell him of the problem, and, between the two of us, cover the cost. If the compact was still there, [perhaps we could] buy it for Mom. That little cracked mirror could be a reminder for [Mom] as long as she owned it that her little girl was unfailingly honest and spiritually sensitive. . . .

"The tears gradually stopped, her little body began to relax, and [she] said, 'I think now I can say my prayers' " (quoted by J. Richard Clarke, in Conference Report, Apr. 1984, 86; or *Ensign*, May 1984, 63–64).

- Do you feel this way when you have been dishonest?

- How can we increase our sensitivity to being honest?

Be Ye Clean

Purpose   To help class members understand the importance of being morally clean.

Preparation   1. Prayerfully study Genesis 39:1–20; 1 Corinthians 6:19–20; 2 Nephi 28:8, 20–22; Moroni 7:16–17; Doctrine and Covenants 98:11; 133:5; Articles of Faith 1:13.

2. Additional reading:
   a. *For the Strength of Youth* (34285). You may want to consult the bishop about obtaining copies of this pamphlet for class members who do not have one.
   b. Two addresses given by Elder Richard G. Scott: "Making the Right Choices" (Conference Report, Oct. 1994, 49–53; or *Ensign,* Nov. 1994, 37–39) and "Do What Is Right" (*Ensign,* June 1997, 51–55).

3. Prepare a snapping turtle trap: Pound nails into a two-foot-long piece of board at three- or four-inch intervals. Bend the head of each nail at a 90-degree angle (see the illustration). If it is not feasible to prepare this trap, draw a picture of it on the chalkboard.

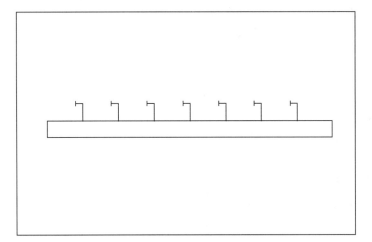

4. Materials needed:
   a. A chart containing the thirteenth article of faith (make your own or use chart 65013 from the meetinghouse library).
   b. A set of scriptures and a scripture marking pencil for each class member. Continue to encourage class members to bring their own scriptures to class each week.

Note to the teacher   *For youth there are few challenges as important, as difficult, or as far-reaching as staying morally clean. Satan is walking among our youth "as a roaring lion, . . . seeking whom he may devour" (1 Peter 5:8).*

Use tact and sensitivity as you help class members understand that sexual intimacy is a gift from God that can bring great fulfillment and pleasure but must be used within the guidelines God has established. He has instructed us that this intimacy should take place only within marriage. Satan tries to convince us that this gift can be used freely, but following his temptations will bring regret, pain, sorrow, and destruction. Teach class members about the happiness and peace of mind that can be theirs if they stand firm against Satan and keep the Lord's standards of moral cleanliness.

You may want to take two weeks to teach this lesson. If you teach the entire lesson in one week, discuss the media and clothing only briefly, or focus on the parts of the lesson you feel are most necessary for your class.

Suggested Lesson Development	**Chastity Is a Precious Gift**
Quotation and discussion	Read the following statement by President Spencer W. Kimball:

"May I talk to you just a moment or two about that which is most dear and precious above all things. Can you think what it would be? Would it be bonds, stocks, or diamonds? Would it be herds or flocks? Would it be automobiles and houses? Would it be medals in athletics?"

• What do you think President Kimball is talking about?

Allow class members a few moments to respond, then continue the statement:

"It cannot be purchased with money, but may be enjoyed by all, even those of humble circumstances as well as the affluent, as much by the high school student as by those who have doctors degrees. . . . That of which I speak is chastity and virtue" (in Conference Report, Sydney Australia Area Conference 1976, 54).

• What is chastity?

Help class members understand that being chaste means keeping the Lord's standard of moral (sexual) cleanliness. Heavenly Father has commanded that we abstain from any kind of sexual intimacy before marriage and be completely faithful to our spouse after marriage. He has also commanded us to avoid immoral forms of entertainment and to keep our thoughts pure.

• President Kimball said that chastity is more important than money, possessions, or awards. Why do you think he felt so strongly about chastity?

Scripture story and discussion

Point out that the scriptures contain many examples of people who understood the importance of chastity. One of these people was Joseph, who was sold into slavery by his brothers and became the servant of Potiphar, a prosperous Egyptian (see Genesis 37; 39).

Have class members read Genesis 39:7–12. Explain that Joseph knew the Lord's standard of chastity and recognized that Potiphar's wife was trying to persuade him to violate that standard (see Genesis 39:9).

• What did Joseph do when his chastity was threatened? (Genesis 39:12.) What did he risk by doing this?

Explain that Joseph had held a high position in Potiphar's household. However, when Potiphar's wife lied about the incident and said Joseph had made improper advances to her, Joseph was thrown into prison (see Genesis 39:13–20).

• Why do you think Joseph was willing to risk so much in order to stay chaste?

Ask class members to think about the following questions without answering them out loud:

• What would you have done in a similar situation? How important is chastity to you?

___

We Must Resist Satan's Temptations

Object lesson

Display the snapping turtle trap (or refer to the drawing on the chalkboard).

• What do you think this object might be?

After class members have had a chance to respond, explain that it is a trap to catch snapping turtles. Give the following information in your own words:

Delicious soup can be made from the meat of snapping turtles. However, these turtles are very smart and very mean, so they are difficult to catch. When they are in the water, they can use their beak-like mouths to steal the bait used to lure them without even touching the hook holding the bait. In the water they are safe and in control. If you can lure them out of the water, however, they are easier to catch.

Hold up one end of the trap so that the bent nails are pointing upward.

If you put raw meat on the top of this trap and set the bottom end of the trap in the water, the turtle will smell the meat and climb up the trap to eat it. When you move toward the trap, the turtle, sensing danger, will pull into its shell and try to slide back into the water. But its shell will catch on one of the nails and it will be stuck. Then you can take it home and make it into turtle soup.

Explain that a man who fished for snapping turtles compared the turtles' safety in the pond to our safety in the gospel. Then he made the following statement:

"Television, movies, magazines, and other media of our day scream out that good times are associated with immorality, alcohol, and violence. Some seemingly good kids in your school may smoke marijuana and use drugs. The attractive young men and women in beer commercials seem to be having fun.

"It's bait. Just like the smelly meat on the plank in my Georgia pond, this bait can be used to trick and betray you. If we allow ourselves to be tricked into leaving the safety of the Church and gospel, we may also be trapped. You simply cannot afford to take the risk of becoming turtle soup!" (Ron Whipple, "Catch a Snapping Turtle," *New Era,* July 1996, 26–27).

Discussion

• Why does a turtle climb up on the trap?

Point out that the turtle is seeking something desirable—food. In other circumstances, it would be good for the turtle to eat the food. In this case, however, the food is being improperly offered, and it results in death to the turtle. Similarly, sexual pleasure is not inherently bad, but when sought in the wrong circumstances—in any situation outside of marriage—it becomes destructive and can result in spiritual death.

Explain that when Satan designs bait to lure us into improper behavior, he is very subtle. He does not begin by immediately tempting us to commit serious sins. Instead, he tempts us into seemingly innocent thoughts and activities that can easily lead to more serious sins (see 2 Nephi 28:8, 20–22).

- What are some kinds of bait that Satan uses to lure us into immorality? (Answers may include immodest clothing, unclean movies or television programs, dirty jokes, and immoral music.)

Satan Uses the Media to Lure Us into Immorality

Quotation and teacher presentation

Explain that some of Satan's bait comes through the media. Read the following statement from *For the Strength of Youth* (if you brought copies for class members, have them follow along on page 11):

"Whatever you read, listen to, or watch makes an impression on you. Public entertainment and the media can provide you with much positive experience. They can uplift and inspire you, teach you good and moral principles, and bring you closer to the beauty this world offers. But they can also make what is wrong and evil look normal, exciting, and acceptable."

Point out that many popular movies, television programs, books, magazines, and music reflect the world's standards, which are very different from the Lord's standards. Not only do worldly standards promote the use of alcohol, tobacco, and violence, they incorrectly suggest that sexual intimacy should be available to anyone at any time. Media that promote worldly standards usually fail to show the physical and spiritual harm that comes from breaking God's commandments.

Quotation

Have a class member read the following statement by President Gordon B. Hinckley:

"There are storms blowing around you. There is the clever exploitation of sex and violence to be seen on television and through videotapes, [pornographic] magazines, long distance telephone services, and even the Internet.

"My plea to you . . . is to distance yourselves from these things. You can [change the channel] on the TV set. You can shun like a plague the renting or acquisition of videotapes designed to titillate and lead you into regrettable paths. . . . You don't have to read sleazy literature of any kind. It will not help you. It will only injure you" ("True to the Faith," *Ensign,* June 1996, 4).

Discussion

- Have you ever said or heard someone else say, "This movie is OK because it only has one bad scene" or "I like the music but I never listen to the words"? What is wrong with these justifications for watching or listening to immoral things?

Point out that even a small amount of evil can affect us negatively by making us temporarily unable to feel the promptings of the Holy Ghost. Accepting a small amount of evil will also make us more susceptible to greater evil. If we watch movies with "just one" bad scene, we will become less concerned about movies with several bad scenes and will accept more immorality and evil into our lives. When we listen to music, even if we do not consciously notice the lyrics, our subconscious mind may be listening to them and recording them in our memory.

- How can you make sure that the movies, television shows, music, books, magazines, and other media that influence you are reflective of the Lord's standards, rather than the world's?

Scripture discussion

Have class members read Moroni 7:16–17 and discuss what these verses teach about how to evaluate what is good and what is evil.

Then display the chart containing the thirteenth article of faith, and refer to the last sentence, which can help us in our selection of movies, music, and other media.

Help class members understand that we should do more than just avoid evil. We are instructed to "forsake all evil," but at the same time to "cleave unto all good" (D&C 98:11). The thirteenth article of faith says that we should "seek after" good things—make an effort to find them, study them, and discover their beauty. We should shun media that do not meet the Lord's standards, but we should also seek out media that support the Lord's standards.

Invite class members to tell about ways they have sought out and found worthy movies, music, books, and other media.

Satan Uses Fashion to Lure Us into Immorality

Quotation

Explain that another way Satan lures us into immoral behavior is by encouraging us to wear immodest clothing. Have a class member read the following statement from *For the Strength of Youth* (if you brought copies for class members, have them follow along on page 8):

"Servants of God have always counseled his children to dress modestly to show respect for him and for themselves. Because the way you dress sends messages about yourself to others and often influences the way you and others act, you should dress in such a way as to bring out the best in yourself and those around you."

Story and discussion

To illustrate the point that how a person dresses affects how he or she behaves, tell the following story in your own words:

A coach of a professional sports team was very disturbed by the actions and language of team members when they were traveling by chartered airplane to their various destinations. They harassed the flight attendants, threw food, and yelled the length of the airplane to one another. The airlines had a difficult time getting flight attendants that would work when this team was flying.

After much thought, the coach came up with a solution. From that point on, the team members were required to wear a suit, tie, and dress shoes when traveling, instead of the casual attire they had been allowed to wear before. Their behavior improved greatly. It seemed that when they were dressed like gentlemen, they behaved like gentlemen. Flight attendants even began requesting to work on flights chartered by this team.

- What helped the team members improve their behavior?

- How does your behavior change depending on what you are wearing? How do you act when you are wearing your oldest, dirtiest clothes? How do you act when you are wearing your Sunday best?

Explain that when we wear immodest clothing—clothing that is too short or too tight or that draws inappropriate attention to our bodies—we may begin to think and act immodestly as well.

Point out that how we dress also affects those around us. Immodest clothing may encourage those who see us to pay too much attention to our bodies. It may also lead them to believe untrue things about our standards and our behavior.

Discussion

You may need to point out that the styles that are most fashionable are not always modest. Ask class members for suggestions on what they can do when the clothing that is currently fashionable is immodest. Help them understand that sometimes fashionable styles can be modified so that they are modest (for example, a skirt can be lengthened or a shirt can be made out of a similar but heavier fabric). If the styles cannot be modified, however, we should always choose modesty over fashion.

Read again the statement from page 8 of *For the Strength of Youth*.

- How can you show your respect for God and for yourself by the way you dress? How can you "dress in such a way as to bring out the best in yourself and those around you"?

Satan Appeals to Natural Desires to Lure Us into Immorality

Teacher presentation

Present the following information in your own words, being sensitive to the maturity level of the members of your class (some 12- and 13-year-olds are very interested in members of the opposite sex and need guidance in forming appropriate relationships with them, while others of the same age may be uninterested or even embarrassed by the suggestion of interest in the opposite sex):

Physical attraction to members of the opposite sex is natural and normal. Heavenly Father has given us these feelings, but he has also instructed us to control them until the appropriate time and circumstance for expressing them.

To help control these feelings, Church leaders have counseled youth not to date until they are at least 16 years old. Some physical expressions of affection may be appropriate in dating situations, but they should be reserved for specially selected people at the proper time in your life, not indulged in casually. These expressions are not appropriate before you are old enough and mature enough to date properly.

Other expressions of affection are only appropriate with your spouse after you are married. These expressions include sexual intercourse and any actions that lead to it, such as intense kissing, touching any part of another person's body under their clothing, or touching another person's "private parts" on top of or underneath their clothing. A good rule of thumb is that any thoughts or actions that increase your interest in or desire for another person's body are inappropriate. These thoughts and actions are sinful outside of the marriage relationship.

Remind class members that if they have already participated in inappropriate behavior, they should talk with the bishop. He can counsel them about how to repent. If class members have concerns about what is or is not appropriate, encourage them to talk privately with their parents or the bishop.

Joy Awaits the Pure

Story and
discussion

Point out that keeping the Lord's standards of moral cleanliness will not necessarily make us popular. But it will lead us toward eternal happiness, which is much more valuable than the approval of the world.

Tell the following story in your own words:

Hal had always done his best to serve the Lord. He tried to keep the commandments and do what the Lord would have him do. Sometimes this was not easy.

Many of Hal's friends and acquaintances were uninterested in religion and lived a lifestyle that seemed to mock Christian teachings. Everyone knew Hal was a Latter-day Saint, and sometimes his companions ridiculed him for his beliefs. Usually Hal ignored their teasing, but sometimes it made him feel isolated and rejected. He sometimes wondered if working so hard to keep the commandments and maintain his integrity was worth it.

During his dating years, Hal dated several girls who were attractive and made him feel less isolated and rejected. When he became aware that these girls desired physical affection from him, Hal often wondered, "Am I really different from the others? Why should I keep trying to stay morally clean? It would be so easy not to." But Hal knew what the Lord expected of him. He knew that he should continue the pattern of righteousness he had established in his life. He lived the law of chastity, although it was painful when some girls seemed to lose interest in him because he maintained the Lord's standards.

When Hal found the young woman who was right for him, he was worthy to marry her in the temple for eternity. Years later, Hal looked back at his early life and realized that all that made him happy—his wife, his family, the Church—were his because he had maintained his standards and sought to live righteously. He thanked Heavenly Father for giving him the strength to do what was right. Now he understood what happiness could come from keeping himself morally clean.

- What might have happened if Hal had not remained morally clean?
- What blessings do we receive in this life for staying morally clean?
- What blessings will we receive in eternity for staying morally clean?

Testimony

Explain that our bodies are temples and the Lord has commanded us to keep these temples clean (see 1 Corinthians 6:19–20; D&C 133:5), which includes being clean in body, mind, and spirit. Bear your testimony of the importance of staying morally clean.

Urge class members to keep the Lord's standards and be morally pure and clean.

**Enrichment
Activities**

You may want to use one or more of these activities during the lesson.

1. Ask the bishop to recommend a young adult whom class members can look up to. This person could be someone who has recently received a mission call or is preparing for a temple marriage. Invite him or her to come to class and share his or her feelings about living a clean life and the peace and joy that come from keeping the law of chastity.

2. If the following video segments are available, show one of them:

   a. "Morality for Youth," a 22-minute segment of *Come unto Me* (53146).
   b. "Chastity: As a Man Soweth," a 2-minute segment of *Family Home Evening Video Supplement 2* (53277).

3. Discuss with class members the article "You Promised," by Elder M. Russell Ballard (*New Era,* Feb. 1994, 4–7). You may want to make a copy of this article for each class member to take home and study.

4. Explain that in today's world, we are often led to believe that important expressions of affection should always be physical. However, there are many ways we can express affection or appreciation without violating the Lord's standards. Ask class members to suggest righteous and wholesome ways they can show affection or appreciation for members of the opposite sex. List responses on the chalkboard.

5. If you feel class members need more emphasis on avoiding the evils of pornography, read or tell the story "The Enemy in the Gutter" (John Bytheway, *New Era,* Mar. 1992, 8).

Be of Good Cheer

Purpose	To help class members avoid discouragement and follow the Savior's counsel to "be of good cheer" (John 16:33).

Preparation	1. Prayerfully study John 16:33; 1 Peter 1:7; 2 Nephi 2:17–18, 27; Ether 12:6; Doctrine and Covenants 121:1–9; 122:5–9.
	2. Materials needed:
	a. Two to four hymnbooks for the activity on page 231.
	b. A set of scriptures and a scripture marking pencil for each class member. Continue to encourage class members to bring their own scriptures to class each week.
Note to the teacher	*In our premortal life we shouted for joy because of the opportunity to progress to our second estate (see Job 38:4, 7). We were aware that during mortality we would experience sorrow, pain, disappointment, problems, and trials, as well as happiness and joy. With all this knowledge we felt peace and security, because we knew that our Father in Heaven would always be mindful of us. Help class members see Christ's admonition to "be of good cheer" as a reminder that, regardless of our circumstances, we can find peace and joy in life.*

Suggested Lesson Development	**Trials Are Part of the Plan of Salvation**
Discussion	Ask class members to imagine that they are in the premortal existence and that they will soon be born on earth. They are talking with one another about what might happen to them, knowing that life on earth will bring many opportunities and challenges. Then read the statements below, one at a time, and have class members discuss their feelings about each statement as they prepare to come to earth.
	1. You will have disappointments, trials, and problems while in mortality.
	2. You will also experience joy.
	3. Satan will tempt you.
	4. Our Father in Heaven wants you to succeed and be happy.
Scripture discussion	Ask the following question, allowing class members to look up the accompanying scriptures to help them answer it:
	• Why are disappointments, problems, and other trials part of the plan of salvation? (See 1 Peter 1:7; Ether 12:6; D&C 122:7.)

Chalkboard presentation	Draw the following diagram on the chalkboard:

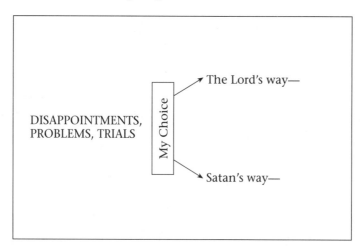

Point out that everyone experiences trials and disappointments. Much of our success in life depends on how we respond to trials. We can choose one of two basic responses to trials: the Lord's way or Satan's way.

Satan Wants Us to Be Discouraged

Quotation and scripture discussion	Read the following statement by Elder Marvin J. Ashton, who was a member of the Quorum of the Twelve Apostles:

"One of Satan's most powerful tools is discouragement" (in Conference Report, Apr. 1988, 73; or *Ensign*, May 1988, 63).

Add *Be discouraged* to the chalkboard after *Satan's way—*.

Have class members read and mark 2 Nephi 2:17–18, 27.

- How does discouragement help Satan accomplish his goal to make us "miserable like unto himself"? How are your efforts to obey the commandments and do well at school and in other activities affected when you are discouraged?

Read the continuation of Elder Ashton's statement:

"Whisperings of 'you can't do it,' 'you're no good,' 'it's too late,' 'what's the use?' or 'things are hopeless' are tools of destruction. Satan . . . wants you to quit trying. It is important that discouragement is cast out of [our lives]. This may take a decided amount of work and energy, but it can be accomplished" (in Conference Report, Apr. 1988, 73; or *Ensign*, May 1988, 63).

The Lord Has Taught Us to Be of Good Cheer

Quotation and scripture discussion	- What trials did the Savior experience?

Point out that the Savior suffered greater trials than we will ever experience, yet he did not get discouraged. Read the following statement by Elder Jeffrey R. Holland of the Quorum of the Twelve Apostles:

"Even with such a solemn mission given to Him, the Savior found delight in living; He enjoyed people and told His disciples to be of good cheer. . . .

230

"Remember the unkind treatment He received, the rejection He experienced, and the injustice . . . He endured. When we, too, then face some of that in life, we can remember that Christ was also troubled on every side, but not distressed; perplexed, but not in despair; persecuted, but not forsaken; cast down, but not destroyed (see 2 Corinthians 4:8–9)" (in Conference Report, Oct. 1995, 90–91; or *Ensign,* Nov. 1995, 68–69).

Have class members read and mark John 16:33.

• How does the Lord want us to feel when we have disappointments, problems, and trials?

Add *"Be of good cheer"* to the chalkboard after *The Lord's way*—. The chalkboard should now look like this:

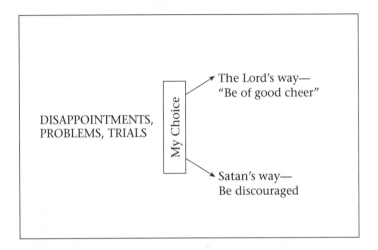

• How has the Savior "overcome the world"?

• How does this knowledge help us "be of good cheer"?

We Can Be of Good Cheer Even in Difficult Times

Activity

Divide the class into four groups, with a leader for each group, and give each group a hymnbook. Assign each group one of the verses of the hymn "Count Your Blessings" (*Hymns,* no. 241; also printed below). If you have a small class, you may wish to divide into two groups and assign each group two verses. Have each group find the message of their verse (or verses). Encourage them to think of examples from scripture stories, Church history, or personal experiences that teach the same message. After each group has had time to think of ideas, have the leader read the verse to the class and then share the ideas the group discussed. (You may want to use the first enrichment activity in place of or in addition to this activity.)

"When upon life's billows you are tempest-tossed,
When you are discouraged, thinking all is lost,
Count your many blessings; name them one by one,
And it will surprise you what the Lord has done.

"Are you ever burdened with a load of care?
Does the cross seem heavy you are called to bear?
Count your many blessings; every doubt will fly,
And you will be singing as the days go by.

"When you look at others with their lands and gold,
Think that Christ has promised you his wealth untold.
Count your many blessings; money cannot buy
Your reward in heaven nor your home on high.

"So amid the conflict, whether great or small,
Do not be discouraged; God is over all.
Count your many blessings; angels will attend,
Help and comfort give you to your journey's end."

Story and
discussion

Read the following story told by President Gordon B. Hinckley about the first few weeks of his mission in England. Have class members listen for things that helped him overcome discouragement.

"I was not well when I arrived. Those first few weeks, because of illness and the opposition which we felt, I was discouraged. I wrote a letter home to my good father and said that I felt I was wasting my time and his money. He was my father and my stake president, and he was a wise and inspired man. He wrote a very short letter to me which said, 'Dear Gordon, I have your recent letter. I have only one suggestion: forget yourself and go to work.' Earlier that morning in our scripture class my companion and I had read these words of the Lord: 'Whosoever will save his life shall lose it; but whosoever shall lose his life for my sake and the gospel's, the same shall save it.' (Mark 8:35.)

"Those words of the Master, followed by my father's letter with his counsel to forget myself and go to work, went into my very being. With my father's letter in hand, I went into our bedroom in the house at 15 Wadham Road, where we lived, and got on my knees and made a pledge with the Lord. I covenanted that I would try to forget myself and lose myself in His service.

"That July day in 1933 was my day of decision. A new light came into my life and a new joy into my heart. The fog of England seemed to lift, and I saw the sunlight. I had a rich and wonderful mission experience, for which I shall ever be grateful" ("Gospel to Great Britain," *Ensign*, July 1987, 7).

- What are some things that helped Elder Hinckley overcome discouragement? What other things have helped you overcome discouragement?

List class members' answers on the chalkboard under *"Be of good cheer."* Answers should include the following:

    Follow the counsel of parents
    Read the scriptures
    Forget ourselves (be selfless)
    Give service
    Pray

Scripture
discussion

Explain that the Prophet Joseph Smith faced trials even greater than those Elder Hinckley experienced in England. During a particularly difficult time, when Joseph was a prisoner in the jail at Liberty, Missouri, he cried to God, asking how long God would permit the Saints to be persecuted (see D&C 121:1–6).

Have class members read the Lord's reply to Joseph's prayer in Doctrine and Covenants 121:7–9 and 122:5–9. Encourage them to mark words and phrases in these verses that they feel are important.

- Which words or phrases did you mark? Why did you mark them?

- What does it mean that "all these things shall give thee experience, and shall be for thy good"? (D&C 122:7). How have you seen that trials can be for our good?

- How do you think Joseph Smith felt when he was told, "Fear not what man can do, for God shall be with you forever and ever"? (D&C 122:9). How can this promise help you overcome discouragement? How can we be worthy of this promise?

Testimony

As appropriate, tell about a time when the Lord helped you overcome feelings of discouragement. Testify that as we follow the Savior, we will be able to "be of good cheer," even during difficult times.

Encourage class members to respond to trials by being of good cheer. Refer again to the list on the chalkboard of ways to overcome discouragement, and encourage class members to do one or more of these things if they feel discouraged this week.

Enrichment Activities

You may want to use one or more of these activities during the lesson.

1. Give each class member a piece of paper and a pen or pencil. Ask class members to list on their papers at least three blessings they have. Help them understand that gratitude helps bring true happiness. Suggest that they take time to list some of their blessings the next time they become discouraged. This will help them "be of good cheer" by reminding them of how good life actually is.

2. Give each class member a copy of the scripture-matching activity on page 234. Have class members draw a line from each scripture to its correct reference. Encourage them to mark the passages in their scriptures as they complete the exercise.

3. Prepare for each class member a card with the following statement on it (quoted by John Henry Evans, in *Joseph Smith, an American Prophet* [1946], 9):

   "Never be discouraged. If I were sunk in the lowest pit of Nova Scotia, with the Rocky Mountains piled on me, I would hang on, exercise faith, and keep up good courage, and I would come out on top." —Joseph Smith

   Encourage class members to keep the cards where they can see them often. This will help class members remember to "be of good cheer," even during difficult times.

4. Tell the story "Beyond the Mud" (LaDawn S. Dalley, *New Era*, Apr. 1996, 8–9). In this true story, a missionary's love for the people she serves helps her overcome discouragement.

"Be of Good Cheer"

Draw a line from each scripture to its correct reference.

"Be of good cheer; it is I;
be not afraid."   Psalm 100:2

"A merry heart maketh a
cheerful countenance."   Matthew 14:27

"Be of good cheer, for I will lead
you along."   Doctrine and
                                                         Covenants 78:18

"Lift up thy head and rejoice, for
thou hast great cause to rejoice;
for thou hast been faithful in
keeping the commandments."   Proverbs 15:13

"Be of good cheer, and do not fear,   Doctrine and
for I the Lord am with you, and will   Covenants 68:6
stand by you."

"In the world ye shall have tribulation: Alma 8:15
but be of good cheer."

"Serve the Lord with gladness."   John 16:33

Home: A School for Eternity

Purpose	To help class members understand that home is the best place to prepare for the challenges of earthly life and the blessings of eternal life.
Preparation	1. Prayerfully study 4 Nephi 1:2–3, 15–16; Doctrine and Covenants 88:119.
	2. Write each of the following words or phrases on a separate strip of paper:

> Work
> Faith
> Love
> Prayer
> Controlling anger
> Service
> Selflessness
> Scripture study

3. Write the following statement on a card or small piece of paper for each class member (from "Blueprint for Family Living," *Improvement Era,* Apr. 1963, 252):

> *"I believe that the best place to prepare for . . . eternal life is in the home."*
> —*President David O. McKay*

4. Make a copy of the house diagram found at the end of the lesson (page 240). Then cut out the different parts of the diagram to make a puzzle.

5. Materials needed:
   a. The picture Latter-day Prophets (62575; Gospel Art Picture Kit 506) and any pictures of members of the current First Presidency or Quorum of the Twelve Apostles (available from the meetinghouse library or in conference issues of the *Ensign*).
   b. A set of scriptures and a scripture marking pencil for each class member. Continue to encourage class members to bring their own scriptures to class each week.

Note to the teacher

Nothing we do while on the earth is of greater importance than what we do in our homes with our families. What we do with our families is important not only because it prepares us for eternity, but also because it helps us meet the challenges of everyday life. No relationships are as important as family relationships. President Harold B. Lee, eleventh President of the Church, emphasized that "the most important of the Lord's work that you will ever do will be the work you do within the walls of your own home" (Strengthening the Home [pamphlet, 1973], 7).

During the lesson be sensitive to the feelings of class members who do not come from gospel-centered homes. You may want to focus on important principles class members can learn from their families, such as honesty and hard work, even when family members are not members of the Church. Encourage class members to decide now that when they are adults, they will establish gospel-centered homes of their own.

Families Are Important to Our Heavenly Father

Picture discussion
and quotation

Display the pictures of latter-day prophets and apostles.

- Who are these men? (If class members cannot identify the men, state their names and their callings in the Church.)

- What are some of the main responsibilities of prophets and apostles?

Invite a class member to list on the chalkboard the responses to this question. After class members have had time to give their answers, tell them that all of the great responsibilities of the prophets and apostles have one main purpose. Then read the following statement by President Boyd K. Packer of the Quorum of the Twelve Apostles:

"The ministry of the prophets and apostles leads them ever and always to the home and the family. . . .

"The ultimate purpose of all we teach is to unite parents and children in faith in the Lord Jesus Christ, that they are happy at home, sealed in an eternal marriage, linked to their generations, and assured of exaltation in the presence of our Heavenly Father" (in Conference Report, Apr. 1995, 8; or *Ensign,* May 1995, 8).

- What does this statement say about the importance of homes and families?

Point out that this statement explains how important families are to our Heavenly Father. Tell class members that today's lesson discusses why families are important and how we can contribute to our families' efforts to learn and apply gospel principles.

Family Life Helps Us Learn Gospel Principles

Story

Explain that home is an important place for us to learn the gospel. Read or tell the following story shared by a young Latter-day Saint about how an experience at home helped him learn gospel principles:

"The Book of Mormon . . . is where you find the best discourse on serving ice cream in a truly righteous family. Actually it doesn't talk much about ice cream. . . . But it does teach you a lot about proper technique in *serving* ice cream.

"Maybe you could understand better if I told you how I used to serve ice cream and then explain the difference.

"Since I am a teenager, when dad or mom would ask me to serve everyone some ice cream, the first thing I would do was find me a [large] bowl and stack the ice cream to the teenager level, which is about two inches above the rim. Then I would dish up the ice cream for the rest of my family. However, my brother and sisters are smaller than I, so of course the small ice cream dishes are just about right for them.

"Well, my dad showed me in the Book of Mormon where it explains that my method [wasn't right].

"In 4 Nephi it tells what it was like after the Savior visited the people in America following his resurrection. After his visit, the people really lived righteous lives. And the way they lived can help us understand how to develop celestial families. It even teaches us how to serve ice cream."

Scripture discussion

Have class members read and mark 4 Nephi 1:2–3, 15–16.

• What might these verses have to do with serving food to your family?

Story continued

Continue the story:

" . . . My dad gently explained to me that when I have the standard teenager's portion, it makes [my sisters] jealous and envious. When they get like that, they start giving me all kinds of reasons why they should have as much as I do. Of course, I have to explain to them, loud enough for them to understand, that teenagers need more nourishment than 'little girls.' Then they always have a response for that. And I have to reply—in a slightly louder tone, of course.

"Well, when I read 4 Nephi, I could see that we were having one of those 'disputations' that Nephi was talking about; and the disputation had been caused by a 'contention;' and the contention was caused by 'envying.'

"So you can see that there is a certain way you have to serve ice cream in a family desiring to be more righteous.

"Mom also pointed out something else. If everyone is allowed to have a fair share, according to their needs, then there are really no rich ice cream eaters and no poor ice cream eaters. Having no rich or poor means that everyone has as much as he needs, but he does not have so much more than [others] that they get envious and cause contentions which lead to disputations.

"When these disputations are avoided, there really is 'peace in the land.' At least there is peace in the [home], and everyone is happier!" (R. Todd Hunt, "Serving Ice Cream in a Celestial Family," *New Era,* Jan.–Feb. 1982, 9).

Discussion

• What did the author of the story learn when he served ice cream to his family? (Answers may include that he learned about the damaging effects of contention and the helpful effects of love, and he realized that his actions influenced the degree of happiness in his home.)

Activity

Show the strips of paper you have prepared and explain that each strip contains a gospel principle that has been discussed in this year's Sunday School class. Point out that we also learn about these principles at home. Have class members take turns selecting a strip of paper, reading the principle that is written on it, and handing it back to you. Then have all class members suggest ways family life can help us learn that principle.

Family Life Prepares Us for the Challenges of Life

Activity

Explain that when we learn gospel principles at home, we are better prepared to successfully meet the challenges of life. For example, if the young man in the story applies the lesson he learned when he was serving ice cream, he will be able to establish and maintain good friendships at school.

Following the same procedure as before, have class members read again the principles written on the strips of paper. As each principle is read, ask class members how it can be applied to meet the challenges they may face outside the home, such as at school or with their friends.

As appropriate, tell about a time when something you learned at home helped you successfully meet a challenge that you experienced outside the home.

Family Life Prepares Us for Eternal Life

Quotation

Point out that family life prepares us for more than just the challenges of everyday life. Hand out the copies you have made of the statement by President David O. McKay, eighth President of the Church, about family life preparing us for eternal life. Have a class member read the statement.

Activity

Explain that class members are going to do an activity to show how family life prepares us for eternal life. Divide the pieces of the house diagram among class members and have them work together to assemble the puzzle.

Have class members read and mark Doctrine and Covenants 88:119. Explain that this verse is part of a revelation instructing the early Latter-day Saints to build a temple. Point out that although this verse is about the temple, it can be applied to the home also, because "only the home can compare with the temple in sacredness" (Bible Dictionary, "Temple," 781).

Discuss with class members why the qualities listed in this verse are essential characteristics of a "house of God." For example, you may want to remove the puzzle piece labeled "Prayer" and ask class members why a home without prayer is incomplete.

Chalkboard discussion

• What are some actions our families can take to make our homes houses of God?

Write class members' answers on the chalkboard. Answers may include the following:

Have family prayer.
Help each other.
Forgive each other.
Read the scriptures together.
Work together.
Be considerate of each other.
Hold family home evening.

• What can youth do to help their parents make their homes houses of God? What can youth do when their parents are not members of the Church or are not enthusiastic about holding family prayer or family home evening or about attending Church meetings?

Quotation

Read the following statement by Elder Boyd K. Packer:

"The most sacred place on earth may not be the temple, necessarily. The chapel, the stake house, and the temple are sacred as they contribute to the building of the most sacred institution in the Church—the home—and to the blessing of the most sacred relationships in the Church, the family" (*That All May Be Edified* [1982], 234–35).

238

Testimony

Testify of the importance of the home and family in learning gospel principles and preparing for eternal life.

Encourage class members to think about President McKay's statement (on their pieces of paper) and to contribute to their family's efforts to have a gospel-centered home.

Enrichment Activities

You may want to use one or more of these activities during the lesson.

1. With class members, sing or read the words to "Home Can Be a Heaven on Earth" (*Hymns,* no. 298).

2. Help class members memorize Doctrine and Covenants 88:119. Write the verse on the chalkboard as shown below:

> Organize yourselves;
>
> prepare every needful thing;
>
> and establish a house,
>
> even a house of prayer,
>
> a house of fasting,
>
> a house of faith,
>
> a house of learning,
>
> a house of glory,
>
> a house of order,
>
> a house of God.

Have class members repeat the verse a few times, reading from the chalkboard rather than their scriptures. Then erase one line and have them repeat the verse again. Continue the process until class members can recite the entire verse from memory.

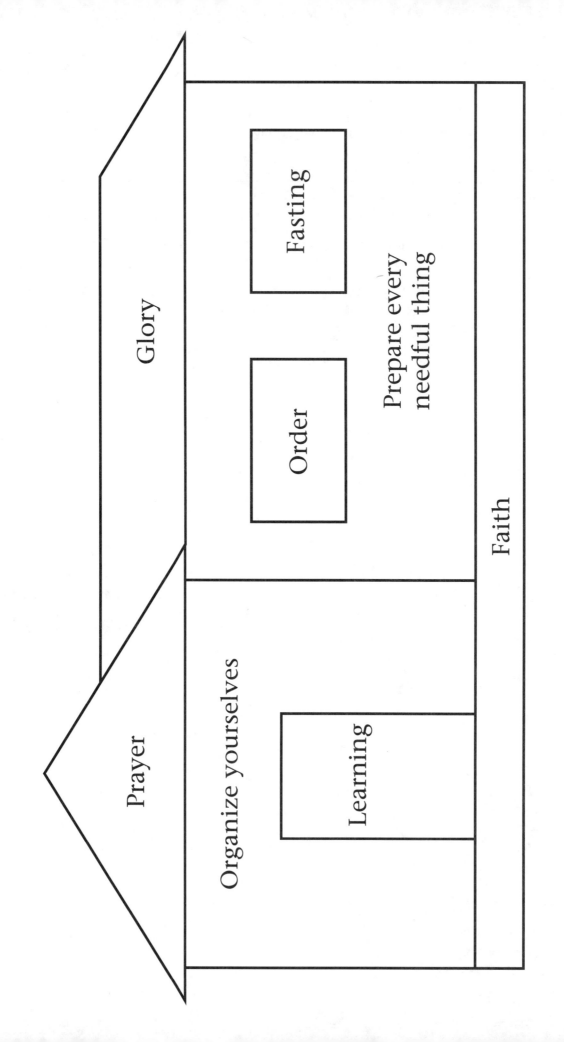

Eternal Marriage

Purpose	To help class members understand how to prepare now for eternal marriage in the future.

Preparation	1. Prayerfully study Genesis 2:24; Doctrine and Covenants 49:15; 131:1–4; Moses 3:24.
	2. Additional reading: "The Family: A Proclamation to the World," *Ensign,* Nov. 1995, 102.
	3. If *Old Testament Video Presentations* (53224) is available, prepare to show "Marriage in the Covenant," a six-minute segment.
	4. Materials needed: a. The plan of salvation chart you made for lesson 2 (or the copy of the chart found in the picture section of the manual). b. A picture of a temple (such as picture 8 in the picture section of the manual). c. A set of scriptures and a scripture marking pencil for each class member. Continue to encourage class members to bring their own scriptures to class each week.
Note to the teacher	*Temple marriage opens the door to exaltation in the celestial kingdom. After a husband and wife have been sealed in the temple, they must keep the covenants they have made and live the principles of love and obedience to achieve an eternal marriage. Those who live for eternal marriage will realize great blessings here on earth and in the next life.*
	During the lesson be sensitive to the feelings of class members whose parents are divorced or have not been married in the temple.

Suggested Lesson Development	**Families Can Be Together Forever**
Story and discussion	Tell class members that throughout today's lesson you are going to share a true story about a young woman named Chris (from Chris Geilman, "As Long As You Both Shall Live," *New Era,* Jan. 1994, 9–11). Then read the beginning of the story:
	Chris and her husband were first married in a civil ceremony conducted by their branch president. Later Chris said of that ceremony: "I remember nothing of what was said except the final words: 'as long as you both shall live.' We were in love, and the fact that we had not been married in the temple seemed unimportant."
	At the time Chris did not plan on being married in the temple. She said: "I had joined the Church five years earlier and had received several lessons concerning

the importance of temple marriage. But . . . eternity seemed such a long way off. . . . I also felt temple marriage was for the 'elite' of the Church, not for someone like me who was still stumbling about with a youthful testimony."

Five months after the wedding, Chris and her husband discovered that they were expecting their first child.

- How do you think this news affected Chris's feelings about eternity and temple marriage?

Continue reading the story:

Chris said: "My greatest jolt about the nearness of eternity came . . . when I discovered that we were expecting our first child. I felt nauseated, thrilled, humbled, and terrified all at the same time. As the months passed, a deep love for that little person inside of me began to grow and fill my very being. As this love grew, so did the reality that I wanted this child to be ours for all eternity. . . .

"My love for my husband was also blossoming beyond anything I had ever imagined. . . . The words 'as long as you both shall live' began to haunt me. Eternity was creeping ever closer, and I wanted our happiness to last forever."

- What did Chris and her husband need to do so their happiness could last forever? (They needed to be married in the temple.)

Explain that in the temple, through the power of the priesthood, Chris and her husband could be married for eternity, not just until death. Their children would then be "born in the covenant," which means that they could be sealed together as a family forever.

Point out that many people consider marriage to be only a social custom or a legal agreement between a man and a woman that they will live together. Others see marriage as outdated and unnecessary. To Latter-day Saints, marriage is much more. God ordained marriage from the very beginning (see Genesis 2:24; D&C 49:15; Moses 3:24). Marriage is the most sacred relationship that can exist. Our Heavenly Father has given us eternal marriage so we can become like him.

- Why did Chris feel at first that getting married in the temple was unimportant? (She felt that "eternity [was] a long way off"; she thought that only the "elite" members of the Church were sealed in the temple.)

- What convinced Chris that it was important to be married in the temple? (Her love for her husband grew, and she wanted their child to be born in the covenant. She wanted to be with her family forever.)

Video presentation

Explain that one reason for getting married in the temple is that we love our family members and want to be with them forever. Show the video segment "Marriage in the Covenant."

After you have shown the video segment, ask:

- How will your decision to marry in the temple affect your children and grandchildren in the future?

Eternal Marriage Is Essential for Exaltation

Story and discussion

Continue with the story about Chris:

The members of the ward where Chris and her husband lived often went on trips to the temple. Chris later recorded how she felt when she could not go with them: "I was learning that unless I made the covenants that are part of the temple ceremony, I would be on the outside looking in for the rest of eternity."

- What do you think Chris meant when she said that she "would be on the outside looking in for the rest of eternity"? (She and her husband would not be able to receive exaltation in the highest degree of the celestial kingdom. Use the following discussions to help class members understand this.)

Chart and chalkboard discussion

Display the plan of salvation chart. Briefly review the plan of salvation.

In the top left corner of the chalkboard, write *Celestial Kingdom.*

- What are some things we must do to be able to enter the celestial kingdom?

Below the words *Celestial Kingdom,* list class members' answers to this question. Answers may include the following:

Be baptized
Receive the gift of the Holy Ghost
Exercise faith in Jesus Christ
Obey the commandments

Scripture and chalkboard discussion

Have class members read Doctrine and Covenants 131:1–4.

To the right of the words *Celestial Kingdom,* write the word *Exaltation.* Explain that exaltation is life in the highest of the three degrees of the celestial kingdom.

- In addition to the requirements to enter the celestial kingdom, what ordinance must we receive to reach exaltation?

On the chalkboard, write *Be married in the temple* under the word *Exaltation.* The chalkboard should look something like this:

CELESTIAL KINGDOM	EXALTATION
Be baptized	Be married in the temple
Receive the gift of the Holy Ghost	
Exercise faith in Jesus Christ	
Obey the commandments	

Testify that only those who have been married in the temple and have lived worthily can receive exaltation.

Preparation for Temple Marriage

Quotation

Read the following statement by President Spencer W. Kimball:

"Marriage is perhaps the most vital of all the decisions and has the most far-reaching effects for it has to do not only with the immediate happiness, but eternal joys. It affects not only the two people involved, but their children and . . . their children's children down through the latest generations.

"In selecting a companion for life and for eternity, certainly the most careful planning and thinking and praying and fasting should be done to be sure that of all the decisions, this one must not be wrong. . . .

"We recommend then that all boys and girls from their infancy up plan to be married only in the temple, to keep their lives spotless so that this can be accomplished" (*The Matter of Marriage* [address delivered at the Salt Lake Institute of Religion, 22 Oct. 1976], 4–5).

Picture and discussion

Display the picture of the temple, and write on the chalkboard *Aspire to something higher.* Explain that when we aspire to obtain something, we are willing to work diligently to obtain it.

- What can you do at this time in your life to prepare to be married in the temple?

Explain that preparation for eternal marriage takes obedience, thought, and prayer. Only members of the Church who live righteously are permitted into the temple.

Story and discussion

Continue with the story about Chris:

After Chris decided that she wanted to marry her husband in the temple, her outlook on life changed. "All of my thoughts became centered around what I would have to do to be worthy of entering the temple," she said.

- How do you think it helped Chris to center all her thoughts on being worthy to enter the temple?

- How would remembering the temple so often influence the things we do and say?

Quotation and discussion

Read the following statement by President Howard W. Hunter, fourteenth President of the Church:

"I invite the Latter-day Saints to look to the temple of the Lord as the great symbol of your membership. It is the deepest desire of my heart to have every member of the Church worthy to enter the temple. . . . The things that we must do and not do to be worthy of a temple recommend are the very things that ensure we will be happy as individuals and as families.

"Let us be a temple-attending people. Attend the temple as frequently as personal circumstances allow" (in Conference Report, Oct. 1994, 8; or *Ensign,* Nov. 1994, 8).

- What do you think it means to "look to the temple of the Lord as the great symbol of [our] membership"?

- How can you follow President Hunter's counsel to be a temple-attending member of the Church?

Explain to class members that they can go to the temple to perform baptisms for the dead (see lesson 45, page 271).

- How can serving in the temple now help you prepare to be married in the temple later?

Point out that serving in the temple brings us great joy and helps us draw nearer to our Heavenly Father. Then remind class members that they need a temple recommend to be able to enter a temple and perform baptisms for the dead. To obtain a temple recommend, they must have an interview with their bishop or branch president to determine whether they are worthy to enter the temple. Read the questions listed below, which give a general idea of the questions that are asked in an interview for a temple recommend. Invite class members to think about how they would answer each question:

1. Do you have a testimony of Heavenly Father, Jesus Christ, and the Holy Ghost?

2. Do you sustain the prophet and other Church leaders?

3. Do you strive to keep the commandments?

4. Do you treat your family members with love and respect?

5. Do you attend your Church meetings?

6. Are you honest with those around you?

7. Do you keep the Word of Wisdom?

8. Are you morally clean?

- Why do you think it is necessary to demonstrate worthiness to be able to enter the temple?

Qualities of Eternal Marriage

Chalkboard discussion

Explain that to be exalted in the highest degree of the celestial kingdom, a husband and wife should strive to have a celestial married life as well as a temple ceremony. The continued righteousness of those married in the temple is as important as the marriage ceremony itself.

Draw a sunburst on the chalkboard. In the center, write *Qualities of Eternal Marriage* (see the illustration on the next page).

- What qualities might help a husband and wife strive to have a "celestial" relationship? (If class members have difficulty answering this question, ask what qualities help them in their family relationships right now. Then point out that these same qualities will help them when they marry.)

Write class members' answers on the lines that move out from the circle. The completed diagram will look something like this:

Choose three or four qualities listed on the chalkboard, and discuss each by asking, "How can this quality strengthen marriages?"

Emphasize that these qualities will help class members now, as they relate with other people. As class members develop these qualities, they will also be more prepared to be good, loving husbands and wives in the future.

Eternal Marriage Brings True Happiness

Story

Read Chris's testimony of temple marriage:

"Finally, one year and two days after our civil marriage, my wonderful husband and I knelt across the altar from each other in the Ogden Temple, surrounded by smiling friends and family members. We gazed on our 'eternal' reflection in the mirrors, tears cascading down our cheeks.

"Four weeks later, our first beautiful baby was born in the covenant. Never had we seen such a living miracle, and she was ours for eternity.

"Over 16 years have passed since that day in the Ogden Temple. The doubts and fears of our first year have been replaced by the peace of knowing ours is a forever family. I shudder to think of the chance we took, and of what these past 16 years would have been like if we had not been sealed in the temple. Many of the couples who begin as we did never do go to the temple.

"I cherish being able to return often to the temple. Within its walls I am reminded that I now possess all I need to be truly happy—forever."

Testimony

Testify of the beauty and importance of temple marriage. Express your gratitude for the promise that we can be together forever with our family members.

Encourage class members to choose a quality from the list on the chalkboard that they can develop now to help them prepare for an eternal marriage later.

**Enrichment
Activities**

You may want to use one or more of these activities during the lesson.

1. If *Doctrine and Covenants Video Presentations* (53912) is available, show "Temples Unite Families," a five-minute segment. The first part of this segment is an excerpt from the conference talk in which President Howard W. Hunter made the statement quoted in the lesson (see page 244).

2. With class members, sing or read the words to "Families Can Be Together Forever" (*Children's Songbook,* 188).

3. Give each class member a piece of paper and a pen or pencil. Then give class members three or four minutes to write down some of the qualities they would like their future husband or wife to have. After they have done this, have them write down a few things they can do that will prepare them to be able to marry someone like the person they have described.

4. Read the short story "What Is It?" (Laura Gough, *New Era,* July 1994, 26–27). In this story, a young woman on a bus trip tells her companions about the purpose of the temple they have just passed.

Honor Thy Father and Thy Mother

Lesson 42

Purpose	To inspire class members to honor their parents by living righteously and by expressing appreciation to their parents.

Preparation	1. Prayerfully study Exodus 20:12; 1 Samuel 1–4; and 3 John 1:4.
	2. If *Old Testament Video Presentations* (53224) is available, prepare to show "Hannah's Faith," a three-minute segment.
	3. Materials needed: a. Envelopes, paper, and a pen or pencil for each class member (see the activity on page 252). b. The picture Boy Samuel Called by the Lord (62498; Gospel Art Picture Kit 111). c. A set of scriptures and a scripture marking pencil for each class member. Continue to encourage class members to bring their own scriptures to class each week.
Note to the teacher	*The love of parents for their children and children for their parents is one of the strongest influences for good in the world. Many people have been motivated to live good lives because of their love for their parents. Help class members see that their lives may bring honor or shame not only to themselves but to their parents as well. Help them commit themselves to honor their parents by living righteously and expressing gratitude to their parents.*
	Be sensitive to the feelings of class members who have a deceased parent. Help them understand the importance of honoring their parents, even if they cannot express this honor directly to them right now.

Suggested Lesson Development	**Our Parents Care About Us**
Role play and discussion	Choose two class members to be the parents and another to be their daughter. Without any preparation, have them dramatize the following scene:
	The daughter has been invited to a party by some of the most popular girls at her school. They plan to see a movie that has received very good reviews. However, the parents are concerned because this movie contains bad language, violence, and immorality. The parents have always taught their daughter to avoid these things, but the daughter doesn't want to lose this chance to be friends with the popular girls.
Note to the teacher	*For help with role plays, see* Teaching—No Greater Call, *141–42.*
	Let the three class members act out the situation without interference. After the role play, ask all class members the following questions:

- How would you have handled the situation if you were the daughter? If you were the parents?

- Why do you think parents care about what their children do?

Tell the following story:

Abraham Lincoln, who became the sixteenth president of the United States, once traveled in a stagecoach with a military man, a colonel, from the state of Kentucky. "After riding a number of miles together, the colonel took a bottle of whiskey out of his pocket, and said, 'Mr. Lincoln, won't you take a drink with me?'

"Mr. Lincoln replied, 'No, Colonel, thank you, I never drink whiskey.'

"They rode along together for a number of miles more, visiting very pleasantly, when the gentleman from Kentucky reached into his pocket and brought out some cigars, saying, 'Now, Mr. Lincoln, if you won't take a drink with me, won't you take a smoke with me? . . .'

"And Mr. Lincoln said, 'Now Colonel, you are such a fine, agreeable man to travel with, maybe I ought to take a smoke with you. But before I do so, let me tell you a little story—an experience I had when a small boy.' And this was the story:

"'My mother called me to her bed one day when I was about nine years old. She was sick, very sick, and she said to me, "Abey, the doctor tells me I am not going to get well. I want you to promise me before I go that you will never use whiskey or tobacco as long as you live." And I promised my mother I never would. And up to this hour, Colonel, I have kept that promise. Now would you advise me to break that promise to my dear mother, and take a smoke with you?' . . .

"'No, Mr. Lincoln, I wouldn't have you do it for the world. It was one of the best promises you ever made. And I would give a thousand dollars today if I had made my mother a promise like that, and kept it as you have done'" ("Abraham Lincoln Keeps His Promise," *A Story to Tell,* comp. Primary Association General Board and Deseret Sunday School Union Board [1945], 256–57).

- Why do you suppose Lincoln's mother asked her son to make this promise?

- When has your parents' counsel helped you know how to act in a certain situation?

Emphasize to class members that our parents love us and want what is best for us. Ask class members to think of how much time and effort it takes to raise a son or daughter. Our parents have made a commitment to help us live a happy, healthy life. When our parents try to guide us, they are trying to help us be our best and be worthy of exaltation with our family.

Heavenly Father Wants Us to Honor Our Parents

Have class members read and mark Exodus 20:12.

- How do you honor someone? (Answers may include by showing them respect, obeying their wishes, listening to them, asking their advice, and following their example.)

- How did Abraham Lincoln honor his mother?

Quotation and discussion	Read the following statement by President Gordon B. Hinckley:

"Be true to your parents and your heritage. Regrettably there are a few parents who act in a way that does serious injustice to their children. But these cases are relatively few. No one has greater interest in your welfare, in your happiness, in your future than do your mothers and fathers. . . . They were once the age that you are now. Your problems are not substantially different from what theirs were. If they occasionally place restrictions on you, it is because they see danger down the road. Listen to them. What they ask you to do may not be to your liking. But you will be much happier if you do it" ("Stand True and Faithful," *Ensign,* May 1996, 92–93).

- What does it mean to you to be true to your parents?

- How can honoring your parents help you enjoy greater blessings and happiness in your life? (Our parents can teach us how to succeed at our goals and how to receive the blessings they have received. Because of their experience, our parents can also help us avoid many of the mistakes they have made or seen others make.)

- What are some ways you can honor your parents? (Ask a class member to list the responses on the chalkboard.)

We Can Honor Our Parents by Living Righteously

Scripture stories and video presentation	Tell the story of Samuel and the story of Eli and his sons (1 Samuel 1–4). (If you are going to show the video segment "Hannah's Faith," show it before you tell the story of Samuel). Ask class members to listen for ways that the people in the stories honored or dishonored their parents.

Samuel

Elkanah lived in Israel during the time of the judges. Hannah, one of Elkanah's wives, did not have any children. Each year when Elkanah took his family to the tabernacle, Hannah prayed and asked God to bless her with a child. Finally, Hannah promised the Lord that if he would bless her with a son, she would give that son back to serve the Lord all his life.

The next year, Hannah had a son and named him Samuel. When Samuel was a young child, Hannah took him to the tabernacle and had him stay there and live with the high priest Eli. Samuel grew up in the tabernacle.

One night, as Samuel was going to sleep, he heard a voice call his name. (Display the picture of Samuel.) He thought that it was Eli. He jumped out of bed and ran to see what Eli wanted. Eli told Samuel that he had not called him and told him to go back to bed. This happened three times. Finally Eli realized that it was the Lord that was calling Samuel. He told Samuel that the next time the voice called he should say, "Speak, Lord; for thy servant heareth." Samuel did so. It was then, in his youth, that Samuel received the first of many revelations he received throughout his life. Samuel became a great Old Testament prophet.

Eli's Sons

Eli was the high priest in Israel during Samuel's childhood. As Eli grew old, his two sons helped him in the tabernacle. Even though they worked in the tabernacle,

Eli's sons were evil men. They forcefully took the best meat away from the men who came to the tabernacle to make sacrifices to God. And they were immoral with the young women who came to the tabernacle to worship. The people of Israel hated to come to the tabernacle because of the wicked things Eli's sons were doing. Although Eli did not approve of his sons' behavior, he did not stop them from doing evil in God's house.

Finally the Lord prophesied that because Eli honored his sons more than he honored God, he and his sons would die. There would not be a priest left in Eli's family.

A short time after this prophecy, there was a war. Both of Eli's sons were killed and the Ark of the Covenant was captured by the Philistines. When Eli heard about the death of his sons and the loss of the ark, he fell off his chair. He was old, and the fall broke his neck and killed him.

Discussion

- Did Samuel honor his parents?

- Did Eli's sons honor their parents?

- How did Samuel honor his parents? (By keeping God's commandments.)

- How do you think Hannah and Eli each felt about their children's behavior?

Write on the chalkboard *We can honor our parents by living righteously.*

To emphasize how parents feel when their children honor them by living righteously, have class members read 3 John 1:4.

Point out that sometimes parents make mistakes. When this is the case, children should still honor them by being respectful to them, living an honorable life, and obeying the commandments.

We Can Honor Our Parents by Expressing Appreciation for Them

Discussion and story

Write on the chalkboard *We can honor our parents by expressing appreciation for them.*

- Do you think your parents need to feel that you honor and appreciate them? Why?

Read the following experience of a father and his son:

"I was suffering from depression. No matter how hard I tried, I always felt sad and worn out. My 14-year-old son was like a light at the end of the tunnel. During those dark days when I would come home from work, cross and irritable, he would often be there playing the piano. He would always greet me with a cheerful hello, a hug, or some funny remark. He always made the weight on my shoulders feel a little lighter.

"There was not a specific thing that he did to show his appreciation. He just let me know that he loved me, that he appreciated how I tried to be kind and patient, and that he was willing to trust and obey me. And even more importantly, he seemed always to do what was right. That wasn't easy to do. I was not easy to get along with at the time. But as a parent, I needed his confidence. I thank God that he was there to love me.

251

"Now my illness has been cured. But still, there are few things in this world that build a parent's spirit like a child's expression of love or appreciation or his decision to do something good and right."

- How can showing our appreciation for our parents help them?

<table>
<tr><td>Quotation</td><td>Have a class member read the following statement by President Spencer W. Kimball:</td></tr>
</table>

Quotation

Have a class member read the following statement by President Spencer W. Kimball:

"No gift purchased from a store can begin to match in value to parents some simple, sincere words of appreciation. Nothing we could give them would be more prized than righteous living for each youngster" (*The Teachings of Spencer W. Kimball,* ed. Edward L. Kimball [1982], 348).

Activity

Give each class member an envelope, a piece of paper, and a pen or pencil. Have class members write a letter to one or both of their parents (or guardians) and express their love and appreciation. Depending on individual circumstances, you may need to give each class member more than one envelope. (You may want to use the first enrichment activity in place of this activity.)

When they have finished writing their letters, have them address the envelopes and seal their letters inside. Assure them that no one but their parents (or guardians) will see what they have written. Collect the envelopes, and mail or deliver them to the appropriate people.

Testimony

Testify of the importance of honoring our parents and of the blessings we can receive by doing so. As appropriate, share a personal experience that taught you the importance of honoring your parents.

Urge class members to consider the consequences of their acts and how they will affect their parents. Encourage them to show appreciation to their parents and also to think, when they consider some action, "Am I doing my best to honor my parents?"

Enrichment Activities

You may want to use one or more of these activities during the lesson.

1. You may want to use this activity in place of the letter activity in the lesson. Give each class member a copy of the Parent Award on page 254. Have them fill out the award and take it home to present to their parents. (The award is worded in such a way that it can be used in either one-parent or two-parent families.)

2. Help class members prepare a plan for a Parent Honor Night for their own parents with the participation of their brothers and sisters or other family members. (This Parent Honor Night could be held during family home evening or at another time convenient for all family members.)

   Class members could use one or more of the following ideas (or their own ideas) in planning their Parent Honor Night:

   - Pretend to be nominating your parents for the "National Parent of the Year" and tell the reasons why they deserve the award (the Parent Award could be given at this time).

- Prepare a talent show and have your parents be the honored guests at the family theater.

- Plan and carry out a home project in your parents' honor.

- Have a "Happy Memories" night and tell some of your most cherished memories of your parents.

3. Have class members answer the following questions to themselves:

Do I honor my parents?

1. Am I respectful in the way I treat my parents? In my choice of words and tone of voice when I speak to them? In what I tell my friends about them?
2. Do I honor them by the way I live? Am I trustworthy? Am I a good example?
3. Do I help my parents, even before they ask? Do I do my best work?
4. Am I grateful for what they have done for me? Do I say "Thank you"? Do I forgive mistakes they make? Do I show that I care?
5. Am I honoring my parents by living a Christlike life? Am I honest? Am I clean? Am I trying to be like Jesus Christ?

$\mathcal{P}$arent Award

the Best of the Best Parents anywhere

for being

awarded to

_____

To mention only a few of your many honorable qualities:

_____

_____

_____

You will be held in honor forever by your loving and dutiful

(Son/Daughter) _____ .

Signed and delivered this _____ day of _____ ,

Being Friends with Our Brothers and Sisters

Purpose	To encourage class members to develop bonds of friendship and love with their brothers and sisters.

Preparation	1. Prayerfully study Genesis 37:15–30; 45:1–15; 1 Nephi 2:16–17; Doctrine and Covenants 135:1, 3.
	2. Materials needed: A set of scriptures and a scripture marking pencil for each class member. Continue to encourage class members to bring their own scriptures to class each week.
Note to the teacher	*We often take for granted our relationships with our brothers and sisters. We may harm these relationships by taking advantage of each other and being the most unkind to those that we ought to love and respect the most. The scriptures tell of many situations where love and respect between brothers and sisters was a great mutual blessing. Help class members understand that the family can be the source of strength and encouragement if brothers and sisters develop bonds of friendship and love.*
	Be sensitive to the feelings of class members who do not have brothers or sisters. You may want to expand the theme of the lesson to include other family members, such as cousins.

Suggested Lesson Development	**Brothers and Sisters Can Be Friends**
Chalkboard discussion and story	Without revealing the subject of the lesson, ask class members to suggest things they could do to strengthen a friendship. List their responses on the chalkboard.
	Then tell the following story:
	"I walked into sacrament meeting late that Sunday, and as usual sat on the back row. I didn't know it at the time, but when I walked out of that meeting I would be a different person. It wasn't just an ordinary meeting—it was the missionary farewell for my brother who's a year older than I am. He was the fourth one in the family to go on a mission, so it was nothing new to me, but I was closer to Chuck than the others. . . .
	"As the speakers in the meeting started talking, I thought about how much I would miss Chuck. We'd grown up together. In fact, we'd shared the same bedroom until just a year before when he had moved into mom's sewing room because I wouldn't keep the room clean. We'd worked together almost every day of our lives since I was six years old. . . . But all of a sudden he'd be gone. In two days he'd be in the MTC learning Spanish, and then on to Spain for two years to teach the gospel.

"I left my daydreaming as I heard Chuck's voice come over the loudspeaker. He was always a joker and started this talk with a joke that had everybody laughing. Then he talked a little about Spain and what his mission would be like. Then for a few seconds everything was quiet and Chuck's face clouded with emotion. And he said, 'I want to talk to my little brother Dean for a few minutes.

"'Throughout my life I've done everything I could to make my brother proud of me. I've always kept the Word of Wisdom and been the best person I could. And as I accept this call to serve the Lord on a mission, I hope that he'll be proud of me.'

"I couldn't believe what I was hearing. He had been trying to make me proud of him? . . . For the first time since I was a kid tears filled my eyes and I started to cry. . . .

"As Chuck talked, I thought back on our lives. . . . He'd always lived a Christlike life and been a good example of a member of the true Church of Jesus Christ. Then I thought back on my own life and how I'd fallen short of his example. He'd never put me down for my shortcomings, though. Sitting in that sacrament meeting, I made a promise to myself that I would someday make my brother proud of me.

"It's been a year and a half since that meeting, and I have not forgotten the promise I made. I have turned my life around and am now serving a mission for my Heavenly Father—the best decision I have ever made in my life. As I kneel every night in prayer, I thank the Lord for the great examples I have had in my life, like my brother, who have had the courage to live the teachings of the Church and act like the sons and daughters of God that they are" ("My Brother the Example," *New Era*, Nov. 1981, 6–7).

Discussion

- How did the friendship between these two brothers benefit both of them?

- What lessons can we learn from this story?

Refer to the question you asked at the beginning of the lesson and the responses written on the chalkboard. Ask the following questions:

- Do you consider your brothers and sisters to be your friends?

- Would your answers to the original question have been different if you were asked how to develop friendships with your brothers and sisters? Why?

Emphasize that we often forget that our brothers and sisters can be our closest and most reliable friends. If we will treat our brothers and sisters as we treat our best friends, we can create more love, unity, and support within our families.

Brothers and Sisters Can Help and Support Each Other

Scripture stories and discussion

The scriptures provide several examples of love and friendship between family members. Select one or two of the following scripture stories. Have class members read and mark the scriptures. Discuss the stories using the questions.

1. Nephi and Sam (1 Nephi 2:16–17)

   • What effect did Nephi have on his brother Sam?

   • Why do you think Nephi shared what he had learned with his brothers?

   • How could your love and friendship help your brothers or sisters?

2. Reuben and Joseph (Genesis 37:15–30)

   • What did Reuben do that showed he cared about his brother Joseph?

   • When has a brother or sister's love and friendship helped you?

3. Joseph and his brothers (Genesis 45:1–15)

   • What did Joseph do that showed his love for his brothers?

   • How did his friendship bless their lives?

Story and discussion

Read or tell the following account from Church history:

Speaking of his brother Hyrum Smith, the Prophet Joseph Smith wrote:

"Brother Hyrum, what a faithful heart you have got!" (quoted by Joseph Fielding Smith, in Conference Report, Apr. 1930, 93).

Throughout his life, Hyrum was a true friend and brother to Joseph. After hearing Joseph's account of the First Vision, Hyrum made a commitment to help Joseph with his responsibilities. He kept this commitment, becoming one of the first six members of the Church and always following the counsel Joseph received through the Lord.

In June 1844 a mob was determined to take the life of Joseph Smith. Hyrum Smith and others met with Joseph and carefully planned what he could do to avoid being killed. But Joseph seemed more concerned for his brother Hyrum's safety than he was for his own. He told Hyrum to take his family to Cincinnati, but Hyrum refused to leave. He followed Joseph to the Carthage Jail.

On 27 June 1844 at about 5:00 P.M., the mob came to the jail. After members of the mob had surrounded the building, some of them went past the guard and up the stairs and began shooting through the door. Others stayed outside and fired through the open windows. Hyrum was standing by the door when a bullet struck him on the side of his nose. He fell to the floor saying, "I am a dead man!" When Hyrum fell, Joseph exclaimed, "Oh! my poor, dear brother Hyrum!" (*History of the Church*, 7:102).

As the mob continued to fire their guns, Joseph went to the window, where he was struck by four bullets. As he died, he fell out of the window, exclaiming, "O Lord my God!" (D&C 135:1).

Though Hyrum could have saved his own life, he chose to stay with his brother. As Elder John Taylor wrote, "In life they were not divided, and in death they were not separated!" (D&C 135:3).

   • How did Hyrum show his brother Joseph that he loved him?

   • What could you do to support your brothers and sisters?

I Will Be a Friend to My Brothers and Sisters

Story

Tell the following story:

Marety was the only girl in a family of four brothers. She was often lonely for someone to talk to and play with. Most of the time she played alone, except when she could talk her little brothers into playing dolls with her, which was not very often.

When Marety said her prayers at night, she would say, "Please, Heavenly Father, send me a little sister." Marety's parents wanted another girl in the family, too, so they adopted a seven-year-old girl from Korea. Her name was Arnetta.

For the next 10 years Marety and Arnetta played together and were not only sisters but best friends.

As they grew up, Marety became very popular at school. She became more interested in her new school friends than she was in the Church and her family. She started missing school classes and stopped doing things with the girls in her ward. She was having a hard time. Her parents were constantly talking with her and trying to get her to do better in school and to be more active in the Church. But Marety was not interested in their counsel because she felt they did not understand her.

So it was Arnetta that Marety talked to about all her frustration and troubles. Arnetta was still her good friend. Although Marety did not think her parents or her brothers could understand or help her, Arnetta continued to encourage her to participate in family activities. After Arnetta had asked her several times, Marety agreed to come to a family home evening.

During this particular family home evening, Marety's father asked the children to bear their testimonies. When it was Marety's turn to bear her testimony, she began to cry. She told her family that she was sorry for the way she had been acting. Then she reminded the family about her prayers when she was a little girl. She told Arnetta that she loved and admired her and was thankful that God had answered her prayers and sent her such a good sister and friend.

Discussion

- How was Arnetta a good friend to Marety?

- Are you able to confide in your brothers and sisters?

- How could the ability to love and trust your brothers or sisters be important to you?

Note to the teacher

In the following discussion, keep the focus on the solutions, rather than the obstacles. For each obstacle the class members bring up, have them think of one or more possible solutions.

Chalkboard discussion

Explain to the class that there can be obstacles in the way of brother and sister friendships.

- What are some of the things that make it difficult for brothers and sisters to become good friends?

Let class members respond freely. List their answers on one side of the chalkboard.

- How can you overcome these obstacles to friendship?

List the solutions on the other side of the chalkboard.

Situation discussion

Read the following three situations. Ask class members what they would do if the person in each situation were a friend. Then ask them what they would do if the person were a brother or sister.

1. John has borrowed something of yours without asking your permission.

2. You spill a glass of water. Mary says, "Good work, clumsy!" and starts laughing at you.

3. You are ready to get on the bus when Robert drops his money. While he is trying to find the money in the grass, the bus drives away, leaving you both.

- Why do we often treat our brothers and sisters differently than we do our friends?

- How would our lives be blessed if we treated our brothers and sisters more as we treat our friends?

Quotation

Conclude by reading the following statement from Elder L. Tom Perry, a member of the Quorum of the Twelve Apostles:

"Continue building lasting, loving relationships for all family members. Listen to one another, be united, work together, play together, pray together, study together. Live celestial principles together, serve the Lord together" (in Conference Report, Apr. 1985, 29; or *Ensign*, May 1985, 23).

Testimony

Testify of the importance of developing close friendships within our families. As appropriate, share a personal experience in which you or a family member was blessed because of this kind of friendship.

Encourage class members to choose one of the solutions listed on the chalkboard and use it during the coming week to strengthen the bonds of friendship between themselves and their brothers and sisters.

Enrichment Activities

You may want to use one or more of these activities during the lesson.

1. Ask class members to choose one of their brothers or sisters with whom they would like to have a better friendship. Invite them to be an anonymous friend to that brother or sister this week. Ask them to think of kind things they could do for their brother or sister. Write their responses on the chalkboard. When you have written several responses, ask class members to do at least three of these kind things secretly for their brother or sister during the next week. Possible anonymous acts of service could include:

- Doing a brother's or sister's jobs around the house.

- Leaving a treat on a brother's or sister's bed.

- Saying something nice about him or her to someone else.

- Writing him or her a note of congratulations or encouragement.

2. Explain that a boomerang is a curved, flat implement that is thrown as a weapon or for sport. The boomerang, if thrown correctly, spins forward, then rises and begins a curved path back to the thrower.

   The actions we send out return to us like a boomerang. The best way to get someone to be happy to see you is for you to be happy to see them. The best way to get someone to be a friend to you is for you to be a friend to them.

   Encourage class members to try this "boomerang" principle on the members of their family by being a friend to each family member. Ask class members to try the principle for one week and then evaluate how well they are doing at making their brothers and sisters their friends.

3. Obtain a piece of lightweight cardboard. Glue a picture of the world on one side of the cardboard (see page 261 for a picture you can copy), and then glue a magazine picture of a family on the other side. Cut the cardboard into a puzzle. Make the puzzle fairly simple so that little time will be required to put it together.

   Lay the puzzle, family side up, where all class members can see it. (Use a table or the floor.) Ask class members to study the pieces. When someone sees two pieces that fit together, have that class member give a suggestion of how families can make the world a better place. Then have the class member place the two pieces together. As the pieces of the family picture are put together, use clear tape to secure their position so the puzzle will hold together when it is turned over. Continue until the picture of the family is complete.

   When the picture of the family is finished, turn the picture over so the picture of the world is displayed. Discuss with class members how strengthening family friendships can make the world a better place.

Turn Your Heart

Purpose	To inspire class members to learn about their ancestors and to keep their own records for posterity.

Preparation	1. Prayerfully study Malachi 4:5–6; Doctrine and Covenants 110:13–16.
	2. Invite a class member or a special guest to display his or her journal or book of remembrance and read an entry to the class.
	3. Materials needed: a. Examples of different kinds of personal records (such as birth or marriage certificates, photographs, family histories, journals, books of remembrance, or scrapbooks). b. A set of scriptures and a scripture marking pencil for each class member. Continue to encourage class members to bring their own scriptures to class each week.
Note to the teacher	*Everyone can do family history work. Help class members see that getting to know our family members, both past and present, can be enjoyable and rewarding.*

Suggested Lesson Development	**Discovering Our Ancestors**
Story and discussion	Tell in your own words the following story:

In Fred and Marion's home, a plaque hangs where everyone can see it. It is written in beautiful script and reads, "God is the head of this house, the unseen guest at every meal, the silent listener to every conversation."

The family loves the spiritual atmosphere the thought adds to their home, but cherishes even more the story behind it.

Marion's ancestors were pioneers. She grew up hearing and reading stories about how her grandparents and great-grandparents loved the Lord, were converted to the gospel, and overcame trials on the journey to Utah.

When Marion married Fred, she was very interested in learning about his ancestors and heritage. But Fred's mother had come from England as a young child with her parents, who were the only members of their families to join the Church. Fred's mother had been so young when she came that she grew up with little knowledge about her grandparents. An occasional letter was the only link between families for many years.

Marion and Fred wrote to ask relatives in England for information about Fred's mother's grandparents and the old family home. They learned of a kind grandmother, very proper in her black satin dress and gold brooch, and of Sunday visits to a tidy cottage where children had to remember their manners and sit quietly on the prickly horsehair-covered chairs. The family honored the Sabbath by attending church and refraining from any unnecessary labor.

One elderly cousin wrote of an inscription, written in an old style of lettering, that had hung above the fireplace of his parents' humble cottage. The inscription had remained vivid in his mind, although time had dimmed his recollection of other events.

Marion was excited when she read the letter and the words of the inscription. Here was a clue to help her identify with her husband's heritage. His great-grandparents' home had been one in which God had been revered, and seeds were planted there that would eventually prepare souls to accept the restored gospel.

This simple inscription has helped Marion and her family feel a closeness to Fred's ancestors. By preserving the inscription on a plaque, this family has developed a new perspective of reverence toward God and appreciation for their ancestors.

- Why is the inscription on the plaque so important to Fred and Marion's family? How does it help them feel closer to their ancestors?

Feeling the Spirit of Elijah

Scripture discussion

Explain that the desire to learn about our ancestors is sometimes referred to as the Spirit of Elijah. Elijah was the last prophet before the time of Christ to hold the sealing power of the Melchizedek Priesthood, which allows us to be sealed to our family members for eternity.

Have class members read and mark Malachi 4:5–6. Explain that this passage contains a prophecy that Elijah would return to the earth to restore the sealing power. This prophecy was fulfilled in 1836 when Elijah appeared to Joseph Smith and Oliver Cowdery in the Kirtland Temple (see D&C 110:13–16).

- What does it mean to "turn the heart of the fathers to the children, and the heart of the children to their fathers"?

Explain that this means to seal us to all our ancestors—our "fathers"—and to all our posterity—our "children"—forever. Because of the sealing power of the priesthood and temple ordinances for the living and the dead, families can be bound together for eternity (note that temple ordinances for the dead will be discussed in the next lesson). Turning "the heart of the fathers to the children, and the heart of the children to their fathers" also refers to the love we feel for our ancestors when we learn about them.

Quotation

Have a class member read the following statement by President Gordon B. Hinckley:

"There are millions across the world who are working on family history records. Why? Why are they doing it? I believe it is because they have been touched by the spirit of this work, a thing which we call the spirit of Elijah. It is a turning of the hearts of the children to their fathers" ("A Century of Family History Service," *Ensign,* Mar. 1995, 62).

- How were the hearts of Fred, Marion, and their family turned to the hearts of their "fathers"?

- What do you know about your ancestors? How does your knowledge of your ancestors turn your heart to them?

- If you could sit down with your ancestors and talk with them, what would you want to know about them?

- What are some things you can do to learn more about your ancestors?

List class members' answers on the chalkboard. You may want to share the following suggestions if class members do not mention them:

1. Ask your parents to tell you about your grandparents and great-grandparents.

2. Write letters to your grandparents asking them to tell you some stories about themselves, their children, their parents, or their grandparents. Ask them to include details such as dates, places, and names of people in the stories. When they send letters to you with stories and information, keep those letters in a safe place.

3. If there is a Church Family History Center™ near your home, go there with your family and use the computers and other resources to find the names of more of your ancestors.

4. Prepare a pedigree chart of your family (see the fourth enrichment activity).

5. If your ancestors are from a different country, read about the customs of that country and try some of them in family home evening.

Read or have a class member read the following story:

Linda was a convert to the Church. She envied her friend's Latter-day Saint pioneer heritage and the many pages of pedigrees, biographies, and stories he had in a book of family records, but she could see nothing very exciting or glamorous in learning about her own ancestors. Then her friend said something that made her look at her situation in a different light.

"'Linda, I envy you!' . . . My friend closed his book and continued, 'All the work that's in here was done by someone else. . . . But you—*you* get to start fresh and snoop around for yourself! Just think how close that will bring you to your mothers and fathers! You'll really get to know them!'

"Knowing my mothers and fathers! I had never thought of it that personally before. Mothers and fathers don't have to be glamorous or royal—they just have to be mine and I theirs! I repented of my envy and scurried home with the spirit of Elijah fluttering around me and some blank pedigree charts in my hand.

"I filled in the information for my parents and me but didn't have much beyond names for my grandparents. Then I remembered some old boxes of family things my mother mentioned once. In the basement covered with dust and smelling like the 19th century, two cigar boxes lay wedged in behind some old tires. I had found treasure chests! I sat down on the cold concrete, surrounded by hardware and hoses and mold, and began to get acquainted with my ancestors. In those boxes I found a 1907 newspaper clipping of my great-grandfather's obituary, my granduncle's report card from Sweden in 1883, a 14-inch swatch of my grand-mother's golden hair, an envelope with five generations of parents' names diagrammed on the back, lots of unlabeled photographs, and a small, brittle bundle of Swedish letters from my great-grandfather to my great-grandmother when they were courting in the 1860s. I offered a teary prayer of gratitude there in that damp, musty sanctuary, and I knew I was not alone in that prayer or that place.

"I studied those treasures in the months that followed. I pumped my mother for anything she could recall about her family. She helped me label photographs and sort out relationships. I studied old Swedish customs. I examined old maps of the areas where my family had lived. I listened to Swedish folk music. I even learned a little of the language. I discovered what kinds of people my ancestors really were: Gerda, my mother's mother—the sensitive, industrious, beautiful nurse; Carl Johan—the stationmaster with the flowing beard who would give advice and settle disputes like a lawyer; Maria Christina—the sturdy, stocky, devoted wife to Carl Johan and a diligent student of the scriptures; Agnes Sigrid Alfreda who had volunteered for the earliest experimental polio immunizations and was unfortunately left crippled; and my dear great-great-grandfather Anders who wrote in 1880, 'If I am now welcome I intend to travel to see you if the Lord will grant me health, and take with me my fishing yarn and the material for wooden clogs.' I loved them all as living people, as my parents" (Linda K. Hoffman, "Gerda, I Love You, or The Spirit of Elijah Is for Simple Folk Too" *New Era,* Aug. 1976, 28–30).

Keeping Personal Records

Quotation

Explain that in addition to learning about our ancestors, we should keep personal records so our family members will be able to learn about us in the future. It will be difficult for future generations to turn their hearts to us if they know nothing about us.

Have a class member read the following statement by President Spencer W. Kimball:

"We may think there is little of interest or importance in what we personally say or do—but it is remarkable how many of our families, as we pass on down the line, are interested in all that we do and all that we say. Each of us is important to those who are near and dear to us—and as our posterity read of our life's experiences, they, too, will come to know and love us. And in that glorious day when our families are together in the eternities, we will already be acquainted" (in Conference Report, Oct. 1979, 5; or *Ensign,* Nov. 1979, 5).

Discussion

- What would you like your children and grandchildren to know about you?

- What challenges do you think your children and grandchildren will have to face? How could knowing about you and your experiences help your children and grandchildren when they face these challenges?

- What kinds of records can we keep? (Answers may include birth certificates, photographs, journals, family records, and scrapbooks.)

Show the examples of different kinds of records.

- What things could you record in a journal to help your descendants love and remember you, even if they never knew you in this life? (Answers may include personal experiences and feelings, testimonies, difficulties, family events, missionary calls, joyful occasions, and funny things that happen to you.)

Quotation

Explain that journals do not need to be fancy. The words we write in them do not need to be fancy, either. But the things we write in our journals will come together to record memories that will be valuable to us and to our posterity. Even things that seem insignificant now, like the clothes we wear, the food we eat, and the things we do at school, may be important to us and to others in the future. Encourage class members to follow this counsel from President Kimball:

"Get a notebook, my young folks. . . . Begin today and write in it your goings and comings, your deepest thoughts, your achievements and your failures, your associations and your triumphs, your impressions and your testimonies" ("The Angels May Quote from It," *New Era,* Oct. 1975, 5).

Journal presentation

Have the previously assigned class member or special guest display a journal or book of remembrance and read a personal entry that might be of interest to the group. Have this person also express his or her feelings about the importance of this record.

After this presentation, ask the assigned class member or special guest the following question:

- How has it helped you personally to keep this record?

Discussion

Explain that our records help our children and grandchildren, but they also help us personally. Then ask class members the following question:

- How can keeping a journal help us?

You may want to share the following suggestions if class members do not mention them:

1. We can remember our experiences by reading things we wrote in the past.

2. We can look back and see how we have changed.

3. We can write about our testimonies and about experiences and feelings that are difficult to share with other people.

Testimony

As appropriate, share an experience you have had with learning about your ancestors or with keeping personal records. Testify of the importance of turning our hearts to our "fathers" and to our "children."

Encourage class members to do all they can to learn about their ancestors. Also encourage them to write consistently in a journal and to save important pieces of information in a book of remembrance, scrapbook, or file.

Enrichment Activities

You may want to use one or more of these activities during the lesson.

1. With class members, sing or read the words to "Genealogy" (*Children's Songbook,* 94).

2. Have class members write a letter to the children they will have in the future. Encourage them to leave it unopened and in a safe place until they are married and have children.

3. If *Old Testament Video Presentations* (53224) is available, show "Marriage in the Covenant," a six-minute segment. This segment is about temple marriage. It shows how our actions today affect our ancestors and our descendants. (Do not show this segment if you showed it during lesson 41.)

4. Give each class member a copy of the pedigree chart found on page 268. Encourage class members to complete the chart at home.

Pedigree Chart

Chart no. _____

No. 1 on this chart is the same as no. _____ on chart no. _____.

Mark boxes when ordinances are completed.

- B Baptized
- E Endowed
- SP Sealed to parents
- SS Sealed to spouse
- F Family Group Record exists for this couple
- C Children's ordinances completed

8

(Father of no. 4) B E SP SS F C   Cont. on chart no.

When born
Where
When married
When died
Where

4

(Father of no. 2) B E SP SS F C

When born
Where

When married
Where

When died
Where

9

(Mother of no. 4) B E SP SS   Cont. on chart no.

When born
Where
When died
Where   _____

2

(Father) B E SP SS F C

When born
Where

When married
Where

When died
Where

10

(Father of no. 5) B E SP SS F C   Cont.on chart no.

When born
Where
When married
When died
Where   _____

5

(Mother of no. 2) B E SP SS

When born
Where

When died
Where

11

(Mother of no. 5) B E SP SS   Cont. on chart no.

When born
Where
When died
Where   _____

1 _____

(Name) B E SP SS F C

When born
Where

When married
Where

When died
Where

_____

(Spouse) B E SP SS

3

(Mother) B E SP SS

When born
Where

When died
Where

12

(Father of no. 6) B E SP SS F C   Cont. on chart no.

When born
Where
When married
When died
Where   _____

6

(Father of no. 3) B E SP SS F C

When born
Where

When married
Where

When died
Where

13

(Mother of no. 6) B E SP SS   Cont. on chart no.

When born
Where
When died
Where   _____

7

(Mother of no. 3) B E SP SS

When born
Where

When died
Where

14

(Father of no. 7) B E SP SS F C   Cont. on chart no.

When born
Where
When married
When died
Where   _____

15

(Mother of no. 7) B E SP SS   Cont. on chart no.

When born
Where
When died
Where   _____

Published by The Church of Jesus Christ of Latter-day Saints   3/96   Printed in USA   31826

Salvation for the Dead

Purpose	To help class members gain an appreciation of God's eternal plan and a desire to participate in the salvation of their ancestors.

Preparation	1. Prayerfully study Malachi 4:5–6; John 3:5; Doctrine and Covenants 138:30; Articles of Faith 1:4.
	2. Additional reading: *A Member's Guide to Temple and Family History Work* (34697).
	3. Materials needed: a. The plan of salvation chart you made for lesson 2 (or the copy of the chart found in the picture section of the manual). b. A set of scriptures and a scripture marking pencil for each class member. Continue to encourage class members to bring their own scriptures to class each week.
Note to the teacher	*The requirements for obtaining exaltation and entering the highest degree in the celestial kingdom include many ordinances that must be done on the earth. Because billions of people have died without any knowledge of these saving ordinances, Heavenly Father has provided a way for all his children to receive them. President Joseph Fielding Smith calls this plan of salvation for the dead "one of the grandest, most reasonable, and soul satisfying doctrines ever revealed to man" (Doctrines of Salvation, comp. Bruce R. McConkie, 3 vols. [1954–56], 2:143). Help class members understand this doctrine and become enthusiastic about participating in this work.*

Suggested Lesson Development	**Ordinances are Necessary for Entrance into the Celestial Kingdom**
Chart and scripture discussion	Display the plan of salvation chart throughout the lesson.

- What are the first principles and ordinances of the gospel?

Invite a class member to recite the fourth article of faith to help answer the question.

- Why are the ordinances of baptism and the laying on of hands for the gift of the Holy Ghost important to us?

Have class members read and mark John 3:5. Point out that these ordinances are necessary for entrance into the celestial kingdom. Explain that these are earthly ordinances that must be performed here on earth.

- How many people do you think have lived on the earth and then died without hearing the gospel, being baptized, or receiving the gift of the Holy Ghost?

- What will happen to these people?

Explain that if these people never receive earthly ordinances, they will be unable to enter the celestial kingdom, regardless of their righteousness. However, Heavenly Father's plan of salvation applies to all his children, and he has provided a way for these people to hear the gospel and receive the ordinances, even though they were unable to do so when they were on the earth.

We Can Help Those Who Have Died without Gospel Ordinances

Story

Relate the following story told by Elder Royden G. Derrick, who was a member of the Seventy:

"When I was a young child, our family was anxious for the return of Uncle Orson. My mother had deep feelings about the matter, which she implanted in her children. For some reason I always watched for Uncle Orson to come to the back door of our home. I remember on a number of occasions when a peddler would come to the back door. I would pull on my mother's dress to get her attention and ask, 'Is this Uncle Orson, huh?' But the answer was always no.

" . . . Uncle Orson was born in 1881. Fourteen months later his father died, leaving him without the guidance of a father during those critical early years. When he was 17 years old, he, with a group of other boys his own age, went to Saltair, a dance pavilion on the shores of the Great Salt Lake. Before the evening was over, they became drunk and ended up in the county jail.

"The following morning, parents and family members came to the jail house and obtained their sons' releases. Many of them put their arms around their sons and built them into pillars in the community. But unknown to my grandmother, Uncle Orson was released from jail, given a one-way ticket to the Northwest, and told never to return.

"Mother said that on occasions she would hear her mother sobbing in her bedroom during the night. When she went to her mother's side, her mother would say, 'I wonder where my wandering boy is tonight.'

"Uncle Orson likely worked in the lumber camps of the Northwest in an atmosphere that was not conducive to living the principles of the gospel. If he were living today, he would be very old. It is most likely that he has gone to the world of spirits by now. . . .

"My good friend, Joseph S. Nelson, died a few months ago at age 86. He was a great missionary during his life. He served four missions. . . . I've been searching the scriptures to find [what he is doing now]—and here he is:

" 'I beheld that the faithful elders of this dispensation, when they depart from mortal life, continue their labors in the preaching of the gospel of repentance and redemption, through the sacrifice of the Only Begotten Son of God, among those who are in darkness and under the bondage of sin in the great world of the spirits of the dead' (D&C 138:57). . . .

"I have loved Uncle Orson from childhood because I inherited a longing for him. I want so much to buy him a return ticket home to his eternal family. . . .

"I wonder if my good friend Joe Nelson might find Uncle Orson and teach him the gospel truths that his father would have taught him in mortality had he been here to do so" ("Find Them," *New Era,* Sept. 1981, 4–6).

Scripture
discussion

Have class members read and mark Doctrine and Covenants 138:30. Remind them that after Christ died, he went to the spirit world and organized righteous members of the Church to teach the gospel to those who had died without hearing it. Once these spirits are taught the gospel, they have the same opportunity to accept or reject it as those who are taught on earth.

- If these spirits accept the gospel, what else is required before they can enter the celestial kingdom? (Baptism, bestowal of the gift of the Holy Ghost, and other earthly ordinances.)

- How do those who have died receive earthly ordinances? (We can perform these ordinances for them in the temple.)

Write the words *vicarious* and *proxy* on the chalkboard. Explain that to do something vicariously means that a person does something in place of someone else. The person doing the work or activity for another person is called a proxy. In the temple we can be baptized and receive other ordinances for people who have died without receiving the ordinances. We are the ones who go down into the waters of baptism or who have hands placed on our head, but they are the ones for whom the ordinances are in effect.

- What ordinances are performed for the dead in the temple? (Baptism, confirmation and bestowal of the gift of the Holy Ghost, ordaining to the priesthood for the men, endowment, marriage, and sealing of children to parents.)

- Which of these ordinances can you participate in for someone who is dead?

Explain that any worthy Church member who is at least 12 years old can receive a recommend from the bishop and go to the temple to be baptized and confirmed for the dead. When class members are older and have received their own temple ordinances, they can return to the temple to receive other ordinances for the dead.

If there is a temple nearby, encourage class members to talk to their parents or Young Men and Young Women leaders about arranging a trip to the temple to do baptisms for the dead.

How We Can Start Helping Those Who Have Died without the Gospel

Chalkboard
discussion

Explain that we are each responsible for helping our own ancestors receive temple ordinances.

- What is the first step in performing temple work for our dead? (Finding out who they are.)

- What kind of information do we need to know about our ancestors in order to do their temple work? (The minimum essential information is each person's name; sex; and one identifying date, such as a birth or death date. However, the more information we can provide, the better. Other helpful information includes birthplace, parents' names, marriage date, spouse's name, and place of death. All this information should be as accurate as possible.)

- What are some things we can do to find out more about our ancestors?

List class members' responses on the chalkboard. Responses might include asking living relatives for information and copies of records that they may have; doing research at family history centers; writing letters to request copies of birth certificates; looking at census records; and going to cemeteries. You may want to remind class members of the things they discussed in lesson 44 about how to learn about our ancestors.

Encourage class members to discuss with their families, perhaps in family home evening, activities they can do as a family to learn about their ancestors.

Teacher presentation

Explain that when a person has the necessary information on an ancestor, he or she can submit the ancestor's name to the temple. If family members want to do the temple work for their own ancestors, the information is held in the family file at a specific temple for a short time until the family members can come to the temple. If family members are unable to do the work, other members of the Church will perform the ordinances.

Story and discussion

Read or tell the following story:

While 11-year-old Cindie and her father were taking a walk together, they found an old tombstone. They cleared the moss from it and found the following inscription:

MARYANN DEMING
wife of Rufus Deming
died Jan. 5, 1855
in the 56th year
of her age

"Cindie said, 'Oh, dad, I can just see what happened. There were Mormon pioneers crossing the plains, and poor Maryann [died], and her husband and children were heartbroken, and they buried her here and sadly left her and went on to Utah. It was so tragic!'"

Cindie's dad replied, "'I don't think so. . . . The Mormon pioneers didn't pass through Lake County, California, in 1855 or any other time. More likely she and her family were here as part of the gold rush or to find a good farm or something like that. But I'm sure you're right about her family being very sad when she died.'"

Cindie was very excited about the thought of using this information to help Maryann's descendants do her temple work:

"'Oh, dad, I can just see it now: one of her great-grandchildren has been looking for her records for just years and years, and they need her death date, and they're praying that someone will find her tombstone and send in the information to the [Family History] Library.'"

Cindie and her parents spent three days collecting information from local cemeteries. They then compiled a book and sent it to the Family History Library in Salt Lake City.

"A few weeks later . . . Cindie came home from school to discover an impressive-looking envelope in the mailbox. Excitedly, she called [her father at work] and read, 'The Genealogical Society wishes to thank you for your 41-page booklet, *Cemetery Inscriptions of Lake County, California.* You have provided important information which we did not have in our collection—information which will no doubt be very useful to many of our patrons in the years ahead. We congratulate you, at age 11, on having your own author card in our card catalog'" (Terry J. Moyer, "An Author Card for Cindie," *New Era,* May 1981, 14–17).

- Why was Cindie so excited to find the tombstone, even though the woman was not one of her ancestors? (Although Cindie was not searching out her own ancestors, she was inspired by the Spirit to help others.)

- What can we learn from Cindie's enthusiasm and determination?

Emphasize that there is much we can do to help our ancestors and others through family history and temple work.

Scripture discussion

Have class members read Malachi 4:5–6. Remind them that they discussed these verses during the previous lesson.

- What does it mean to turn our hearts to our fathers? (As we learn about our ancestors and dedicate ourselves to do temple work for them and for others who have died without the gospel, we are turning our hearts towards them.)

- How can this work for the dead help us and them to become perfect? (By being baptized for the dead, we help them fulfill the principles and ordinances of the gospel. This work blesses us as we obey the Lord's commandment to turn our hearts to those who have died without the gospel.)

Quotation

Read or have a class member read the following statement by President Joseph Fielding Smith:

"By this means [doing temple work for the dead] we may help to save those who have gone before and in our limited way become *saviors to many people.* How great shall be the satisfaction of the man and the woman who have performed those ordinances for their dead, when they stand in the presence of their dead, and see their joy and hear expressions of gratitude" (*Doctrines of Salvation,* 2:143).

Testimony

Bear testimony, as the Spirit directs, of the importance of doing temple work for the dead. Encourage class members to choose one activity to do this week, by themselves or with their families, that will help them find out more about their ancestors.

You may want to use one or more of these activities during the lesson.

1. Before class, write on a card, in the most beautiful writing possible, the text of John 3:16 ("For God so loved the world, that he gave his only begotten Son, that whosoever believeth in him should not perish, but have everlasting life") and Doctrine and Covenants 14:7 ("And, if you keep my commandments and endure to the end you shall have eternal life, which gift is the greatest of all the gifts of God"). Place the card in a box and wrap it nicely.

   Have class members sit or stand in a circle. Pass the wrapped box around the circle, having each class member tell what the nicest gift he or she could receive would be before passing the box to the next person. When the box comes back to the first class member who spoke, have him or her open it and read the card.

   Explain that when we help provide temple ordinances for our ancestors, either by participating in the actual ordinances at the temple or by finding and submitting information so the ordinances can be done by others, we are helping to make "the greatest of all the gifts of God" available to those ancestors.

2. Invite a ward or branch member who has participated in temple work for family members to come to class and share his or her feelings about temple work for the dead. Or invite the ward or branch family history consultant to teach class members more about how to prepare and submit names for temple work.

Course Review

If you have extra time after a lesson or an extra lesson period at the end of the year, you may want to review the doctrines and principles that have been taught in this course. One way of doing so is described below.

Create a game board like the one illustrated and review the questions on the next page. (If you are going to play the game for an entire class period, you will need to create additional questions and play several rounds of the game.)

Divide class members into two or three teams. Have one team select a category and the number of points they want to earn (the higher the point reward, the more difficult the question). Ask the corresponding question, and give the team the appropriate number of points if they answer correctly. (You are the judge of how exact an answer must be to receive credit. For example, you may want to allow one or two minor errors in a scripture being quoted.) Have the teams take turns doing this until all the questions have been asked or you run out of time. As each question is answered, make a mark in the appropriate box so it will not be chosen again.

Plan of Salvation	Principles of the Gospel	Ordinances of the Gospel	Gospel Teachings	Prophets and Temples
100	100	100	100	100
200	200	200	200	200
300	300	300	300	300
400	400	400	400	400
500	500	500	500	500

Plan of Salvation

100 Name the three degrees of glory. (Telestial, terrestrial, celestial.)

200 What is our "second estate"? (Mortality, or earth life.)

300 What is spiritual death? (Separation from Heavenly Father.)

400 What two conflicting commandments were given to Adam and Eve in the Garden of Eden? (To multiply and replenish the earth; to not eat the fruit of the tree of knowledge of good and evil.)

500 Recite from memory Moses 1:39.

Principles of the Gospel

100 How many times should we forgive those who have sinned against us? ("Seventy times seven" [Matthew 18:22]; in other words, every time.)

200 What is charity? (The pure love of Christ; see Moroni 7:47.)

300 Name at least two steps of repentance. (Recognize the sin and desire to change; confess; forsake the sin; make restitution; keep the commandments.)

400 How did Naaman demonstrate faith? (He bathed in the river Jordan when the prophet Elisha told him it would cure his leprosy.)

500 What is the "first law of heaven"? (Obedience.)

Ordinances of the Gospel

100 How do we renew the covenants we made at baptism? (By taking the sacrament every Sunday.)

200 What priesthood must a man have to bestow the gift of the Holy Ghost? (Melchizedek Priesthood.)

300 How do members of the Church most often receive personal revelation? (Through inspiration, or promptings, from the Holy Ghost.)

400 Recite from memory the fourth Article of Faith.

500 Who is the one person on earth who holds all the keys to perform all the ordinances of the gospel? (The President of the Church.)

Gospel Teachings

100 How much is a full tithe? (Ten percent of our increase, or income.)

200 For each member of your team, name two gifts or talents he or she has.

300 What was the "iron rod" of Lehi's dream? (The word of God.)

400 Where is the Word of Wisdom written down? (Doctrine and Covenants 89.)

500 What is the three-part mission of the Church? (To proclaim the gospel, perfect the Saints, and redeem the dead.)

Prophets and Temples

100 Who is the current living prophet?

200 How old do you have to be to go to the temple and participate in baptisms for the dead? (12.)

300 Name the prophet whose mother promised him to the Lord. (Samuel.)

400 Which prophet restored the sealing keys of the Melchizedek Priesthood to the Prophet Joseph Smith? (Elijah.)

500 Name two ordinances that can only be performed in the temple. (Baptism for the dead; eternal marriage or sealing; the endowment.)

Notes

Notes

Notes

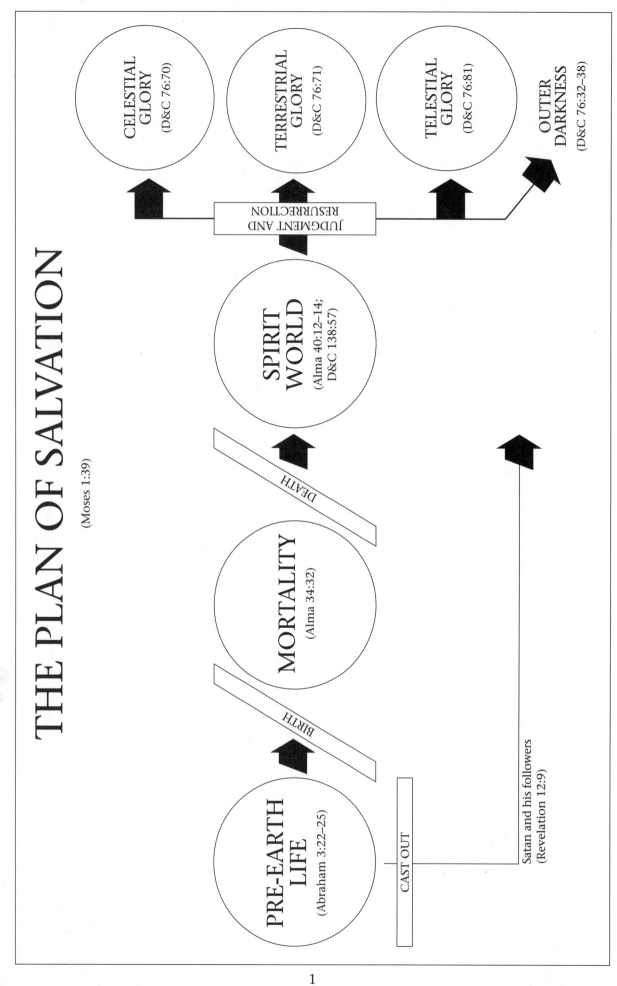

THE PLAN OF SALVATION

(Moses 1:39)

CELESTIAL GLORY (D&C 76:70)

TERRESTRIAL GLORY (D&C 76:71)

TELESTIAL GLORY (D&C 76:81)

OUTER DARKNESS (D&C 76:32–38)

JUDGMENT AND RESURRECTION

SPIRIT WORLD (Alma 40:12–14; D&C 138:57)

DEATH

MORTALITY (Alma 34:32)

BIRTH

PRE-EARTH LIFE (Abraham 3:22–25)

CAST OUT

Satan and his followers (Revelation 12:9)

1

3

4

7